INSPIRE / PLAN / DISCOVER / EXPERIENCE

CROATIA

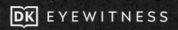

CROATIA

CONTENTS

DISCOVER 6

EXPERIENCE 60

NEED TO KNOW 250

Left: A beach on Dugi Otok, Northern Dalmatia
Previous page: City of Šibenik at sunset
Front cover: The harbour in Dubrovnik's Old Town

DISCOVER

Plitvice National Park, Kvarner Area

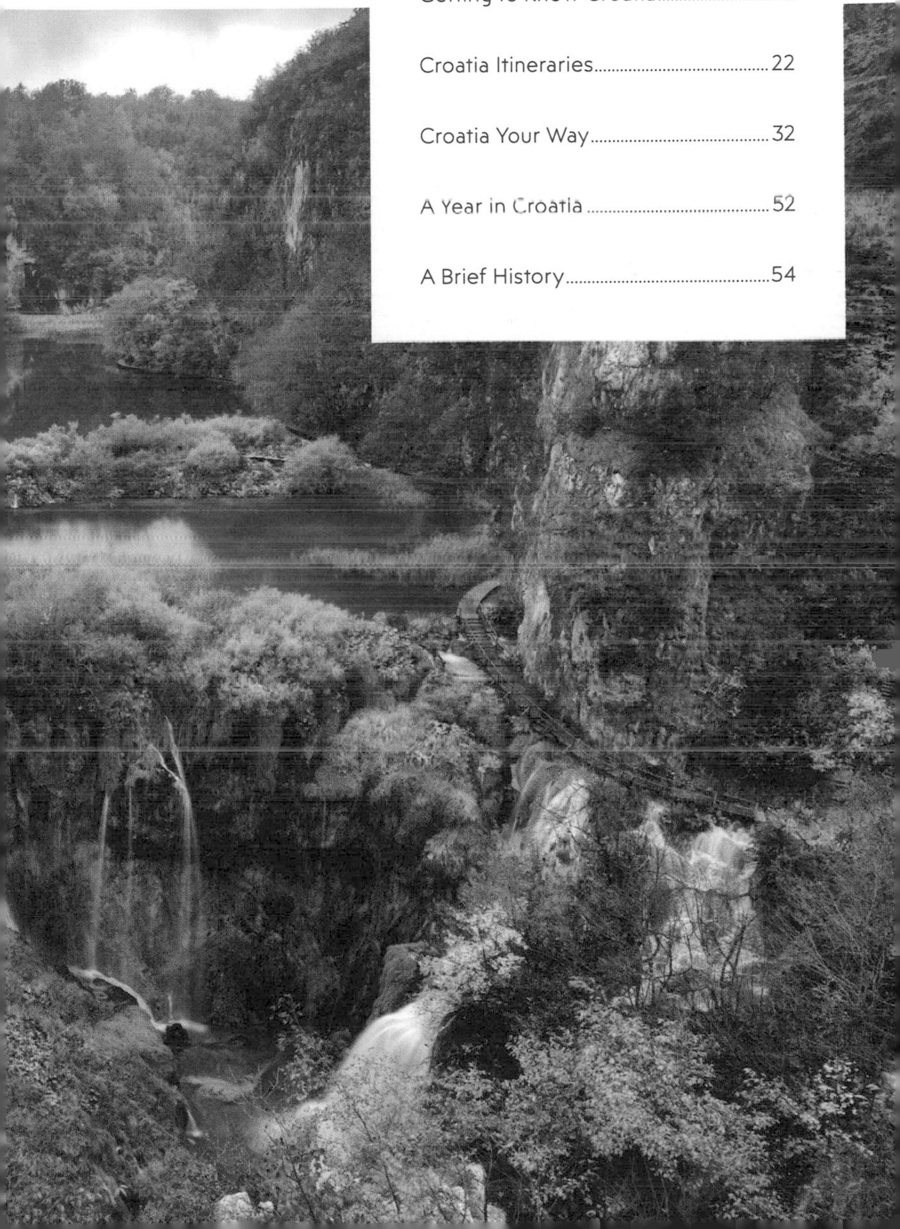

WELCOME TO
CROATIA

Sparkling waves lapping sultry, sun-drenched beaches. Crumbling castle walls shading cobbled city piazzas. Verdant vegetation fringing tranquil lakes and thundering waterfalls. Croatia has it all, and more. Whatever your dream trip to Croatia includes, this DK Eyewitness Travel Guide is the perfect companion.

① Sailing at sunset in Brela, Central Dalmatia.

② Pausing to tuck into Croatia's delectable cuisine.

③ Dubrovnik's famously charming Old Town, popular with Croatians and sightseers alike.

Ancient mythology permeates Croatia, and nowhere more so than across the constellation of islands along Dalmatia's coastline. Follow the course of Greek hero Odysseus and negotiate the Adriatic Sea, before taking a dip in Calypso's cave on mystical Mljet. Celebrate Mother Earth with every season in Croatia; cross the footbridges of photogenic Plitvice Lakes National Park in summer, cycle around Slavonia's Kopački Rit Nature Park and watch birds feed here in autumn, or build snowmen in Kvarner's Risnjak National Park in winter. You'll need sustenance after your adventures. Try Pag cheese in Dalmatia, succulent scampi in Kvarner, and head to Istria for wine tastings.

Craving the bustle of a city? You're spoiled for choice. Traverse the medieval walls of magnificent Dubrovnik, today recognised for their starring role in *Game of Thrones*. Make like an emperor and explore the Palace of Diocletian in ancient Split before unwinding in a bar in the city's labyrinthine streets. Follow in the footsteps of Roman gladiators at Pula's amphitheatre, which today hosts less gruesome film festivals. Inland, explore the open-air cafés in Zagreb before visiting its unique museums, like the emotive Museum of Broken Relationships.

With so many regions and experiences on offer, Croatia can seem overwhelming. We've broken the country down into easily navigable chapters, with detailed itineraries and comprehensive maps to help plan the perfect adventure. Add insider tips, and a Need To Know guide that lists all the essentials to be aware of before and during your trip, and you've got an indispensable guidebook. Enjoy the book, and enjoy Croatia.

REASONS TO LOVE
CROATIA

Its coastline is stunning. It's a gourmet's delight. It's soaked in history. Ask any Croatian and you'll hear a different reason why they love Croatia. Here, we pick some of our favourites.

1 DUBROVNIK

Dubrovnik is one of Europe's most iconic cities, famous for its tightly wound warren of stone alleys. It can be evocative, romantic and inspirational whatever the season *(p66)*.

LAKES AND WATERFALLS 2

From the tumbling waterfalls of the Plitvice Lakes *(p184)* to the cataracts and canyons of the river Krka *(p136)*, Croatia's national parks are strong on heart-stopping natural beauty.

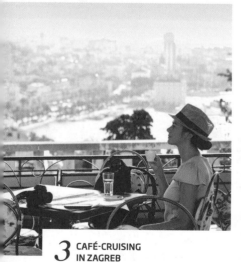

3 CAFÉ-CRUISING IN ZAGREB

Coffee-drinking is the glue that keeps Croatian society together and nowhere is this more evident than in Zagreb, where the pavement cafés are open from morning till night *(p196)*.

BEACHES 4

Croatia has a staggering variety of beaches, from beaches backed by pinewoods to swathes of grey-gold pebble. Wherever you find yourself, the water is crystal-clear.

PULA AMPHITHEATRE 5

Once used for gladiatorial combat, this magnificently preserved 1st-century arena is nowadays used as a venue for live music and film festivals *(p154)*. See the relic for yourself.

THE ADRIATIC DIET 6

Seafood, olive oil and seasonal vegetables form the backbone of Croatian coastal cuisine, while fish is accompanied by *blitva* (Swiss chard), famous for its mineral-rich leaves.

ISLAND-HOPPING *7*

It's on the islands that you'll find the Adriatic at its most unspoiled, and stringing a few islands together in a succession of scenic sea voyages is an essential experience.

CROATIAN NIGHTS *8*

The open-air nightlife is vivacious. Promenaders throng past pavement cafés and busy bars, and a schedule of summer fiestas and arts festivals add spice to the party.

9 THE UNDERSEA WORLD

Whether snorkeling just off the beach or scuba diving in the depths you'll find the waters of the Adriatic full of wonders, from starfish to multi-coloured shoals.

10 COASTAL DRIVES

Stretching from Istria down to Dubrovnik, Croatia's coastal highway is among the most dramatic in the Mediterranean, and offers fantastic views of the country's islands.

CAVES AND GROTTOES 11

According to myth, Odysseus met the nymph Calypso in one of Croatia's caves. Filled with ethereal turquoise light, Biševo's Blue Cave is the best known of Croatia's mesmerizing sea caves. Will you glimpse a nymph?

WINE 12

From the velvety reds of the Dalmatian islands to the light crisp whites of the southeast, Croatia's characterful local wines are finally getting the recognition they deserve.

EXPLORE
CROATIA

This guide divides Croatia into
eight colour-coded sightseeing
areas, as shown on this map.
Find out more about each area
on the following pages.

Krapina

SLOVENIA

Zagreb

ZAGREB
p196

Karlovac

Glina

Opatija

Rijeka

Ogulin

Poreč

ISTRIA
p146

Krk

Rovinj

Krk Town

Senj

Pula

Cres

Rab

KVARNER AREA
p170

Bihać

Unije

Adriatic
Sea

Mali Lošinj

Lošinj

Gospić

Pag Town

Pag

Premuda

Gračac

Molat

Zadar

Benkovac

ZADAR AND
NORTHERN
DALMATIA
p116

Knin

Dugi Otok

Biograd na Moru

Drniš

Kornat

Šibenik

Vis

EUROPE

DENMARK

RUSSIA

UNITED
KINGDOM

NETHER-
LANDS

BELARUS

GERMANY

POLAND

BELGIUM

CZECH
REP.

SLOVAKIA

UKRAINE

FRANCE

SWITZ.

AUSTRIA

HUNGARY

CROATIA

ROMANIA

ITALY

BOSNIA
HERZ.

SERBIA

BULGARIA

MACEDONIA

SPAIN

ALBANIA

TURKEY

GREECE

TUNISIA

CYPRUS

ALGERIA

LIBYA

EGYPT

GETTING TO KNOW
CROATIA

A crescent-shaped country that arches across the borders of Mediterranean, central and southeastern Europe, Croatia offers a staggering diversity of landscapes and lifestyles. From the island-speckled Adriatic coast to the green and mountainous interior, each region has its own distinct personality.

PAGE 62

DUBROVNIK AND SOUTHERN DALMATIA

With its narrow, photogenic alleys overlooked by historic monuments, the walled city of Dubrovnik has few equals in Europe. It's no wonder it is frequently seen on the silver screen. The city's sophisticated seafood eateries are well worth splashing out in, and the nation's boutique wine and beer scene is eloquently showcased in Dubrovnik's growing number of chic, open-air bars. Quaint passenger-only ferries chug their way around the unspoiled Elaphite Islands, while sun-soakers head for the beaches of sandy Lopud and rocky Sveti Jakov.

Best for
Soaking up history, screen-worthy scenes and beaches

Home to
Dubrovnik, Mljet National Park

Experience
The sunset over the Adriatic from the summit of Mount Srđ

PAGE 80

SPLIT AND
CENTRAL DALMATIA

Split is one of the great Mediterranean cities, brimming with both historical sights and the bustle of contemporary life. It's certainly unique, with the 3rd-century palace of Roman Emperor Diocletian forming the very heart of the modern city. Accessible from Split by ferry, the islands of Hvar, Brac, Vis and Korčula attract the well-heeled with their quaint fishing villages, mouthwatering cuisine, quiet pebbly coves and outstanding wines, not forgetting their outdoor nightlife.

Best for
Island-hopping and traditional Dalmatian food

Home to
Split, Hvar, Vis, Trogir, Korčula

Experience
Gambolling dolphins by catching one of the early morning ferries between Split and Korčula

$\rightarrow$

PAGE 116

ZADAR AND NORTHERN DALMATIA

From cities steeped in history and culture to the rocky canyons and cascading waters of national parks, Northern Dalmatia has it all. Ultra-hip Zadar and stylish Šibenik attract the crowds thanks to their mix of medieval fortresses, cutting-edge museums and urban landscape art. Both make great bases from which to explore stunning natural sights in the Med, such as the Kornati Islands and the Krka National Park. Those looking to take a break from sightseeing can chill on its plethora of beaches.

Best for
Roaming castle ramparts, urban art and national parks

Home to
Zadar, Šibenik, Kornati National Park, Krka National Park

Experience
Swimming in freshwater pools below the waterfalls of Skradinski Buk

PAGE 146

ISTRIA

In Istria, chic cosmopolitan coastline segues into a beautiful green interior dotted with ancient walled towns. Established resorts like Rovinj and Poreč combine evocative medieval town centres with modern complexes. The port city of Pula contains an unmissable Roman relic in the shape of its fabulous amphitheatre. Just inland, hilltop settlements like Motovun and Grožnjan loom above misty valleys famed for their truffle-bearing forests. Foodies flock here for the region's irresistible traditional cuisine.

Best for
Fortified hilltop towns, Roman ruins and truffles

Home to
Pula, Brijuni National Park, Euphrasian Basilica

Experience
The flavour of local truffle-flavoured dishes in traditional taverns and inns

KVARNER AREA

The island-scattered gulf of Kvarner is a place of compelling contrasts. At its heart stands Rijeka, a gritty post-industrial city that has reinvented itself as a cultural hub. Leafy Lošinj is the pick of the islands, while the medieval town of Krk and the beaches of Rab provide additional excuses for island-hopping. Adventurers head for Plitvice Lakes to traverse the park's snaking walkways and feel the cooling spray of thundering waterfalls. Not forgetting the food. Kvarner's modern take on Adriatic cuisine is best tasted in the restaurants of Opatija, where famously succulent shrimps reigns supreme.

Best for
Fresh shrimps, waterfalls and family-friendly beaches

Home to
Rijeka, Krk, Rab, Plitvice Lakes National Park, Lošinj

Experience
A sunset walk along the luxurious white sand beaches of Rab island

→

PAGE 196

ZAGREB

A central European city with a Mediterranean soul, Croatia's capital mixes Austrianate architecture with a southern European appetite for outdoor living. Celebrated for its pavement cafés, street festivals and abundant green spaces, it's a year-round attraction whose cultural life and nightlife scene never really let up. Above all, it's a city in which to take a break from the sightseeing treadmill and savour urban life without the rush: chill out in Gornji Grad (Upper Town), stroll the city's parks, and browse the many traditional markets.

Best for
Museums and galleries, café culture, nightlife and craft beer

Home to
Gallery of Old Masters, Museum of Broken Relationships

Experience
Saturday morning "špica", when pavement cafés are crammed with locals meeting to socialize over coffee

CENTRAL AND NORTHERN CROATIA

The tone of inland Croatia is delightfully rural, with a picturesque array of villages and towns scattered over its green landscape. The gently undulating terrain is celebrated for its hilltop-hugging castles, whitewashed churches and tumbledown villages. When it comes to urban highlights, Varaždin is a perfectly preserved Baroque town, while Krapina is home to a state-of-the-art museum on evolution. Food is on the hearty side, with meat and game weighing down restaurant tables.

Best for
Fairy-tale castles, meat dishes and a flavour of rural life

Home to
Varaždin, Karlovac, Krapina

Experience
The indulgent samoborska kremšnita, a wobbly vanilla slice that's a speciality of Samobor

EASTERN CROATIA

Carpeted with fields of corn and sunflowers, and dotted with pastel-coloured villages, Eastern Croatia is enchanting. Many of its settlements are steeped in history. Regional capital Osijek is built around the Tvrđa, a fortified Habsburg military settlement that is more or less in its original state. Further east is quaint riverside Vukovar, where the Vučedol Museum showcases local prehistory in spectacular multi-media style. It's also an area of great beauty, from the wildfowl-teeming wetlands of Kopački Rit to the paprika-growing villages of the Baranja.

Best for
Nature and spicy paprika-laden stews

Home to
Osijek, Kopački Rit Nature Park

Experience
Wild swimming off the sandy Danube shore

←

1 The walls of Dubrovnik, fringing the Adriatic.

2 Wandering through the Old Town.

3 Rector Palace pillars.

4 Fish dish at Proto.

Croatia brims with travel possibilities, from two-day tours around its bigger cities to grand odysseys exploring the country's dazzling coastline. These itineraries will help you to chart your own course through this vibrant country.

3 DAYS

In Dubrovnik

Day 1

Morning Rise early before the crowds descend on Dubrovnik's Old Town and join a tour of the perfectly preserved medieval walls (p66). Follow this with a stroll along the Stradun (p68), the Old Town's main street and the site of countless cafés – perfect for morning coffee and a spot for people-watching. At the eastern end of Stradun, the Church of St Blaise (p68) honours the city's patron saint; visit the nearby Dominican Monastery (p69) for quiet cloisters and Renaissance paintings.

Afternoon Enjoy a traditional Croatian lunch at Kopun (p71) before calling in at the former Rector's Palace (p69), home to an impressive collection of paintings and furniture. Also nearby is the Cathedral (p69), its treasury packed full of intriguing relics, plus some of the Old Town's most atmospheric alleyways. A stroll here is a lovely way to while away the afternoon.

Evening Sample fusion cuisine at Azur (www.azurvision.com) before relaxing with a glass or two at D'Vino (p67), one of the wine bars hidden in the Old Town's alleys.

Day 2

Morning
Grab your swimmers (you'll need them later) and start the day with a few hours at the Museum of Modern Art (p71), an impressive collection housed in a stunning waterside mansion.

Afternoon Buy a quick bite from Babić Bakery (Ul Frana Supila 2) before taking a boat across to the gorgeous island of Lokrum (p70), the site of a ruined monastery, botanical gardens and countless idyllic coves, perfect for an afternoon dip. Return to the mainland and check out the medieval Lazareti quarantine buildings (p70).

Evening Ride the cable car to Mount Srđ (p70) in the early evening and stay to catch the dramatic sight of the sun sinking over the Islands. Finally, treat yourself to a slap-up feast at Proto (p71) before joining the locals at Buža Bar (p67)

Day 3

Morning Begin a day of island-hopping by calling at Gruž market (Obala Stjepana Radića 21) to stock up on fresh picnic fare. Catch the local ferry to Suđurađ on the island of Šipan (p79) and set off on foot to explore the lush vegetation and ancient buildings of the interior. There are plenty of shaded spots to eat your picnic if it's a hot day.

Afternoon Catch the ferry from Suđurađ to the tranquil island of Lopud (p79) and head uphill to the fortress for a fantastic panorama of the coast. Continue eastwards to Šunj Bay and enjoy a paddle before returning to Dubrovnik.

Evening Dine on refined Adriatic fare at Amfora (www.amforadubrovnik.com), found opposite Dubrovnik's ferry landing, before heading up the street for a beer or two at the Dubrovnik Beer Company taproom (www.dubrovackapivovara.hr).

←

1 Zagreb illuminated at dusk.

2 Shopping for books at one of Zagreb's many markets.

3 Museum of Contemporary Art.

4 Vaulting of the Cathedral of the Assumption of the Blessed Virgin Mary.

3 DAYS

In Zagreb

Day 1

Morning Walk from Trg bana Jelačića, the perpetually busy central square, to the Neo-Gothic Cathedral (p202), with its trademark twin-towers. Here you'll find crowds of buyers and sellers jostling at Dolac, Zagreb's colourful fruit-and-veg market. A short uphill stroll brings you to a well-preserved quarter of Baroque houses and churches, plus the thought-provoking Museum of Broken Relationships (p212). Enjoy a light lunch in its classy bistro.

Afternoon Take a picture of the Church of St Mark (p206) and its iconic tiled roof before heading for the City Museum (p204) for an insight into Zagreb's eventful history. Scale the Tower Lotrščak (p207) and admire its impressive views of the city skyline. From here descend to Ilica, the main shopping street. Take a look at the murals of the Art Park (p212) before strolling through Grič Tunnel (p213).

Evening Enjoy the night-time buzz of Tkalčićeva (p203), an energetic strip of bistros, bars and pavement cafés.

Day 2

Morning Walk south from the main square to the Archaeological Museum (p210), where you can gaze on the timeless faces of Egyptian mummies. The nearby Gallery of Old Masters (p200) is the city's premier collection of European paintings. Frequent food festivals are held in the gardens of nearby Strosmayerov trg; otherwise, Teslina and Masarykova streets are lined with tempting bistros.

Afternoon Begin the afternoon with the pretty Trg Hrvatske Republike, home to the Croatian National Theatre (p208) before admiring the fantastic array of furnishings and ceramics at the Museum of Arts and Crafts (p209). Return towards the main square via Cvjetni trg or "Flower Square", pausing for coffee or an aperitif at one of its many cafés.

Evening Enjoy a Croatian meal at Vinodol (p203) before returning to Cvijetni trg for a post-prandial drink.

Day 3

Morning Take a tram westward towards the woodland delights of Maksimir Park (p211), a beautiful green space offering plenty of opportunities for a leisurely walk and a coffee or ice cream. Head north for more fresh air at Mirogoj Cemetery (p211), with its rich variety of memorial sculptures, before returning to the city centre

Afternoon For a late lunch, sample global bistro fare at Mundoaka (p203) near the main square. Then take a tram south of the river to the Museum of Contemporary Art (p210), a great place to ponder the ambiguities of Croatian modern culture.

Evening Treat yourself to some Japanese-Adriatic fusion at Takenoko (p203) before taking in some live music at one of Zagreb's many jazz bars.

7 DAYS
In the Northern Adriatic

Day 1

Wander the cobbled streets of chic Rovinj *(p161)*, Istria's most charming seaside town, with its well-preserved medieval centre and quirky gallery scene, before enjoying a leisurely lunch in one of the numerous seafood restaurants. Walk off lunch by heading south along the seafront to the Zlatni Rt forest park. If it's been a hot day, consider a dip at Lone Bay before drying off in the last of the sunshine. Settle in to one of the bars along ul svetog Križa for an evening of sipping cocktails beside the lapping waves.

Day 2

Pack your bag and drive to Vodnjan *(p162)* to view the holy relics in the parish church. Enjoy a good lunch at Vodnjanka *(www.vodnjanka.com)*, known for its hearty local fare, before continuing on to Pula *(p150)*. Make straight for the stellar Roman amphitheatre *(p154)* before scaling Kaštel hill to ramble over the fortifications. Alternatively, make for the dramatic rocky beaches on the outskirts of town and contemplate the waves. Eat in the centre, where restaurants are famous for their rich, regional cuisine.

Day 3

Take the coastal road from Pula to the sedate Habsburg-era resort of Opatija *(p188)*, where the fishing-village suburb of Volosko is perfect for a leisurely seafood lunch. Stroll along the Šetalište Franza Josefa, the shoreline path that leads past many of Opatija's belle-époque hotels. The best place for a swim is the pebbly beach at Ičići, midway between Opatija and Lovran. Wind down with an evening of quality Croatian wine and nibbles at Food & Wine Bar Ganeum *(Stari Grad 5)*, in Lovran.

Day 4

It's a short journey from Opatija to Rijeka *(p174)*, leaving most of the morning free to explore the northern Adriatic's biggest metropolis. Check out the exhibitions at the Museum of Modern and Contemporary Art before taking in the colours and aromas of the city market. The streets beside the market are full of inexpensive bistros for lunch. Catch a local bus or walk to Trsat *(p176)*, the hilltop castle that rewards visitors with sweeping views. Relax over

① Pula's Roman amphitheatre.

② Sunrise over Rovinj.

③ Boats in Mali Lošinj harbour.

④ Walking in Plitvice Lakes National Park.

⑤ Colourful houses in Vodnjano.

coffee in one of Trsat's cafés before walking down to Konoba Nebuloza *(www.konoba nebuloza.com)*, with its imaginative menu of local and global seafood.

Day 5

Catch the ferry from Brestova just south of Opatija to Porozina on the bare, tawny-coloured island of Cres *(p188)*. Enjoy the scenic drive down the spine of Cres island, with sweeping maritime views on all sides. Stop off in Cres Town for a quick stroll and lunch in one of the shoreline restaurants. Rejoin the road from Cres Town to Mali Lošinj *(p186)*. Arrive in time for a leisurely amble round the picturesque harbour. Mali Lošinj's fantastic Apoxyomenos Museum is often open late. Conclude with a meal and drinks in one of the harbourside eateries.

Day 6

Retrace your steps along the road from Lošinj to Cres, and take in the stunning views. Cross from Cres to the stark, grey island of Krk *(p178)* via the Merag-Valbiska ferry. Continue to medieval Krk Town in

time for a lunch of home-made pasta at one of the many local restaurants. Roam the alleys of Krk Town, taking time to examine the intricate metalwork on show at the Cathedral Treasury. By late afternoon you'll be ready for the beach; there's a pleasant stretch of pebble just west of town, and a rocky stretch to the east. Grab an ice cream and stroll around the harbour before choosing one of the outdoor bars just outside the Old-Town gates.

Day 7

Get back on the ferry, this time destined for Rab *(p182)*, and grab breakfast in one of Rab town's local restaurants. Spend the morning on the sandy Lopar peninsula, enjoying the popular Veli Mel beach or the quieter coves to the north. Rab's narrow cobbled streets are perfect for a stroll, followed by dinner and drinks on the town square. If you're feeling adventurous, and want to extend your trip, catch the ferry to Jablanac and continue on to Plitvice Lakes National Park, Croatia's most dramatic lakeland landscape.

→

1 Waterfall in
Krka National Park.

2 Congregating at Zadar's
Sea Organ.

3 Traditional Croatian fare.

4 Boats at Skradin.

2 WEEKS

In Dalmatia

Day 1

Start by roaming dynamic Zadar (p120), strewn with Roman monuments as well as bold new public artworks, such as the Sea Organ (p124). Lunch at Pet Bunara (p120) and go on to explore the city's UNESCO fortifications at Queen Jelena Madijevka Park (p125). Take a dip at Kolovare beach, or relax in one of the waterside cafés, before an evening stroll along the promenade – the sunsets here are spectacular. End up at Greeting to the Sun, the art installation that glows at night (p124).

Day 2

Take a boat trip to the Kornati National Park (p134) and spend the morning on deck, marvelling at the views of the mainland and Adriatic islands. A seafood lunch in one of the Kornati-island restaurants will likely be laid on. Enjoy a swim in crystalclear Kornati waters before taking the boat back to Zadar. End the day by putting your feet up with a craft beer or a cocktail at Zadar's legendary Garden Lounge (p123).

Day 3

Follow the coast road southeast to Šibenik (p128), pausing at pretty Lake Vrana (p144), and lunch on pasta at one of Šibenik's shoreline restaurants. Amble the narrow stepped alleys of medieval Šibenik, visiting the stunning Cathedral of St James (p132) before climbing towards the Fort of St Michael (p130), which has lovely views. If there's time, the Barone Fortress (p130) is worth a trip. Be sure to book dinner at Michelin-starred Pelegrini (p129).

Day 4

Drive or catch a bus from Šibenik to Skradin, the entrance point to the spectacular Krka National Park (p136). Don't forget your swimming costume; bathing beside the waterfalls of Skradinski buk is a must. Follow boardwalk trails beside the park's rushing cataracts and visit its old watermills. If time allows, take one of the boat trips into the park's lakes and canyons. Skradin has options for an evening meal.

Day 5

Travel down the coast to Trogir (p98), pausing at the lively peninsula town of Primošten (p140) for a moment of chill on the beach. Wander aimlessly through labyrinthine Trogir and don't miss the town's celebrated Cathedral (p98). Sample *pašticada* (meat stewed with prunes) in one of the local restaurants before sipping cocktails on the waterfront.

Day 6

It's only a short distance from Trogir to Split (p84) but break your journey at the Roman city of Salona (p106), where ruins lie scattered across vineyards and olive groves. On arrival in Split make straight for the Roman palace that now forms the centre of the modern city and can keep you occupied for hours. An early evening paddle at Bačvice beach (p91) will be the ideal prelude to a night in the cafécrammed alleyways of Split's old centre.

$\rightarrow$

Day 7

Linger over a coffee on Split's waterfront before catching a ferry to Supetar on Brač (p110). Admire Supertar's pretty fishing harbour and then head across the island's interior to Bol on the south coast. Walk along Bol's lovely waterside promenade, shaded by towering pine trees, to Zlatni rat, a photogenic spit of shingle jutting into the Adriatic. Seafood aplenty awaits on Bol's harbourfront; after dinner, check what's on at the open-air cinema perched spectacularly above the harbour.

Day 8

Catch a catamaran from Bol to Jelsa on the island of Hvar (p92) and soak up the small-town charm with a coffee in Jelsa's square. Drive or catch a bus to Hvar Town (p94), arriving in time for a quick lunch. Make your way to the string of rocky beaches to the west of the harbour for a dip or a kip. Spend late afternoon climbing to the hill-top fortress above town, and soak up the views of the coast and its scattering of green islets. Reserve a table at welcoming Macondo (www.macondo. com.hr).

Day 9

A coffee on Hvar's yacht-filled harbour is a must before setting off for Stari Grad (p92), a soulful town of stone houses, narrow streets and fishing boats. Visit the Renaissance mansion of Petar Hektorović for an insight into how Hvar nobles once lived, and study the story of Stari Grad's ancient founders in the town museum. Enjoy a drink in one of the harbourfront bars. If you're in the mood for open-air partying, make for Carpe Diem Beach (p95) for a night of DJs and cocktails.

Day 10

On some days of the week you can catch a direct catamaran from Hvar Town to the island of Vis (p96). Otherwise take a ferry back to Split and then travel on to Vis in the afternoon. Strolling along Vis Town's seafront to the suburb of Kut is one of the most gorgeous shoreline walks in all of Croatia. If you still have the legs, climb up to the King George IV Fort on the opposite side of the bay, with its beautiful courtyard café-restaurant and charming museum. Relish well-earned

1. Ferry crossing the water, Korčula.
2. Split lit up at dusk.
3. A beach on Marinkovac island near Hvar.
4. Cookies at Cukarin, Korčula.
5. Dinner with a view in Bol, on the island of Brač.

sustenance at Pojoda (p97), under the shade of the orange trees on its charming patio, or at any other seafood restaurant in Vis Town.

Day 11

Cross the island to Komiža (p96), the main jumping-off point for excursions to the intoxicating Biševo cave. Make an early start: Biševo is busy and there are often queues. Stroll Komiža's harbour or spend the afternoon in Kamenica Bay, a lovely beach just to the south of town. Splash out on a lobster meal at Jastožera (p96) before returning to Vis Town for a nightcap.

Day 12

Travelling from Vis to Korčula (p102) likely involves a catamaran or ferry to Split in the morning, and then again from Split to Korčula in the afternoon. When you arrive, take a stroll around Korčula Town, checking out the Tintoretto altarpiece in the Cathedral before a stroll around Korčula's battlements. Feast on seafood at rooftop Adio Mare (www.konobaadio mare.hr).

Day 13

Take an excursion boat to the island of Mljet, home to the lakes and forests of the Mljet National Park (p74). Hire a bike here and pedal to the turquoise Veliko Jezero lake, where there are snack bars and a pebbly beach. Join a boat trip to the mysterious monastery, cast in the middle of the lake, before taking a dip and returning to Korčula. Laze away the rest of the day on one of the glorious shingle beaches north of Pupnat. Back in Korčula Town, climb the Zakerjan Tower to the rooftop Massimo cocktail bar (Šetalište Petra Kanavelića).

Day 14

Stock up on pastries and sweets at Korčula's famed patisserie Cukarin (www.cukarin.hr) before embarking on the sea voyage to Dubrovnik (p66), enjoying stunning views of the South Dalmatian coast. Arrive in Dubrovnik ready to knit together some of the ideas contained in the itinerary on p22.

Beach Babies

Croatia's long sunny days and warm, emerald waters draw families to its beaches. Fine pebbles beaches such as those in Bol on Brač *(p110)*, in Baška on Krk *(p179)*, and the likes of Brela *(p106)* on the Makarska Riviera are ideal for kids, or better still sandy stretches like Paradise beach in Lopar *(p183)* on Rab. All of these have sun-beds and parasols to hire. Little feet can be sensitive, so it's advisable to buy water shoes for sharp pebbles and rocks.

→

Families enjoying the blue, shallow waters of a beach on Rab, Kvarner

CROATIA FOR
FAMILIES

Croats generally adore children, and their relaxed way of life means Croatia is a brilliant destination for families. Kids can enjoy the great outdoors in summer, whether splashing around in the Adriatic or dancing at a carnival, while puppet shows and interactive museums are ideal for rainier days.

Festival Fun

Each summer, Šibenik *(p128)* hosts the two-week Šibenik Children's Festival, with concerts, plays, puppet shows and exhibitions, as well as educational workshops. Dubrovnik *(p66)*, Split *(p84)* and other seaside towns hold various summer festivals with outdoor cultural events suitable for all the family, while Rijeka *(p174)* and Samobor *(p222)* celebrate *karnival* with costumed processions, during Lent, in the lead up to Easter.

↑

A procession of carnival revellers parading through Rijeka, in Kvarner

Learning Through Play

Croats are big advocates of learning through play, so you'll easily find attractions that are captivating and educational. Budding scientists will love the Tesla Memorial Centre *(www. mcnikolatesla.hr)* in Smiljan and the Technical Museum *(www.tehnicki-muzej.hr)* in Zagreb, both holding demonstrations of Nikola Tesla's inventions. Augmented reality means you can time travel back to the 17th-century at Šibenik's Barone Fortress *(p130)* and at Ivana's House of Fairy Tales in Ogulin *(p223),* you can explore fairy tales, with interactive touch screen presentations and even a magic mirror.

← Mum and child learning how to pan for gold at the fascinating Technical Museum, in Zagreb

↑ Zip-lining over the spectacular Cetina gorge in Omiš, Dalmatia

Thrill-Seeking Teens

It's not just about the little ones; Croatia has plenty to keep teenagers amused, particularly when it comes to adventure sports *(p48).* Burn off steam windsurfing, sea-kayaking, scuba-diving, cycling, rafting and more, with professional instruction and organized tours to keep adventures fun and safe. You'll also find thrilling ziplines in the Cetina gorge near Omiš *(p113)* and near Baška *(p179)* on Krk. There are also adventure parks in Ćilipi near Dubrovnik *(www.cadmosvillage. com)* and in Barban near Labin *(www.glavanipark.com),* where the whole family can join a paintball fight or archery contests.

Did You Know?

Rijeka, Zadar and Split all have puppet theatres, and Zagreb hosts a puppet festival in September.

Hidden Treasures

Istria's undulating hills are planted with fruitful vineyards and olive groves. But the biggest surprises lies below your feet. Hidden underground, Baredine Cave *(p159)* is other-worldly, dripping with stalagmites and stalactites. The beautiful oak forests of the Mirna Valley, around Hum and Buzet *(p169)*, are hunting ground for Istria's culinary delight, *tartufi* (truffles).

$\rightarrow$

Stalactites protruding from mystical Baredine Cave, Istria

Did You Know?

At least 10 per cent of Croatia's land is made up of national parks and nature reserves.

CROATIA FOR
NATURAL BEAUTY

Croatia's landscape is one of contrasts. Dramatic rocky mountains and pastoral fields segue into the spectacular deep blue Adriatic Sea. These countless examples of natural beauty found all across the country can be seen from a boat, car or bike, or simply on foot.

Natives of Nature

Croatia isn't just home to Croats. In Kavarner, the mountains and pine forests of Risnjak National Park *(p190)* are inhabited by lynx, wolves and bears. Kuterevo's Velebit Sanctuary also looks after orphaned bears that would struggle in the wild *(p194)*.

↑ Looking out onto the snowy peaks of Risnjak National Park, Kvarner

Lush and Leafy

Away from the country's famous coastline is the flat, fertile plain of Slavonia, which typifies inland Croatia. Birds feed and nest in the trees of Kopački Rit Nature Park *(p242)* and Lonjsko Polje Nature Park *(p227)*. But the star of the show is Plitvice Lakes National Park *(p184)*, home to crashing waterfalls and colourful foliage.

$\longrightarrow$

Autumn colours in magical Plitvice National Park, and a family of deer in Kopački Rit *(inset)*

TOP 5 GREAT HIKES IN NATURE

Mount Medvenica, Zagreb
6 hours; fairly challenging. Woodland trails lead to 1,035-m (3,396-ft) high Sljeme, a favourite outing for nature lovers from the capital.

Opatija Seafront, Kvarner
3 hours; easy. Waterside walk from Volosko to Lovran and overlooking the Kvarner Gulf.

Anića Kuk, Paklenica National Park
4 hours; fairly challenging. On the lower slopes of Mountt Velebit, Anića Kuk is a sheer rocky outcrop affording magnificent views out over Dalmatia.

Vidova Gora, Brač
3 hours; fairly challenging. The highest peak on the Adriatic islands stands at 780 m (2,559 ft).

Mount Biokovo, Makarska
12 hours; challenging. Trails lead to the 1,762-m summit (5,781-ft).

↑ Photographing Dalmatia's beautifully green island of Mljet

Dynamic Dalmatia

Dalmatia isn't just about beaches. Wild and dramatic, the rugged limestone mountains backing the Adriatic coast attract hikers and free-climbers. Out at sea are the uninhabited rocky islets of Kornati National Park *(p134)* and Mljet National Park *(p74)*, with two interconnected saltwater lakes surrounded in dense forest.

A Stone's Throw

The archetypal Croatian beach is pebbly, slopes into the turquoise waters of the Adriatic, and is fringed by pine trees or tamarisks. Some of the best lie along the Makarska Riviera *(p112)*, notably in Brela *(p106)*, but pride of place is reserved for Croatia's most-photographed beach, the stunning Zlatni Rat, a fine pebble spit, in Bol on Brač *(p110)*.

→

A beach in Brela, Dalmatia, backed by the Biokovo mountain range

Did You Know?

You can get an all-over tan in Croatia thanks to a number of naturist beaches; these are marked "FKK".

CROATIA FOR
SUN WORSHIPPERS

Croatia has a treasure trove of beaches, particularly along the Dalmatian coast. The majority are pebble and rock, and offer great visibility for snorkelling and scuba diving, but there are a clutch of gorgeous sand beaches, and a number of urban beach options too.

A pretty, secluded beach on the Pelješac Peninsula in Dalmatia ↓

Build Sandcastles

Sandy beaches are fairly rare, but there are a number in Dalmatia, and a couple up the coast. Notable sandy beaches are: Rajska plaža (Paradise beach) in Lopar *(p183)* on Rab, Sabunike near Nin *(p142)*, Vela Przina in Lumbarda *(p102)* on Korčula, Saplunara on Mljet *(p74)*, and Šunj on Lopud near Dubrovnik *(p79)*.

Rocky Outcrops

Croatia's coastline is peppered with rocky beaches, perfect for finding a stony throne and burying your nose in a book. The more adventurous flock to Mala Kolombarica on the Premantura Peninsula, near Pula *(p150)*, which has an expanse of flat rocks and steep cliffs, popular for jumping from into the sea. In Dubrovnik *(p66)* Danče is equally rocky but less dramatic.

INSIDER TIP
Picigin

Join the locals on Bačvice beach in Split and play *picigin* (pronounced "pitseegin"). Five players stand in a circle in ankle-deep sea, and pass a ball randomly at high speed. The aim is to keep the ball dry. There are no rules – it's a game of pure fun.

← Sun setting over turquoise waters and a rocky outcrop on the Premantura Peninsula, Istria

TOP 5 CITY BEACHES

Banje, Dubrovnik
This pebble beach is found immediately outside Dubrovnik's City Walls, near Ploče Gate.

Bačvice, Split
A sandy beach in a sheltered bay, just a 10-minute walk from Diocletian's Palace.

Kolovare, Zadar
This pebble beach is a 10-minute walk south of Zadar's Old Town.

Lake Jarun, Zagreb
Swim in the capital at this artificial beach, a 20-minute tram ride south of the centre.

Copacabana, Osijek
On the north bank of the River Drava, opposite Tvrđa, you'll stumble across this sandy beach.

↑ Sun loungers lining a bathing deck on Mulini Beach in Rovinj, Istria

Bathing Decks

Traditional beaches aside, many of Croatia's large and modern seaside hotels have concrete bathing decks in place of natural beaches - perfect for those who just want to relax without travelling to a traditional beach. You'll find bathing decks across Croatia, but two of the best are Hotel Amfora's Bonj le Bain in Hvar Town *(p94)*, and Hotel Lone's Mulini Beach in Rovinj *(p162)*.

Kingly Kvarner

From Rijeka's port, hop on a speedy Jadrolinija catamaran to Mali Lošinj (p186), where 19th-century villas set in lush gardens overlook a deep sheltered bay. If you're on Krk (p178), which is joined to the mainland by a bridge, catch a ferry from Valbiska to the sandy beaches of Lopar (p183) on Rab, or sail to Merag on Cres (p188), with its mountains and seaward cliffs.

The charming Villa Hortensia in Mali Lošinj, in the Kvarner Area

CROATIA FOR
ISLAND
HOPPERS

It's hard to resist the call of the blissful islands speckling Croatia's coastline, from the northern reaches of Kvarner's islands down to the collection of islets in Southern Dalmatia. Ferries and catamarans run by state-owned Jadrolinija mean all are reachable and await exploration.

SAILING

The ultimate way to explore the islands is to charter a private boat. Rentals generally run one-week (Sat–Sat) and can be skippered or bareboat (without a skipper, but one of your crew will need to have a licence). This gives you the freedom to plan your own itinerary. Top charter bases are marinas in Split, Zadar and Dubrovnik.

Sailing Southern Dalmatia

From Dubrovnik you can make day trips to the idyllic Elaphite Islands (p79). Alternatively, catch a catamaran to distant Lastovo (p115), with its sole settlement hidden inland, away from pirates. Catamarans also run to the turquoise lakes of Mljet (p74) and to Split (p84), with stops at Korčula (p102) and Hvar (p92).

→ Blue, tranquil waters surrounding Hvar Town on Hvar island

↑ The tranquil coast-
line around Dugi Otok,
in Northern Dalmatia

Navigating Northern Dalmatia

Explore the Zadar archipelago, taking a Jadrolinija ferry from
Zadar *(p120)* to the sleepy islets of Ist, Molta or Premuda, or head
to remote Dugi Otok *(p138)*, a rocky island and home to Telašićica
Nature Park. Here you'll find a therapeutic salt lake and steep
cliffs rimming a deep blue bay, much loved by yachters. If your
next destination is Istria, catch
a Mia Tours catamaran
from Zadar to Pula
(p150), which stops
at places such as
Silba *(p140)* and
Lošinj *(p186)*.

> 💬 INSIDER TIP
> ## Lighthouses
>
> Fancy having an entire
> island to yourself?
> Company Plovput offers
> 11 lighthouses to rent
> (generally Sat–Sat) along
> the coast, several on
> rocky islets, far from the
> mainland *(www.light
> houses croatia.com)*.

Cruising Central Dalmatia

Split's busy port sees regular
Jadrolinija car ferries running
to nearby islands. Catamarans
also head direct to trendy
Hvar Town *(p94)*, with its
luxurious waterside hotels
and hip beach bars, and to Bol
on Brač *(p110)*, home to the
fantastic Zlatni Rat beach.
There is also the fast Krilo
catamaran from Split to
Dubrovnik, covering the most
beautiful route in Dalmatia's
waters; it makes stops at Hvar
Town, Korčula Town *(p104)*,
and Pomena on Mljet *(p74)*.

↑ Yachts moored in a harbour
on Brač, and a boat sailing from
Hvar into the sunset *(inset)*

Don't Stop the Music

Croatia's clubs famously party well into the night. In Zagreb, international guest DJs play electronic dance music at mega-clubs Aquarius *(Aleja Matije Ljubeka 19)* and Boogaloo *(Ul grada Vukovara 68)*. Club events ramp up in summer, particularly along the coast. Zrće beach in Novalja *(p193)* has a great summer line-up at Aquarius *(www.aquarius.club)*, Kalypso *(www.kalypso-zrce.com)* and Papaya *(www.papaya.com.hr)*. In Dubrovnik, Revelin Club *(www.clubrevelin.com)* plays dance music in a medieval tower, while Carpe Diem Beach *(p95)* on Hvar is famed for its parties.

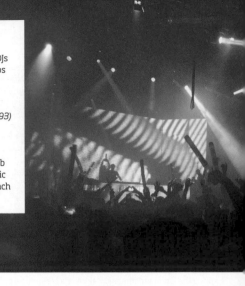

→

DJ Fedde Le Grand playing to crowds at Aquarius, Zagreb

CROATIA
AFTER DARK

Come sunset, hot summer days turn into balmy summer nights, and many Croats head out for a mellow evening below the stars. Aside from its late-night bar and café scene, Croatia offers a lively programme of gigs, parties concerts and cultural events. The question is, where to begin?

Café Culture

In the pedestrian-only old towns of Dubrovnik *(p66)*, Split *(p84)* and Zadar *(p120)*, cafés spill onto paved squares, cobbled alleys and palm-lined promenades during the summer months. Expect outdoor tables, flickering candles, sun-tanned patrons and chilled drinks. Bars are generally open to 1 or 2am at weekends.

→

A late-night café buzzing with patrons in Dubrovnik

 INSIDER TIP
Summer Cinema

Ljetno Kino (summer cinema) sees open-air screenings (mainly in English) at Bačvice in Split, Tuškanac in Zagreb and Slavica in Dubrovnik *(www.kinomediteran.hr)*.

Festival Feeling

It's not just about club music and pricey cocktails. Summer festivals in Croatia's seaside cities encompass classical music, jazz, opera, theatre and dance, frequently staged in truly unique settings. Highlights include Shakespeare at Lovrijenac Fortress *(www.dubrovnik-festival.hr)* in Dubrovnik, the only English theatre festival in south-eastern Europe. In Split, Splitsko Ljeto *(www.splitsko-ljeto.hr)* sees opera performed on the atmospheric setting of the palace's Peristyle *(p85)*. The Klapa Festival *(www.fdk.hr)* in Omiš showcases *klapa* (Dalmatian plainsong), while laid-back Fisherman's Nights on the islands are celebrated with barbecued sardines, local wine and music.

← Fire eaters performing at a festival in Biograd na Moru, Dalmatia

TOP 4 MUSIC FESTIVALS

IN Music, Zagreb
Ⓦ inmusicfestival.com
Alternative rock, with big names such as the Pixies, David Byrne and Nick Cave, at Zagreb's Lake Jarun.

Hideout, Novalja
Ⓦ hideoutfestival.com
Electronic music festival on Zrće beach in Novalja on Pag island.

SunceBeat, Tisno
Ⓦ suncebeat.com
Disco, house and techno music at The Garden in Tisno.

Outlook, Tisno
Ⓦ outlookfestival.com
Underground dance, garage, dubstep, hip hop and reggae at the Garden Resort in Tisno.

Concerts in the Capital

When it comes to live rock and indie concerts, Croatia's capital is king. From autumn to spring, Zagreb *(p196)* hosts national musicians at alternative venues, such as Tvornica *(www.tvornicakulture.com)* and Močvara *(www.mochvara.hr)*, while mainstream bands perform at Arena Zagreb *(www.zagrebarena.hr)*. Spaladium Arena in Split *(p84)* is also great for gigs *(www.spaladiumarena.hr)*.

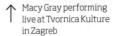

↑ Macy Gray performing live at Tvornica Kulture in Zagreb

Public Art

Croatia has a number of free, modern art installations in its historic cities. On the seaside promenade in Zadar, the harmonic Sea Organ and dazzling Greeting to the Sun *(p124)* are both innovative works by local architect Nikola Bašić. Further north in Pula's industrial port, five cranes – called the Lighting Giants – are bathed in multi-coloured light every day at sunset.

→

Enjoying the colourful Greeting to the Sun installation in Zadar

CROATIA
WITH A
DIFFERENCE

Croatia has beaches, historic cities and adventure sports galore, but those who want to see the country in a different way will find plenty of options to intrigue. Unique museums, stunning public art installations and imaginative hotels mean Croatia can feel like a playground for visitors of all ages.

Zany Zagreb

The dynamic Zagreb has become a top tourist destination. The conceptual Museum of Broken Relationships *(p212)* does as it says on the tin; each object in its collection is given meaning by the significance it held to its donor in a failed love story. When it comes to the city's architecture, award-winning buildings include the turf-roofed Karlovac Aquatika *(www.aquariumkarlovac. com)*, a fresh-water aquarium next to River Korana, and the impressive Arena Zagreb *(www.zagrebarena.hr)*, built for the 2009 World Men's Handball Championships.

←

Exhibits displayed at Zagreb's poignant Museum of Broken Relationships

SHOP

Life According to KAWA
This concept store sells souvenirs with a difference. Splash your cash while also supporting local designers.

⬛F7 ⬛Hvarska 2, Dubrovnik
☎(20) 696 958

Croatian Design

Kuna burning a hole in your pocket? Croatia has a wealth of young designers to tempt you. Zagreb is great for one-off items, such as sunglasses at Sheriff&Cherry *(www.sheriffandcherry.com)*. On Hvar, Isola *(www.isolashop.com)* makes beautiful ties. More designs stylish beachwear for women *(www.morebeachwear.com)* and Baggiz sells leather backpacks *(www.komad.com)*.

← Window shopping outside a boutique store in Korčula Town

Hip Hideaways

Rovinj excels at stylish accommodation. Hotel Lone *(p163)* is Croatia's only official Design Hotels while Hotel Adriatic *(www.maistra.com)* is a 19th-century building with modern artworks. One Suite Hotel *(www.onesuitehotel.com)* just outside of Dubrovnik and D-Resort in Šibenik *(p131)* are both ultra-cool. On a tiny island nearby is back-to-nature retreat Obonjan *(www.obonjan-island.com)*. Croatia's hippest hostel is Zagreb's Swanky Mint *(p209)*.

↑ Stunning, contemporary interior of Hotel Lone, in Rovinj

From Land and Sea

Locals in Kvarner claim their *škampi* (shrimps) to be the best *(p191)*, while seafood in Dalmatia is generally excellent; head to Kamerlengo *(p99)* in Trogir and Pojoda *(p97)* in Vis. A fish dish is, naturally, best enjoyed with a sea view, and the coast offers countless options. Croatia also dishes up delicious meat. Cres *(p188)*, Pag *(p140)* and Brač *(p110)* are all famed for their locally reared and succulent lamb.

→

Dining with a view on Krk island in the Kvarner Area

CROATIA FOR
FOODIES

Croatian cuisine is heavily influenced by historic empires that once occupied the region, particularly Austro-Hungary and Venice. Each region has its own flavours – from paprika seasoning inland to seafood along the coast. Wherever you go, expect dishes prepared with local, seasonal produce.

Hungry for Austro-Hungarian

Let's not forget Austro-Hungarian flavours, in Central, Northern and Eastern Croatia. Dishes inspired by Central Europe include *Bečki odrezak* (Wiener schnitzel) and *gulaš* (goulash). In Slavonia, *kulen* (spicy salami with paprika) and *fiš paprika* (freshwater fish stewed in paprika) are favourites. Head to Gabrek 1929 *(p222)* and Vuglec Breg *(p231)* for hearty fare.

Traditional pots and smoky charcoal used for cooking meat ↑

Sweet Treats

Those with a sweet tooth are in for a treat. Rab *(p182)* is known for *Rapska torta,* a moreish cake made with Maraschino liquor and almonds. Dubrovnik *(p66)* specializes in *rožata,* which is akin to a crème caramel, and Samobor makes *Samoborska kremšnita (p223).* Croatians make festive *fritule* at Christmas, which resemble rum-flavoured doughnuts. Both sweet and savoury strudels can be found across the country all year round.

 INSIDER TIP
Truffle Treasure

Truffles are an Istrian speciality, with woodland around Motovun *(p168)* and Buzet *(p169)* the most fruitful. Eateries in all price ranges serve truffle dishes, and you can buy jars of truffle sauces to take home. A great place to purchase truffle goods is Zigante *(www.zigante tartufi.com).* It also has a restaurant.

← Croatian fritters or *fritule,* typically coated in sugar and eaten at Christmas

 CITY FOOD MARKETS

Dolac Market, Zagreb
Under several historic structures you'll find butchers, fishmongers, fruit and vegetables.

Pula Market
Based in an elegant iron-and-glass building, dating from 1903.

Rijeka's Main Market
Near the port, Rijeka's *tržnica* (market) occupies three halls: one for meat, one for seafood, and another for dairy.

Pazar, Split
An open-air market with daily arrivals of fruit and veg cultivated on nearby islands.

↑ A waiter presenting an Italian-inspired dish in Šibenik, Dalmatia

Inspired by Italy

Mediterranean influences permeate Croatia's cuisine, and Italian refinement is particularly apparent with olive oil and pasta on many menus. In Istria, specialities such as *tartufi* (truffles), handmade *fuži* pasta, *rižot* (risotto), and *brodet* (fish stew) are inspired by Italy. You're spoiled for choice for restaurants but we've made some suggestions on p161.

Hollywood Heavyweights

Finding Croatia's scenery familiar? It's no surprise, given the country has starred in many modern movies. Some prefer to call Dubrovnik *(p66)* "King's Landing" as it was the backdrop for blockbuster TV series *Game of Thrones* (2011-19). *Star Wars: The Last Jedi* (2017) and *Robin Hood* (2018) were also filmed in the historic walled city. Surprisingly, although set in Greece, *Mamma Mia II* (2018) was shot on Vis *(p96)*, its fertile plains and crumbling buildings lending themselves to the silver screen. Rade Šerbedžija (1946–) is Croatia's most famous star, with *Eyes Wide Shut* (1999) and *Harry Potter and the Deathly Hallows* (2010) among his box office hits.

→

Lena Headey filming
Game of Thrones on
Dubrovnik's city walls

CROATIA FOR
INSPIRATION

Balkan beauty can be seen on cinema and TV screens the world over thanks to film-makers choosing Croatia as a movie set. The country has staged numerous blockbusters, and many visit to see the real-life locations of their favourite films and shows. Here, we pick some some inspirational highlights.

Tito and the Movies

President Tito famously loved Westerns. During the 1960's, when Croatia was part of Yugoslavia, a dozen films about Native American hero Winnetou were filmed in the rocky canyons of Paklenica National Park *(p143)*. Tito was also close friends with Richard Burton, who played Tito in the *Battle of Sutjeska* (1973). Elizabeth Taylor, Sophia Loren and Gina Lollobrigida, all visited Tito's presidential retreat on Brijuni *(p156)*. Although you can't visit the villa, there is an exhibition centre behind Hotel Karmen.

←

Richard Burton playing
Josip Broz Tito in
Battle of Sutjeska

Did You Know?
John Malkovich is of Croatian origin and he often holidays in Croatia.

TOP 3 FILMING LOCATIONS

Dubrovnik
The Old Town was the main filming location of King's Landing in the hit show *Game of Thrones*.

Pag
This island doubled as an arctic wasteland in Ridley Scott's TV drama *The Terror* (2021).

Rovinj
Action-comedy film *The Hitman's Wife's Bodyguard* (2021) was filmed in Rovinj, Rijeka, Zagreb and Karlovac.

↑ Jerome Flynn taking a break from filming *Game of Thrones*

🔍 HIDDEN GEM
Ulysses Theatre
Brijuni island *(p156)* welcomes an open-air theatre festival in the summer. Its 19th-century Fort Minor is used to stage plays by Shakespeare and giants of Ancient Greek drama. Founded by Croatian actor Rade Šerbedžija, it attracts stars such as Vanessa Redgrave and Ralph Fiennes. Tickets can be bought online or at the National Park Office, Fažana *(www.ulysses.hr)*.

↑ Pula Film Festival, staged in the city's spectacular Roman amphitheatre

Film Festivals
Croatia offers a fantastic showcase of film festivals, frequently set in unique settings. The start of the show is Pula Film Festival, which premiered in 1954. The one-week festival takes place in mid-July, set in the monumental Roman amphitheatre *(p154)*. Motovun Film Festival has attracted a number of celebs in years gone by. Held in the attractive Istrian hill-town of Motovun *(p168)* in late July, this is an intimate, five-day affair. Zagreb Film Festival, meanwhile, is a larger, one-week event held in early November in Croatia's cosmopolitan capital *(p196)*.

River Rafting

Nothing beats the thrill of negotiating a raft around rocky waters. In Dalmatia, the Cetina river near Omiš (p113) and the Zrmanja near Zadar (p120) have rapids and waterfalls, ideal for rafting and canyoning. In northern Croatia, the Mrežnica near Karlovac (p223) and the Kupa in the region of Gorski Kotar are popular rafting locations. Local providers organize trips.

A group rafting the boisterous waters of the Kupa River ↑

CROATIA FOR
THRILL SEEKERS

Dramatic and unspoiled, Croatia is a fantastic destination for adventure sports, both water-and land-based. Organized tours and lessons can be booked for just about everything, from cycling and rafting to windsurfing and diving. Croats themselves are outdoor enthusiasts and patient instructors.

TOP 5 SITES FOR DIVING

Baron Gautsch, Rovinj
The Adriatic's most impressive wreck, this Austrian passenger ship sank in 1914.

Mali Ćutin, Cres
An underwater canyon and sea wall with coral, sponges and schools of fish.

Katedrala Cave, Premuda
Several inter-connected caves, including a vast cupola-shaped hall with spectacular lighting.

Vodnjak, Hvar
An underwater crag, reached via a canyon of red gorgonians.

Mrkanjac, Cavtat
A sea wall and reef. Look out for electric rays, monkfish and lobsters.

Enjoying stunning scenery while kayaking along Croatia's coastline ↓

Kayak the Coastline

Kayaking is a superb way to explore Croatia's stunning coast. Organised tours range from half-day to one-week, notably around Dubrovnik's Elaphite Islands (p79) of Koločep, Lopud and Šipan. The Makarska Riviera (p112) and around the smaller islands near Zadar (p120) are also great settings.

↑ Kite- and windsurfers flying over the golden sands and blue waters of Brač

Harnessing the Wind

Admire Croatia from a different angle. Winds are optimum for surfing at Bol on Brač *(p110)* and Viganj on the Pelješac Peninsula *(p76)*, with gentle morning winds for beginners, and a stronger wind in the afternoon for experienced surfers. Kite-boarding is popular in the Neretva delta near Ploče.

> 🔍 HIDDEN GEM
> ### Rock Climbing
> Climbers should head for Paklenica National Park *(p143)*, which has more than 400 climbing routes, from single-pitch bolted routes to big-wall routes. The 350 m (1,148 ft) lime-stone Anića Kuk wall is the highlight

Get Pedalling

Croatia's varied landscape is perfect for cycling. A network of marked routes leads through gorgeous scenes, from the plains of Slavonia in Eastern Croatia, through the pine forests of Gorski Kotar at the top of the Kvarner Area, and over the limestone mountains of Dalmatia. The Parenza Cycle Route *(p168)* in Istria is also very pretty, passing through bucolic countryside and pretty villages. Bike hire and cycling maps are readily available, and specialist companies arrange tours.

↑ Cycling through the Ucka mountains, and stopping to admire a coastal view *(inset)*

Invigorating Rakija

Loved throughout the Balkans, *rakija* is a potent spirit infused with local herbs. Flavours include *travarica* (fennel, sage and juniper), *medovača* (honey), and biska (mistletoe). In and around Zadar *(p120)*, *maraschino* is made from marasca cherries, while on Vis *(p96) rogačica* uses carob pods. Something of a social ritual across all of Croatia, *rakija* is consumed as an aperitif and as a digestif.

$\rightarrow$

Line-up of various *rakija* bottles in Motovun, Istria

CROATIA
BY THE GLASS

Croatians enjoy a drink – whether it's a sociable morning coffee, a pre-prandial glass of wine, or a herbal digestif. They have history too – wine production dates back to the ancient Greeks and Romans, who introduced grapes, while beer came later under the 17th-century Habsburgs.

WINE TASTING

Croatia's repertoire of wines continues to grow and improve, and a wine tasting is a great way to support a business while trying local flavours. Wineries open to the public for tours generally begin with an introductory talk about the history of the winery and wine-making process, followed by a walk through the cellars. Afterwards, you'll sample several wines (whites first, then reds, and finally dessert wines) accompanied by local cheeses, olives and bread. Wineries often require you to reserve in advance. Some charge for tastings; others rely on you buying bottles.

Winning Wines

Dalmatia's red wines are made chiefly from Plavac and Mali Plavac grapes. A good place to sample Plavac is Vis, where fertile vineyards around Plisko Polje *(p97)* yield quality grapes. The Pelješac Peninsula *(p76)* is great for Mali Plavac wines. Korčula *(p102)* excels at white wines, with grapes for Pošip wine grown around Pupnat, and Grk around Lumbarda.

$\rightarrow$

Rows of fruitful vines beside the Dalmatian coast

Beer by the Barrel

Croatia has two market-leaders when it comes to mainstream beer, or *pivo*: Karlovačko, which is produced in Karlovac *(p223)*, and Ožujsko made in Zagreb *(p196)*. Pan, produced by Carlsberg, is also common. It's worth seeking out craft brews, particularly as the number of Croatian craft breweries is increasing. Zagreb has a burgeoning craft beer scene *(p204)*, with top brewers like Zmajska pivovara *(www. zmajska pivovara.hr)*. It's worth visiting their taproom for tasters. Across in Split *(p84)* you'll find LAB Split Craft Brewery *(www. lab-split.com)*, which has a handful of zesty pale ales.

←

An open bottle of Dalmation-brewed Pan lager, a member of the brewing empire of Carlsberg

TOP 3 CROATIAN CRAFT BEERS

LAB Barba Imperial IPA
Rated as Croatia's best beer, LAB Barba's Imperial IPA is a spicy pale ale from Split.

The Garden Vanilla and Chocolate Porter
One of several stouts from The Garden Brewery in Zagreb.

Nova Runda C4
This hoppy amber beer is brewed in Zabok, near Krapina, situated north of Zagreb.

↑ Street vendor selling healthy fruit juices

Thirst-Quenchers

Juices and cordials are popular in Croatia, as is Pipi, an orange drink in iconic retro packaging. Coffee is integral to Croatian culture. Zagreb *(p196)* in particular enjoys *špica* – the Saturday morning ritual of people-watching with a cup of coffee. Join the the tradition and grab a coffee along Tkalčićeva *(p203)*.

A YEAR IN
CROATIA

JANUARY

△ **Night of the Museums** (late Jan). Cultural institutions across the country throw open their doors for an evening of exhibitions, music and entertainment.

FEBRUARY

Feast of St Blaise (3 Feb). Dubrovnik honours its patron saint with religious processions, street fairs and plenty of outdoor merrymaking.

△ **Carnival** (weekend before Shrove Tuesday). A massive carnival parade featuring floats and costumed revellers takes over Rijeka's streets.

MAY

Feast of St Dujam (7 May). The protector of Split is honoured with a big outdoor Mass, a huge handicrafts market and an evening concert on the seafront.

△ **Subversive Festival** (mid-May). International festival of political theory, political films and political debate, in Zagreb.

JUNE

Mediterranean Film Festival (late Jun). New films from the across the Med, with popular outdoor screenings above Split's Bačvice beach.

△ **International Children's Festival** (late June). Film, theatre, music, workshops and supervised play in the squares of Šibenik's Old Town.

InMusic (late Jun). Croatia's prime rock-and-pop festival attracts brings top international names to the grassy banks of Zagreb's Jarun lake.

SEPTEMBER

Dimensions (early Sep). Leading festival of electronic music takes over a former Habsburg fortress near Pula. Opening-night concerts are held in Pula's amphitheatre.

△ **Buzet Saturday** (mid-Sep). The start of the truffle-hunting season is celebrated with music and feasting in the Istrian town of Buzet.

OCTOBER

△ **Feast of St Simeon** (8 Oct). A major day of pageantry in Dalmatia's Zadar when the gold-plated casket of St Simeon is paraded through the streets.

MARCH

△ **Zagrebdox** (late March). Zagreb's highly regarded festival of documentary films attracts some big international guests.

APRIL

△ **Easter** (Mar or Apr). The islands of Hvar and Korčula witness solemn processions on Good Friday, while Easter Sunday is the day for family get-togethers.

Tolerance Film Festival (mid-Apr). Films dealing with racism and human rights are shown in Zagreb, with an accompanying programme of workshops and concerts.

JULY

△ **Pula Film Festival** (mid-Jul). Croatia's oldest and most famous film festival sees screenings in the atmospheric Roman amphitheatre.

Dubrovnik Summer Festival (late Jul). A month-long celebration of theatre, music and dance, with many of the performances taking place in the city's historic palaces, squares and fortresses.

Rabska Fjera (late Jul). Medieval-themed fair in the town of Rab featuring food stalls, craft displays, crossbow tournaments and a lot of dressing up.

AUGUST

Sinjska Alka (early Aug). Centuries-old sporting challenge in Sinj, in which horseriders attempt to spear a small metal circle dangling above the track.

△ **Neretva Boat Marathon** (mid-Aug). Local crews row a variety of craft from the riverside town of Metković to the mouth of the river Neretva, cheered on by enthusiastic crowds.

Špancirfest (late Aug). Hugely enjoyable street festival featuring stalls, entertainers, concerts, exhibitions and activities for kids. Takes over the centre of Varaždin for a week.

NOVEMBER

△ **St Martin's Day** (11 Nov). The first new wine of the season is celebrated in towns and villages across northern Croatia.

Zagreb Film Festival (mid-Nov). One of the capital's most popular festivals, with a packed programme of shorts and features from award-winning international directors.

DECEMBER

△ **Advent** (all month) The pre-Christmas season sees Zagreb, Split and Dubrovnik taken over by street stalls, live music, and festive partying.

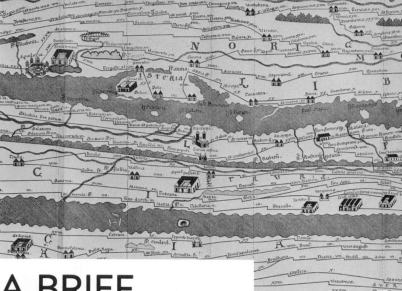

1

A BRIEF
HISTORY

Croatia has long been a point of contact between different worlds and cultures. Despite establishing an independent state in the early Middle Ages, the Croats spent long periods under foreign rule, and national independence was a hard-won affair.

Ancient Origins

The first inhabitants of Croatia are understood to be the Neanderthals, thanks to a hoard of 30,000-year-old Neanderthal bones discovered at Krapina, north of Zagreb, in 1899. The earliest signs of Homo sapiens in Croatia come from the Vela Spila cave on the island of Korčula, inhabited continuously for some 18,000 years. Croatia was an important crossroads of cultures during the Neolithic epoch, when the Danube valley around Vukovar supported a sophisticated population of agriculturalists. Ceramics from this period include the Vinkovci Orion, a decorated pot dated to around 2600 BC.

① Medieval map of the Balkans, based on roads of the Roman Empire. ↑

② Byzantine emperor Heraclius (575–641 BC).

③ The Neanderthal Museum in Krapina.

④ Queen Teuta of Illyria (c 231–227 BC) ordering the deaths of visiting Romans.

Timeline of events

50,000– 30,000 BC

Neanderthals occupy caves near Krapina

2600 BC

Neolithic culture flourishes in south-east Croatia, producing sophisticated earthenware like the Vinkovci Orion

384 BC

Ancient Greeks establish a colony at Stari Grad on Hvar

200 BC– 12 AD

Romans extend control over present-day Croatia

Illyrians and Romans

Some time after 1000 BC, tribal units emerged with an urbanized culture and wider Mediterranean contacts. Known collectively as Illyrians, and ruled over by Queen Teuta, they established cohesive states, such as the Histri in Istria and the Liburnians in the Kvarner Area. The Ancient Greeks established colonies on Vis, Hvar and Korčula in the 4th century BC, occasionally fighting the Illyrians for control. From the 2nd century BC the Romans were increasingly involved in keeping the peace and by the 1st century AD had absorbed all of present-day Croatia into their empire.

The Arrival of the Slavs

Although the Romans were rocked by invasions in the 4th and 5th centuries, the Adriatic coast preserved its Mediterranean culture. However, the 6th century saw an invasion by the Avars from central Asia. Emperor Heraclius invited a Slav tribe known as the Croats to help defend his territory. Migrating from lands north of the Black Sea, the Croats arrived at the same time as other Slav tribes who spoke similar dialects – tribes who would later become known as Serbs, Slovenes and Macedonians.

ROMAN REMINDERS

Croatia is peppered with reminders of Roman rule and you can walk in the footsteps of the ancient civilization. Surviving Roman remnants include the almost intact amphitheatre at Pula (p150), the ancient city of Salona (p106), and the imperial palace at Split (p84); the latter was built as a retirement home for Emperor Diocletian in 305.

81 AD

Construction of the Roman amphitheatre at Pula

550

Poreč's Basilica of St Euphrasius decorated with captivating mosaics

600–700

Slav tribes settle in southeastern Europe, laying the foundations of future Croatian and Serbian states

305

Roman Emperor Diocletian retires to the palace that still forms the centrepiece of present-day Split

The Croatian Medieval State

Croatian leaders gradually carved out autonomous states and converted to Christianity in the 8th century. Croatia's first internationally recognized king, Tomislav (910–928), consolidated the states and established a Croatian archbishopric at Split. Croatia's neighbours fought back, but kings Petar IV Krešimir (1058–75) and Zvonimir (1089–91) once again united the country under firm rule. Due to a shortage of male heirs, however, Croatia fell to the kings of Hungary, and dynastic union was confirmed in 1102. Croatia's autonomy gradually eroded as time went on.

Venice Versus Dubrovnik

With the decline of Byzantine power, Croatia's Adriatic coast was a bone of contention between the Venetians and Croats. Venetian rule was confirmed in 1409, but city-state Dubrovnik slipped out of Venetian control and emerged a major independent power. Both Dubrovnik and Venetian-controlled Dalmatia were open to the ideas of the Renaissance, with Hvar, Šibenik and Zadar centres of Humanism. Ottoman expansion threatened in the 15th and 16th centuries, and fortifications were built at Zadar and Šibenik.

↑ Sculpture of Tomislav, Croatia's first king, in Zagreb

Timeline of events

1091

The Croatian royal line dies out, leading to union with Hungary a few years later

1240

Master Radovan carves the Romanesque portal of Trogir Cathedral

1307

Opening of the Franciscan Monastery's pharmacy in Dubrovnik, the oldest still-working pharmacy in Europe

1409

Venetians extend control over Dalmatia

1493

The Ottomans defeat a Croatian-Hungarian army at Krbavsko Polje

Consolidation of Habsburg Power

Hungary and Eastern Croatia fell to the Ottoman Empire in 1526 and the unconquered Croatian territories turned to the Austrian Habsburg Empire. At the Battle of Sisak, in 1593, the Austrian-Croatians repelled a major Ottoman invasion. The Austrians won back Hungary and Eastern Croatia in the 17th century and re-settled the latter. Croatian nobles Petar Zrinski and Fran Kristo Frankopan were executed in 1671 for plotting against the Austrian court, depriving Croatia of aristocratic leadership.

Nineteenth-Century Croatian Revival

Napoleon defeated Venice and Dubrovnik in the early years of the 19th century, and he briefly ruled the Croatian Adriatic before it was absorbed by the Austrian Empire. The region experienced a cultural rebirth and a Croatian language was developed, over-riding regional dialects. Croatian Colonel Josip Jelačić fought for Croatian autonomy following the revolutions of 1848, but these hopes were dashed by the Austrians. After 1867, Inland Croatia found itself in the Hungarian-ruled half of the Habsburg Empire while most of the Adriatic coast remained in Austria.

1 *Allegory of the Battle of Sisak* by Hans von Aachen (1604).

2 *Arrival of Napoleon in Venice* by Giuseppe Borsato (19th century).

3 A 19th-century draw-ing of a Dalmatian woman.

Did You Know?

Epoch-defining inventor Nikola Tesla was born in the Croatian village of Smiljan in 1856.

1593
Austrian-Croatians resist Ottoman invasion at the Battle of Sisak

1667
A huge earthquake almost destroys Dubrovnik, leading to its reconstruction

1699
The Treaty of Karlowitz confirms the Austrian conquest of Eastern Croatia

1867
The Habsburg Empire is separated into Austrian- and Hungarian-administered halves; Croatian lands are divided between the two powers

A New State

When Austria-Hungary collapsed, in 1918, Croatia joined an independent kingdom of Slovenes, Croats and Serbs – renamed Yugoslavia. Enthusiasm for the new state quickly waned and tensions grew. Nazi Germany overran Yugoslavia in April 1941, creating quisling regimes. The right-wing regime Ustaše killed thousands of Serbs, Gypsies, Jews and Croats. Resistance came from a movement led by communist Josip Broz Tito (1892–1980), who wanted a federation of semi-autonomous republics.

Communist Yugoslavia

Tito emerged victorious in 1945 and set about establishing a one-party state. The early years of his rule were characterized by brutality. In 1948, Stalin expelled Yugoslavia from the Soviet bloc, he and Tito having had an uneasy alliance. Yugoslavian Communism became more liberal; Yugoslavs were allowed to travel and work abroad, and the coast was opened up to mass tourism. Tito's death led to increased instability. The rise of a National-Communist Serbian leader, Slobodan Milošević, forced Croatia to reconsider its relationship with Belgrade.

1 Josip Broz Tito in his Belgrade office, c 1946.

2 German soldiers advance on Yugoslavia, April 1941.

3 A photograph taken on 12 November 1991 shows the city of Dubrovnik in flames after a heavy bombardment by the Yugoslavian Federal Army.

4 Former president Kolinda Grabar-Kitarovićv speaking at the NATO Military Committee Conference in Split.

Timeline of events

1918
Croatia joins the new state of Yugoslavia following the collapse of Austria-Hungary

1941
Hitler's Germany attacks Yugoslavia and Croatia becomes a Nazi quisling state

1971
Liberal voices within the Croatian Communist party are silenced by the crackdown on the 'Croatian Spring'

1991
Fighting erupts between Croats and Serbs

PRESIDENT

4

The End of Yugoslavia

Free elections in 1990 brought the nationalist, pro-independence Croatian Democratic Union (HDZ) to power. A referendum on full independence was held on 19 May 1991, paving the way for a declaration of independence from Yugoslavia on 25 June. Areas with large Serbian populations declared unofficial autonomy from Zagreb, afraid that their rights would be at risk. Autumn 1991 saw the Yugoslav People's Army launch major offensives in eastern Croatia, and pockets under Serb control were ethnically cleansed of Croats. The war saw thousands die and hundreds of thousands flee. Dubrovnik was held under a seven-month siege.

Independent Croatia

In August 1995, land occupied by Serbs was liberated by the Croatian army and the country was largely unified under the Erdut Agreement. Membership of NATO and the EU confirmed Croatia's move to parliamentary democracy and membership of the western alliance. The 2008 financial crisis led to mass unemployment and a high rate of emigration. However, in recent years Croatia has enjoyed a period of peace and relative prosperity.

KOLINDA GRABAR KITAROVIĆ (1968-)

Croatia's former president is a figure of firsts. Elected in 2015, Grabar-Kitarović was the first woman elected since the multi-party elections. She was also Croatia's youngest ever president. Before the election, she was the first female Minister of Foreign Affairs and European Integration. In 2017, *Forbes* named her the world's 39th most powerful woman.

1995

Operation Storm brings the war in Croatia to an end

2009

Croatia joins NATO

2013

Croatia joins the European Union

2018

Croatia reaches the final of the FIFA World Cup

2020

Two deadly earthquakes strike Croatia, first in Zagreb and then in Petrinje

EXPERIENCE

The lively Trg Josip Jelačica Square, Zagreb

DUBROVNIK AND SOUTHERN DALMATIA

Relatively small but packed with enthralling sights, the walled town of Dubrovnik is one of the most visually breathtaking destinations in the Mediterranean. Bordered by rugged mountains and lush islands, it's a good base from which to explore the varied landscapes of Southern Dalmatia. Dubrovnik was for centuries an independent republic, breaking free from the control of Venice in 1358 and going on to prosper as a regional trading power. The governing aristocracy carefully divided up the offices of state between themselves, preventing the dominance of any one family or faction. Skillful diplomacy ensured good relations with both the Ottoman Empire and the Christian states of southern Europe. Seriously damaged by an earthquake in 1667, Dubrovnik was rebuilt by a city government with progressive ideas about social planning and public space. Damage inflicted by Serbian-Montenegrin besiegers during the Homeland War of 1991–5 was soon patched up, and a boom in tourism followed. Increased visitor numbers have not, however, dented the city's essential charm.

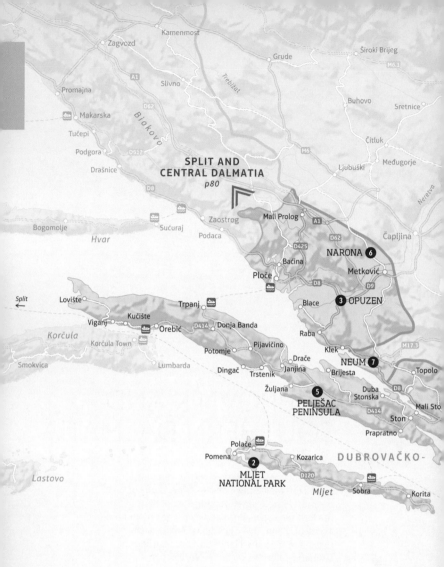

SPLIT AND
CENTRAL DALMATIA
p80

NARONA **6**

3 OPUZEN

NEUM **7**

5
PELJEŠAC
PENINSULA

2
MLJET
NATIONAL PARK

DUBROVAČKO-

*Adriatic
Sea*

**DUBROVNIK AND
SOUTHERN DALMATIA**

↙ *Bari*

DUBROVNIK AND SOUTHERN DALMATIA

Must Sees
① Dubrovnik
② Mljet National Park

Experience More
③ Opuzen
④ Trsteno
⑤ Pelješac Peninsula
⑥ Narona
⑦ Neum
⑧ Cavtat
⑨ Konavle
⑩ Sokol Grad
⑪ Elaphite Islands

↑ Looking out over the Old Town's roof-tops, Dubrovnik

❶ 🍴 🖥 🛍

DUBROVNIK

▲F7 ✈ **Čilipi, www.airport-dubrovnik.hr** 🚌 **Obala pape Ivana Pavla 11, 44A, www.libertasdubrovnik.hr** ⛴ **Harbour Master: (020) 418 988; Jadrolinija: www.jadrolinija.hr** 🛈 **Local: Brsalje (020) 312 011; Regional: Šipčine (020) 324 999; www.tzdubrovnik.hr**

Croatia's most famous city tells a fascinating story. According to Emperor Constantine Porphyrogenitus it was founded by fugitives from Roman Epidaurum (now Cavtat) in the 7th century. It came under Byzantine and Venetian rule and attained independence after 1382, when it became the Republic of Ragusa. It flourished artistically and benefited from new trade routes after the discovery of America. Following the devastating 1667 earthquake, the Old Town was largely rebuilt, and from 1991–2 it was the target of heavy bombing by Yugoslav troops. Undaunted, Dubrovnik has regained its splendour and attracts travellers and film-makers alike.

①

Walls
Gradske zidine

🕐 **Jun-Jul: 8am-7:30pm; Apr-May & Aug-Sep: 8am-6:30pm; Oct: 8am-4pm; Nov-Mar: 9am-3pm**
🌐 **citywallsdubrovnik.hr**

A symbol of Dubrovnik, the walls offer stunning views from the guards' walkway. They were built in the 10th century,

with modifications in the 13th century, and were reinforced at various times. The walls and ramparts are 1,940 m (6,363 ft) long and reach a height of 25 m (82 ft) in some parts. Those facing inland are up to 6 m (20 ft) wide and strengthened by an outer wall with ten semi-circular bastions. Other towers and the Fort of St John, (also called Mulo Tower) defend the part facing the Adriatic and the port. Completing the defences

to the east and west of the city are two fortresses: the Revelin and the fortress of Lovrijenac.

Minčeta Tower (Tvrđava Minčeta) is the most visited of the walls' defensive structures. Designed by Michelozzo Michelozzi in 1461, it was completed by Juraj Dalmatinac. The semicircular tower is crowned by a second tower with embrasures at the top.

Visitors walk anticlockwise round the walls. The main access points are at Pile Gate at the western entrance to the Old Town, and at the Fort of St John at the eastern end of town. Queues for the wall can be long in summer; arrive early in the morning if you want to avoid the crush.

②
Pile Gate
Gradska vrata Pile

This is the main entrance to the old fortified centre. The stone bridge leading to Pile Gate is from 1537 and crosses a moat which today forms a garden. The gate is built on different levels. In a niche above the ogival arch stands a statue of St Blaise, the patron saint of Dubrovnik, by Ivan Meštrović (*p205*).

③
Ploče Gate
Vrata od Ploča

Dating from the 1300s, Ploče gate is reached by an imposing stone bridge. It was the last of the defences to be built, and the city's treasures were brought here for safety in times of difficulty, thanks to the strength of the walls.

---

④
Maritime Museum
Pomorski muzej

🏛 Tvrđa Sv Ivana 🕐 Apr-Oct: 9am-6pm Tue-Sun; Nov-Mar: 9am-4pm Tue-Sun 🌐 dumus.hr

Based in the upper areas of the Fort of St John, this informative museum tells the seafaring history of Dubrovnik through model ships, prints, diaries and portraits.

⑤
Aquarium
Akvarij

🏛 Ul kneza Damjana Jude 2 📞 (020) 323 978 🕐 Jun-Sep: 9am-9pm daily; Oct-May: 9am-1pm Mon-Sat

On the lower level of the Fort of St John is an aquarium, home to a range of Mediterranean marine life.

---

⑥
Big Fountain of Onofrio
Velika Onofrijeva fontana

Standing in the square beside the Pile Gate, this monument was built in 1438-44 by the Neapolitan architect Onofrio de la Cava, who also designed the city's water supply system. The fountain once had two storeys, but the upper level was destroyed in the earthquake.

DRINK

D'vino
A stellar choice among the city's growing roster of wine bars, tucked into one of the atmospheric alleys uphill from the Stradun. Sommelier advice is first class.

🏛 Palmotićeva 4a
🌐 dvino.net

Buža Bar
Located just outside Dubrovnik's seaward walls, Buža Bar offers outdoor seating with stunning sunset views over the sea.

🏛 Crijevićeva ul 9
📞 (099) 660 8258

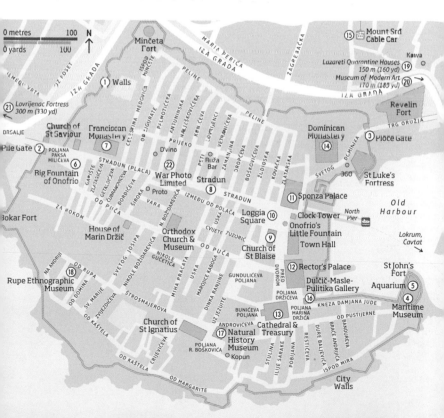

⑦

Franciscan Monastery

Franjevački samostan

🏠 Placa 30 📞 (020) 641 111
🕐 Summer: 9am–6pm daily;
winter: 9am–2pm daily

Construction of the monastery began in 1317 and was finally completed in the following century. It was almost entirely rebuilt after the earthquake in 1667, but the 15th-century south door, cloister and marble pulpit escaped damage.

The cloister leads to the pharmacy (Stara ljekarna), in use since 1317. Here alembics, mortars, measuring apparatus and beautifully decorated jars are displayed. There's also a small museum in the capitular room, housing religious works of art and instruments from the pharmaceutical laboratory.

↑ Dubrovnik's main thoroughfare, Stradun, buzzing at night

⑧

Stradun

Placa

The wide street that crosses the city from east to west was constructed in the 12th century and follows the line of the channel that separated the island from the mainland. A series of stone houses were built after the earthquake of 1667. Today the street is lined with bars and cafés, and is a popular place for socialising, particularly in the evening.

⑨

Church of St Blaise

Crkva sv. Vlaha

🏠 Loža 📞 (020) 324 911 🕐 8am–noon, 4:30–7pm daily

St Blaise was rebuilt in the early decades of the 18th century according to a 17th-century design and contains many Baroque works of art.

On the main altar stands a statue of the city's patron saint, Blaise. Produced in the 15th century in gold-plated silver, it depicts the saint holding a model of the city in the Middle Ages.

⑩

Loggia Square

Luža

This square, the political and economic heart of Dubrovnik, is situated at the eastern end of Stradun and surrounded by important buildings. Today it is still a popular meeting place, in particular around Orlando's Column, built by sculptor Antonio Ragusino (1418).

On the eastern side of the square is a Clock Tower (Gradski zvonik). Repair work carried out in 1929 restored a 15th-century appearance to it. The nearby Loggia of the

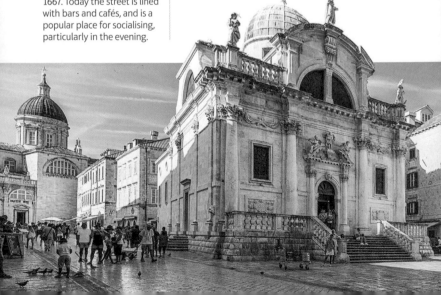

Did You Know?

The city is used as the King's Landing in *Game of Thrones*, and countless scenes were filmed in the Old Town.

Bell dates from 1463, and the bells were rung when danger threatened. Next to this stands the Main Guard House, rebuilt in 1706 after the earthquake of 1667. It has a large Baroque doorway, similar to a city gate. The Small Fountain of Onofrio, dating from 1438, stands alongside the Guard House.

⑪ Sponza Palace
Palača Sponza

🏛 Placa bb 📞 (020) 321 032 ⏰ May-Oct: 9am-10pm daily; Nov-Apr: 10am-3pm daily

Remodelled in 1516-22 Sponza Palace has been used as a mint, an armoury and a school. Today it houses the State Archives. It has an elegantly sculpted Renaissance loggia on the ground floor, a beautiful Venetian Gothic three-mullioned window on the first floor and a statue of St Blaise on the upper floor.

⑫

Rector's Palace
Knežev dvor

🏛 Pred Dvorom 3 ⏰ Apr-Oct: 9am-6pm daily; Nov-Mar: 9am-4pm daily 🌐 dumus.hr

The Rector's Palace was, for centuries, the seat of the most important government institutions of the Dubrovnik Republic. It housed the Upper and Lower Council, as well as the rector's quarters and rooms for meetings and audiences. The building was constructed in the 15th century on the site of a medieval fortress, and designed by Onofrio de la Cava.

The rooms of the palace house the Cultural Historical Museum (Kulturno-povijesni muzej), comprising various collections of historic items from the 16th to 20th centuries. On the ground floor a jail space, court, notary and archives have been preserved. Coins, medals, ancient weapons and works of art are on display on the mezzanine floor. On the first floor, rooms contain valuable objects from the 16th–18th centuries. Also of great interest are the portraits of illustrious personalities from Dubrovnik. During the Festival of Dubrovnik concerts are held in the atmospheric internal courtyard.

Next door is the 1863 Town Hall, home of the Gradska Kavana café and Civic Theatre.

⑬

Cathedral and Treasury
Velika Gospa

🏛 Kneza Damjana Jude 1 📞 (020) 323 459 ⏰ Apr-Oct: 8am-5pm Mon-Sat, 11am-5pm Sun; Nov-Mar: 8am-noon & 3-5pm Mon-Sat, 11am-noon & 3-5pm Sun

Built in 1667, the cathedral has paintings by Italian and Dalmatian artists from the 16th–18th centuries and *Assumption* by Titian (c 1552). The Cathedral Treasury (Riznica Katedrale) houses reliquaries and sacred objects.

⑭

Dominican Monastery
Dominikanski samostan Bijeli fratri

🏛 Od sv Dominika 4 📞 (020) 322 200 ⏰ 9am-6pm daily (Nov-Apr: to 5pm)

The monastery is arranged around the Gothic cloister by Maso di Bartolomeo, and features the Dominican Museum (Muzej Dominikanskog samostana). It contains works from the so-called "Dubrovnik school" and Venetian school.

SHOP

Kawa

An Aladdin's cave of cool gifts, Kawa offers everything from clothing to deli products. There's a café too.

🏛 Ul Hvarska 2 ⏰ 9am-6pm Mon-Fri (from 10am Sat)

←
Attractive Church of St Blaise, standing amidst restaurants and cafés

A cable car returning to the city from Mount Srđ at sunset

the underground silos ("holes" or "rupe") from which the building gets its name.

On display are costumes from around the region. The most colourful are the blouses worn by people from the Konavle region. Visit the museum for the seasonal exhibitions relating to folk culture and social history.

 Mount Srđ

🏛 **Dubrovnik Cablecar: Ul Kralja Petra Krešimira IV**
🌐 **dubrovnikcablecar.com**

The towering summit of Mount Srđ can be reached by a cable car, or can be climbed via a zig-zagging path known as the "serpentina". Visit the **Museum of the Homeland War** (Muzej domovinskog rata), which is devoted to the 1991-2 siege.

Museum of the Homeland War

🏛 Srđ ul 2 📞 (020) 324 856
🕐 8am-10pm daily

 Dulčić-Masle-Pulitika Gallery

🏛 Držićeva poljana
🕐 10am-8pm Tue-Sun
🌐 ugdubrovnik.hr

An art galley that conveys a great deal in a small space, the

Dulčić-Masle-Pulitika Gallery (Galerija Dulčić-Masle-Pulitika) celebrates three artists who gave a distinctive style to local painting. Ivo Dulčić (1916–75), Antun Masle (1919–67) and Đuro Pulitika (1922–2006) used bold Expressionist styles to paint local landscapes and city scenes.

 Natural History Museum

Prirodoslovni muzej

🏛 Androvićeva 1 🕐 10am-5pm Mon-Fri, 10am-2pm Sat 🌐 pmd.hr

The Natural History Museum displays traditional taxidermy collections alongside modern multimedia exhibits highlighting environmental issues.

 Rupe Ethnographic Museum

🏛 Od Rupa 3 🕐 9am-4pm Wed-Mon 🌐 dumus.hr

The Rupe Ethnographic Museum (Etnografski muzej Rupe) occupies a large slope-hugging building that was once used to store the city's vital grain supply. Wheat was kept on the upper floors until dry, when it was sent by chute to

 Lazareti Quarantine Houses

🏛 Ul Frana Supila bb
🌐 lazareti.com

Just beyond the Ploče Gate, at the eastern entrance to the Old Town, the row of buildings known as the Lazareti were used as quarantine houses for merchants. The complex was completed in 1642. Dubrovnik was prone to outbreaks of plague (the last great epi—demic occurring in 1526), and the Lazareti made a major contribution to the decline of such infections.

The Lazareti now provide rehearsal and performance space for cultural institutions as well as housing the Club Lazareti alternative nightlife space and an art gallery run by Art Radionica Lazareti.

 Museum of Modern Art

🏛 Frana Supila 23
🕐 9am-8pm Tue-Sun
🌐 ugdubrovnik.hr

Located in a gorgeous villa constructed in the 1930s

→
Winding walls of Lovrijenac Fortress, on the city's water edge

 INSIDER TIP
Extend Your Trip

Venture beyond the city if you are spending a few days here to explore the island of Lokrum and Trsteno, an arboretum northwest of Dubrovnik.

by ship owner Božo Banac, Dubrovnik's Museum of Modern Art (Umjetnička galerija Dubrovnik) contains a representative selection of Croatian paintings and sculpture dating from the late 19th century onwards. Particularly well represented is the Cavtat-born Vlaho Bukovac (1855–1922), an extraordinary talent who excelled in Realist landscapes and portraits. He subsequently moved on to styles influenced by Symbolism and Post-Impressionism. Seasonal exhibitions feature works by local and international contemporary artists.

㉑

Lovrijenac Fortress

📍 Ul od Tabakarije 29
🕐 Summer: 8am-7:30pm daily; winter: 9am-3pm daily 🌐 citywalls dubrovnik.hr

Built on a rock just west of the Old Town, Lovrijenac Fortress once guarded the approaches to the city by both sea and land. Above the main entrance is the inscription "Non Bene Pro Toto Libertas Venditur Auro", which means "freedom is not to be sold for all the gold in the world." This pithy expression reflects the city's centuries-long resistance to foreign powers. A triangular fort, with walls 12 m (39 ft) thick in places, Lovrijenac is approached via a steep flight of steps. It has frequently been used as one of the outdoor drama venues during the Dubrovnik Festival and is often associated with Shakespeare's *Hamlet*, which has been performed here several times, with well-known faces in the cast. It has also been used as a location for the TV series *Game of Thrones* and *Knightfall*.

㉒

War Photo Limited

📍 Antuninska 6
🕐 Apr & Oct: 10am-4pm Wed-Mon (May-Sep: to 6pm daily) 🗓 Nov-Mar
🌐 warphotoltd.com

This gallery showcases photojournalism from war zones around the world. There's a permanent display about the bloody break up of Yugoslavia, along with ever-changing temporary exhibitions focusing on global conflict and its emotional toll on the communities involved. Recent shows have featured war photography from Afghanistan, Gaza, Iran, Iraq and Myanmar.

EAT

Proto
Traditional Dalmatian seafood dishes are served with care at elegant Proto. The first floor terrace is an evocative eating spot.

📍 Široka 1 🌐 esculap restaurants.com

Kopun
Roast capon is the speciality here. Pick of the lunchtime dishes is *Šporki makaruli*, a pasta dish classic to the city.

📍 Poljana Rudera Boškovića 7
🌐 restaurantkopun.com

360
Relish seafood, wine and extravagant cocktails at this Michelin-starred restaurant, found in the Old Town fortifications.

📍 Svetog Dominika 1
🌐 360dubrovnik.com

A SHORT WALK
DUBROVNIK

Distance 500 m (547 yds) **Time** 10 minutes

Set in the limpid waters of the Adriatic, Dubrovnik had been one of the top international tourist destinations of Dalmatia, renowned for the beauty of its monuments, its magnificent walls and welcoming atmosphere. This was until war broke out. During the siege of 1991–2, around 2,000 bombs and guided missiles fell on Dubrovnik, damaging some of the most significant symbols of Dalmatian culture. After 1995, UNESCO and the EU set up a special commission for the reconstruction of the city, and in a remarkably short space of time much of the damage was repaired. It's no wonder that tourists have once more returned to this beautiful Mediterranean city, nor that it can frequently be seen on the silver screen. Negotiate the historic, winding streets of the Old Town for yourself – you might even spot a camera crew.

Did You Know?

Dubrovnik was against slavery long before the rest of the world – it officially banned it in 1416.

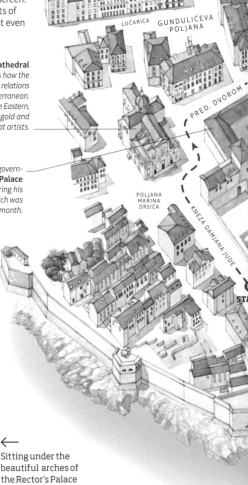

LUĆARICA GUNDULIĆEVA POLJANA

PRED. DVOROM

POLJANA MARINA DRŽIĆA

KNEŽA DAMIANA JUDE

STA

The provenance of the objects in the **Cathedral Treasury** *(p69) clearly demonstrates how the Dubrovnik merchants developed trading relations with the principal cities of the Mediterranean. It holds works from the Byzantine, Middle Eastern, Apulian and Venetian schools. There are gold and enamel objects and works by great artists.*

The highest level of city government met at the **Rector's Palace** *(p69). The rector lived here during his period of office, which was limited to one month.*

← Sitting under the beautiful arches of the Rector's Palace

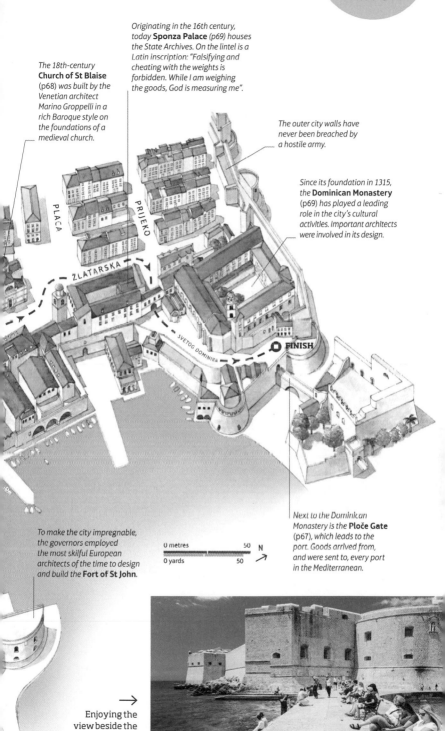

The 18th-century **Church of St Blaise** (p68) was built by the Venetian architect Marino Groppelli in a rich Baroque style on the foundations of a medieval church.

Originating in the 16th century, today **Sponza Palace** (p69) houses the State Archives. On the lintel is a Latin inscription: "Falsifying and cheating with the weights is forbidden. While I am weighing the goods, God is measuring me".

The outer city walls have never been breached by a hostile army.

Since its foundation in 1315, the **Dominican Monastery** (p69) has played a leading role in the city's cultural activities. Important architects were involved in its design.

PLAČA

PRIJEKO

ZLATARSKA

SVETOG DOMINIKA

☐ **FINISH**

To make the city impregnable, the governors employed the most skilful European architects of the time to design and build the **Fort of St John**.

Next to the Dominican Monastery is the **Ploče Gate** (p67), which leads to the port. Goods arrived from, and were sent to, every port in the Mediterranean.

0 metres 50 N
0 yards 50 →

→ Enjoying the view beside the Fort of St John

2 〈〉 〈〉

MLJET
NATIONAL PARK

⚠ E7 🚌 From Dubrovnik 🛈 Polače (020) 744 186; National Park: (020) 744 041 🌐 np-mljet.hr

An Arcadian paradise, bewitching Mljet is shrouded in myth. At the western tip of the island is a national park, frequented by day-trippers boating around the aqua blue waters and calling in at the quaint villages of Pomena, Polače and Goveđari. The national park is also home to a wealth of wildlife and woodland paths.

The island of Mljet, called Melita by the Romans and Meleda by the Venetians, covers an area of 100 sq km (38 sq miles). It is mountainous, with two limestone depressions in which there are two saltwater lakes linked by a channel. In Roman times, galleys would take shelter on Polače bay and a small settlement formed here – some ruins can still be seen today. In 1151, Duke Desa gave the island to the Benedictines of Pulsano in Gargano (Italy), who founded a monastery here. Two centuries later Stjepan, the Ban (governor) of Bosnia, gave it to Dubrovnik, to which it belonged until 1815. In 1960 the western part was declared a national park to save the forest of Aleppo pine and holm oak. The park can be visited on foot or by bike, following the trails. Boats must be authorised; call for more information.

Tranquil lakes and lush vegetation in Mljet National Park ↑

① Boats moored along a bay close to Polače.

② A couple enjoying dinner on Pomena's illuminated harbourfront.

③ Dried palm umbrellas shade sunloungers on a sandy Mljet beach, just outside the national park.

Did You Know?

Mljet is where Odysseus is believed to have had an affair with the nymph Calypso.

TOP 3 VILLAGES IN THE NATIONAL PARK

Pomena
This harbourside hamlet was originally a fishing village. Today it has just 50 residents and serves tourists to the national park with its clutch of souvenir shops and family-run restaurants.

Polače
Most day-trippers arrive first at this charming port village. The harbour waters are good for swimming, and neaby are the remains of a Roman palace.

Goveđari
Clinging to a hillside, this village was Mljet's main settlement and protected the island from pirates in the 18th century. Today it has 200 residents and a number of charming accommodation options.

 Boats floating on the crystal clear blue waters off Trsteno

EXPERIENCE MORE

❸
Opuzen

 E6 🚌 Metković; (060) 365 365 🛈 Trg kralja Tomislava 1; www.tz-opuzen.hr

At the edges of the delta of the River Neretva stands Opuzen, fortified for centuries and long considered something of a border town.

Towards the end of the 15th century, the Hungarian-Croat king, Matthias Corvinus, built the fort of Koš here. There are also traces of a 13th-century castle and the remains of a fort (Fort Opus), built by the Venetians during their 17th-century rule and from which the town takes its name.

❹
Trsteno

F7 🚌 Metković; www.libertasdubrovnik.hr

Clinging to a coastal hillside 20 km (13 miles) north of Dubrovnik, Trsteno village is home to one of Croatia's most picturesque botanical gardens. It circles the former summer house of the noble Gučetić family, who laid out an extensive, palm-dotted Renaissance garden. The property remained in the family until 1950 and much of the garden still survives. It now forms part of **Trsteno Arboretum**, established by the Croatian Academy of Sciences and Arts, and perhaps most famous for being a filming location for the TV series *Game of Thrones*. Near the entrance are two ancient plane trees, brought here by a Dubrovnik ship's captain more than 450 years ago.

Trsteno Arboretum
❀ 🏛 Potok 20, Trsteno 📞 (020) 751 019 🕙 Summer: 7am-7pm daily; winter: 8am-4pm daily

❺
Pelješac Peninsula

E7 🚌 Metković; www.libertasdubrovnik.hr

The peninsula of Pelješac juts out 65 km (40 miles) from the mainland, but it is only 7 km (4 miles) wide at its broadest point. A mountain chain forms its backbone, which peaks at Mount St Elijah. The slopes and plain are covered with vineyards and fruit trees, and the shallow coastal waters are given over to oyster farming.

The town closest to the mainland is called Ston, and today is primarily visited for its spectacular defensive walls, which stretch across the surrounding hillside. Begun in the 14th century, they constituted the Dubrovnik Republic's principal northern line of defence, and remain one of the largest defensive structures in the world. More than 5 km (3 miles) of walls climb from Ston (often referrred to as Veliki Ston or "Great Ston"), the main heart of the town, to Mali Ston ("Little Ston") on the eastern coast of the peninsula. Visitors can walk the whole stretch from Ston to Mali Ston, enjoying superb views along the way. The walls end at Mali Ston's 14th-century Fort Koruna.

Towards the tip of the peninsula, Orebić is the boarding point for ferries to Korčula. It has a **Maritime Museum** (Pomorski muzej) that illustrates the history of its inhabitants, who were the most sought after sea

TOP 3 **LOCAL WINERIES**

Korta Katarina

A large villa and winery on the fringes of Orebić with a highly regarded Plavac Mali *(www. kortakatarina.com)*.

Saints Hills

Head here for tastings and fine dining in an impressive ridge-top setting. Best known for exceptional local reds and a white Chardonnay-Malvazia blend called Nevina *(www.saints hill.com)*.

Matuško

One of the leading producers of Dingač – a velvety red only made with Plavac Mali grapes from the region *(www. matusko vina.hr)*.

by ferry. Divna beach, to the northwest, offers spectacular views back across the mainland.

Maritime Museum

⊕ Trg Mimbelli bb
Jun-Sep: 8am-8pm Mon-Fri, 6-8pm Sat & Sun; Oct-May: 8am-8pm Mon-Fri
muzej-orebic.hr

6

Narona

E6 Metković; (060) 365 365 www.a-m-narona.hr

The Roman walled town of Colonia Julia Narona was founded by the Romans in the 1st century BC. An important road junction and a trading centre with the Adriatic hinterland, it had temples, baths and other buildings grouped around the Forum. It was one of the Balkans' first dioceses, and flourished until the 7th century when it was destroyed by the Avars and the Slavs.

At the end of the 19th century, Austrian archaeologist Karl Patsch began to carry out excavations. Work uncovered objects from pagan and Christian temples, houses and public works. Large parts of the area have yet to be explored, but the Archaeological Museum Narona in Vid gives some idea of the importance of

2,800

The average annual hours of sunlight enjoyed by the Pelješac Peninsula's Dingač wine region.

the town. The museum contains statues of Roman emperors and their families, as well as pottery, glassware and other items found in Narona. Some pieces are also on display at the Archaeological Museum *(p184)* in Split.

The 16th-century Church of St Vitus (Sv. Vid) stands just outside the town on the site of a 5th-century church.

7

Neum

E7 Bosnia-Herzegovina Metković; www.libertas dubrovnik.hr neum.ba

All vehicles taking the coastal road between Dubrovnik and Split pass through the 9-km (5-mile) stretch of coast that is part of Bosnia-Herzegovina. The main town in this area is Neum, Bosnia's only coastal town. A bridge is due to be built that will connect the Pelješac Peninsula to the mainland and resolve this territorial gap. Neum is a border town, and visitors should carry passports when passing through.

captains in the Mediterranean. The sweeping Trstenica bay on the eastern side of Orebić is one of the finest shingle beaches in Dalmatia. Just west of the town is a Franciscan Monastery (Franjevački samostan), founded in the 15th century. The church alongside contains two reliefs: one is a *Virgin with Child* by Nikola Firentinac (1501), who was a pupil of Donatello. Orebić lies at the edge of one of Croatia's most valued wine-growing areas, with the nearby villages producing highly prized reds made from the indigenous Plavac Mali grape.

West of Orebić, the coastal village of Viganj is a windsurfing resort with a fine pebble beach. The main town on the northern side of the peninsula is the pleasant beach resort of Trpanj, linked to the mainland

→

Coastal town of Neum illuminated at dusk

↑ The rooftops of Cavtat, with a cemetery sculpture detail *(inset)*

8
Cavtat

 F7 From Dubrovnik; (020) 478 065 From Dubrovnik; www.liber tasdubrovnik.hr Zidine 6; www.visit. cavtat-konavle.com

Cavtat is the Croatian name for Civitas Vetus, the site of the Roman town of Epidaurum, which was destroyed by the Avars in the 7th century (occasional excavations have revealed the remains of a theatre, several tombs and parts of a road). The beauty of the area, which is dotted with beaches and monuments, attracts many visitors to the present-day village.

Cavtat's most important sights include the Račić Mausoleum, which was built by Ivan Meštrović *(p205)* in 1922, and the House of Vlaho Bukovac, birthplace of one of Croatia's most famous painters. Some of Bukovac's works are a highlight of the Baltazar Bogišić Collection, which was assembled and donated by the 19th-century scholar and jurist after whom it was named. The collection is housed in the 16th-century Rector's Palace.

At the end of the seafront is a Franciscan Monastery and the church of Our Lady of Snow (Gospa Snježna), both dating from the 15th century.

9
Konavle

F7 Zidine 6, Cavtat; www.visit.cavtat-konavle.com

Stretching southeast from Cavtat to the Montenegrin border, the narrow fertile plain of Konavle traditionally supplied the city of Dubrovnik with cattle, vegetables and wine. It remains an agricultural area of green fields broken up by dry-stone walls, with the grey heights of the Dinaric mountains looming further inland. Gruda is the main market centre, home to a handful of traditional country-style restaurants. The nearby, hillside-hugging villages of Pridvorje, Mihanići and Drvenik are particularly picturesque, preserving a rustic character that seems a world away from touristic Dubrovnik and Cavtat. The seaside village of Molunat, in the southeastern reaches of Konavle, has an attractive part-sandy beach.

10
Sokol Grad

 F7 Sokol Grad Jun-Oct: 10am-7pm daily; Apr & May 10am-6pm daily; Nov: 10am-4pm daily; Dec-Mar: noon-3pm daily city wallsdubrovnik.hr

Perched dramatically on a rock 4 km (2 miles) north of Gruda, Sokol Grad ("Hawk Castle") was fortified by local chieftains in prehistoric times. Its current diamond-shaped appearance dates from the 15th century, when it was a crucial point in the southerly defences of the Dubrovnik Republic. The fort was abandoned in the 17th century and its stones carried away by locals for use in village houses and walls. Finally restored in the early 21st century, the fort's crenellated ramparts offer spectacular views of the surrounding countryside.

---

⑪

Elaphite Islands

Ⓐ F7 ➎ From Dubrovnik; www.jadrolinija.hr ℹ Dubrovnik regional tourist office; www. visitdubrovnik.hr

Lying just to the north of Dubrovnik, the Elaphite Islands (Elahtski otoci) can be reached from the city by motorboat. The islands were named by the Roman natural historian Pliny the Elder after the fallow deer then found here. Only three islands are inhabited: Šipan, Lopud and Koločep, while Jakljan is devoted to farming. All the islands have woods of maritime pines and cypresses in the uncultivated areas, and beautiful beaches

and bays. They have long been popular with the aristocracy of Dubrovnik, who built villas here. Some islands had monasteries that were suppressed with the arrival of French troops in 1808. Many of the churches date from the pre-Romanesque period, but few remain intact.

Koločep is the nearest island to Dubrovnik, and has been a summer retreat for city folks since the 16th century. The island is covered in pine trees and subtropical scrubs.

Lopud island, which measures 5 sq km (2 sq miles), has a fertile valley sheltered from the winds by two ranges of hills. There are two ruined forts that date from the 16th century, while the Franciscan Monastery is from 1483. Its church contains works by Pietro di Giovanni, Nikola Božidarević and Leandro da Bassano.

Šunj, in the southeast, draws visitors because of its sandy beach, but the church is also worth visiting for its many works of art.

Šipan is the largest of the Elaphite Islands (16 sq km/ 6 sq miles) and has two towns. In Šipanska Luka stands the pre-Romanesque Church of St Michael and the ruins of a Benedictine Monastery. In Suđurađ there is a castle and the ruins of a bishop's palace.

↑ Perfect water clarity in the bay of Koločep Island, Elaphite Islands

EAT

Bakus

This cosy Dalmatian restaurant is a local favourite, serving excellent seafood at affordable prices. Pride of the dessert menu is Ston Cake: an unusual combination of chocolate and pasta tubes.

Ⓐ E7 Ⓐ B. Angeli Radovani 5 Ston ⓦ bakus.hr

Bota Šare

Adriatic-Japanese crossover dishes combine sushi and tempura with local ingredients, such as Mali Ston bay oysters.

Ⓐ E7 Ⓐ Mali Ston bb, Ston ⓦ bota-sare.hr

Bugenvila

Head here for Croatian-Mediterranean fine dining with a seasonal menu, superb cocktails and sublime desserts.

Ⓐ F7 Ⓐ Put dr. Ante Starčevića 9 Cavtat ⓦ bugenvila.eu

Konoba Koraćeva kuća

This evocative spot is a traditional stone house with a terrace looking towards the mountains of Bosnia-Herzegovina. Feast on fresh seafood and locally reared meats; the bruschetta in particular makes for an outstanding light bite.

Ⓐ F7 Ⓐ Gruda Ⓒ 020 791 557

Ⓚⓝ Ⓚⓝ Ⓚⓝ

SPLIT AND CENTRAL DALMATIA

Split is the hub of Central Dalmatia, a ferry port serving the islands as well as a captivating urban attraction in its own right. Historic towns and splendid beaches draw tourists to the islands of Brač, Korčula, Hvar and Vis. The interior of Central Dalmatia is very different, with stark mountains and arid plateaus offering plenty in the way of wild nature.

Urban life first took off on the islands, with the ancient Greeks establishing colonies on Vis, Hvar and Korčula. It was their successors the Romans who developed the mainland, building harbours, roads, and at least one major city in the shape of Salona just inland from Split. Split itself began life as the retirement home of Roman Emperor Diocletian, whose palace buildings still form the core of the modern city.

Central Dalmatia was originally settled by Croats in the 7th century, although the area fell under the sway of Venice in the Middle Ages, which is why so many of its buildings bear a distinct Venetian stamp. The islands once supported thriving populations involved in fishing, shipping and olive-growing. Emigration to Australia and the Americas in the 20th century led to island depopulation, although a blossoming tourist industry has seen prosperity return.

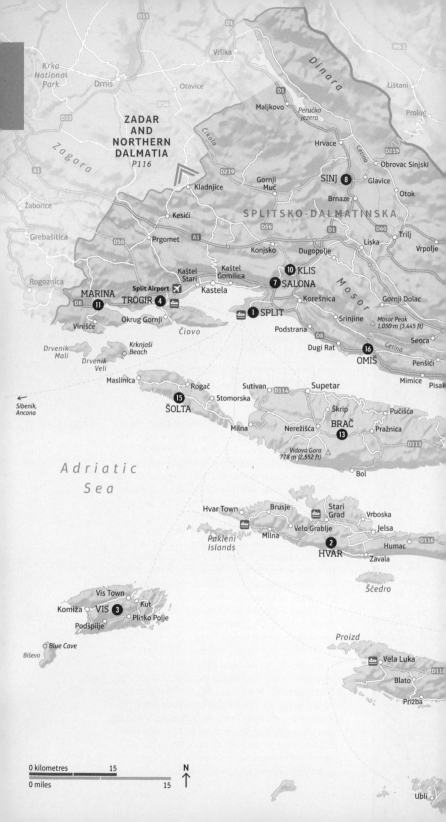

SPLIT AND CENTRAL DALMATIA

Must Sees
1. Split
2. Hvar
3. Vis
4. Trogir
5. Korčula

Experience More
6. Brela
7. Salona
8. Sinj
9. Imotski
10. Klis
11. Marina
12. Gradac
13. Brač
14. Makarska
15. Šolta
16. Omiš
17. Zaostrog
18. Tučepi
19. Podgora
20. Vrgorac
21. Živogošće
22. Lastovo

↑ Marjan hill, overlooking the Old Town of Split at sunset

SPLIT

△D6 ✈Split Airport: Kaštel Štafilić, www.split-airport.hr
🚌Obala kneza Domagoja, (060) 333 444 ⛴Obala kneza Domagoja, (060) 327 777 4; Jadrolinija, www.jadrolinija.hr
ℹ Peristil bb; www.visitsplit.com

Shipyards and a busy port are the modern face of Split but the Roman Emperor Diocletian's vast palace reminds us of the city's ancient roots. In 614, the palace took in refugees from Salona and they breathed new life into Split. Byzantine rule followed before Split became part of the Venetian territories in 1409. Under the Venetians, city walls were built, and the arts flourished.

DRINK

Academia Club Ghetto

One of a handful of bars in the palace area, Ghetto has retained its authenticity and kept a loyal following of local arty types. The garden patio is a great spot in summer.

△Dosud 10
📞(091) 197 7790

---

① Golden Gate
Zlatna vrata

This was the main entrance to the Palace of Diocletian (p88) from the road to Salona. It was the most impressive of the palace gates (all of which were named after a metal), with towers and decorative elements above the arches; its carved niches once housed statues. In the 11th century, the corridor between the palace and the gate was closed and converted into the Church of St Martin (Sv. Martin). An inscription commemorates Father Dominic, the founder.

---

② Split City Museum
Muzej grada Splita

△Papalićeva 1 🕐Apr & May: 8:30am-9pm daily; Jun-Sep: 8:30am-10pm daily; Oct: 8:30am-9pm Mon-Sat, 9am-5pm Sun; Nov-Mar: 9am-5pm Tue-Sat, 9am-2pm Sun
🌐mgst.net

The attractive Gothic Papalić Palace is one of the most interesting of the 15th–16th-century buildings constructed in the abandoned parts of the Diocletian complex. The palace houses the illuminating Split City Museum, which holds various artistic finds, paintings and books illustrating the city's celebrated history from the 12th to the 18th centuries. Highlights include a scale model of the peristyle.

→ A weathered statue in the courtyard of the fascinating Split City Museum

Peristyle

The peristyle (or interior courtyard) of the Palace of Diocletian is an impressive part of the complex where layers of building from across the centuries can be seen. The slim columns bordering three sides rest on a high plinth. The access to the emperor's former private quarters has a tall arched tympanum and relief decorations.

Silver Gate and Church of St Dominic
Srebrna vrata I Sv. Dominik

Beside the Silver Gate is a lovely daily market selling seasonal fruit and vegetables, homemade cheeses, hams and dried herbs. Because of the open space, you will also get a great view of the palace here.

In front of the gate is the Oratory of St Catherine, built in the Middle Ages. It was used by the Dominicans while they built their own monastery (1217). The oratory was rebuilt in the 17th century and became the Church of St Dominic (Sv. Dominik). Inside the church, which was enlarged in 1930, are a *Miracle in Surian* by Palma il Giovane and an *Apparition in the Temple*, attributed to his school.

Baptistry of St John
Sv. Ivan Krstitelj

☎ (021) 345 602
🕓 9am–7pm daily

This small and beautiful building, consecrated in the 6th century, was the palace's Temple of Jupiter. Inside, the baptismal font incorporates a pre-Romanesque panel of King Zvonimir and other dignitaries. The statue of St John on the end wall is by Ivan Meštrović *(p205)* and was added before World War II. The tomb of Bishop John is from the 8th century and the one in front of it, that of Bishop Lawrence, dates from the 11th century.

Iron Gate
Željezna vrata

The Church of Our Lady of the Belfry (Gospa od Zvonika) has the city's oldest early Romanesque bell tower (1081) and was constructed in the outer passageway above this palace entrance.

🔍 HIDDEN GEM
Orson Welles

One of Split's more unusual sights is the statue of film director Orson Welles at the entrance to the Joker shopping mall. It was sculpted by his partner, Zagreb-born artist Oja Kodar. The couple frequently visited Split.

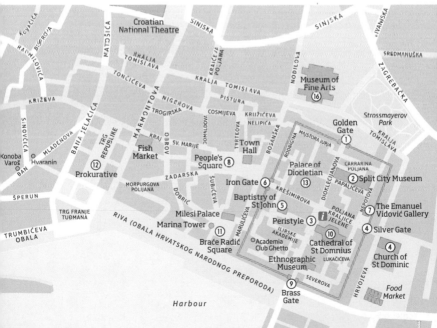

⑦

The Emanuel Vidović Gallery
Galerija Vidović

📍 Poljana kraljice Jelene
🕐 Jun–Sep: 9am–9pm Tue–Fri, 9am–4pm Sat & Sun; Oct–May: 9am–4pm Tue–Fri, 10am–1pm Sat & Sun
🌐 galerija-vidovic.com

The Vidović Gallery honours Split painter Emanuel Vidović (1872–1953) with a career-spanning display of his works. He was famous for his maritime landscapes and seaside city-scapes in dark, atmospheric styles. The Adriatic coast was his prime inspiration, and many of his paintings feature Split and Trogir.

⑧

People's Square
Narodni trg

The People's Square was, as the name in implies, the centre of business and administration from the 15th century, used in place of the Peristyle. The nobility erected prestigious buildings as the space rose in impor-tance; examples include the Venetian Gothic Cambi Palace and the Renaissance Town Hall (Vijećnica), built in the first half of the 15th century, with a loggia with three arches and a Gothic window.

⑨

Brass Gate
Mjedena vrata

📍 Obala Hrvatskog narodnog preporoda 22

The Brass Gate's appearance is deceptive, opening onto the richest façade of the palace. The upper floor had a portico which was later enclosed for living quarters. The vast cellars have been excavated to reveal impressive arched vaults and skilful masonry. Shops occupy some of these while others house an exhibition about the palace and temporary local displays.

⑩

Cathedral of St Domnius
Katedrala sv. Duje

📍 Kraj sv Duje 5 ☎ (021) 345 602 🕐 Apr–Oct: 8am–7pm Mon–Sat, 12:30–6pm Sun; Nov–Mar: 8am–5pm daily

Originally the mausoleum of Emperor Diocletian, the cathedral was consecrated in the 7th century when the sarcophagus containing the emperor's body was removed and replaced – with a certain poetic justice – by the remains

🔍 HIDDEN GEM
Ethnographic Museum

By the Brass Gate, on Severova, this charm-ing museum displays Dalmatian folk costumes in a medieval palace. After you've had a look, climb the stairs to the Renaissance terrace, which has great views (www.etnografski-muzej-split.hr).

of St Domnius (locally St Duje). This 3rd-century bishop was martyred as part of Diocletian's perse-cution of the early Christians. It was the archbishop of Split at the time who trans-formed the mausoleum into a Christian church, and the structure became the city's patron saint.

St Domnius is widely known as the oldest Catholic cathedral in the world that has not been substantially rebuilt at any time. It has remained practically unaltered except for the addition of a Romanesque bell tower and a 13th-century choir. Visitors can climb the bell tower for dizzying views over the old town.

An ancient sphinx in black granite rests at the foot of the bell tower. The entrance doorway has wooden panels from 1214, with scenes from the Gospel in floral frames. The cathedral, built on an octagonal ground plan, has a double order of Corinthian columns, most of them the Roman originals; above is a frieze decorated with scenes of Eros hunting, supporting medallions with portraits of Diocletian and his wife Prisca. In the second niche on the right, with frescoes dating from 1428, is the Altar of St Domnius, the work of Bonino of Milan (1427). The wooden choir stalls in the 17th-century presbytery are an example of Romanesque carving from the beginning of the 13th century. To the side is a chapel housing the Altar of St Anastasius, designed in 1448 by Juraj Dalmatinac. The niche after

Did You Know?

Split is home to Europe's third-oldest, still active synagogue, built into the western wall of Diocletian's Palace.

this was altered in the 18th century to create the Baroque chapel of St Domnius. The 13th-century hexagonal pulpit is supported by thin columns with carved capitals.

The 14th-century building behind the cathedral houses the sacristy and the name of one of the architects, Filotas, is inscribed by the entrance. In the sacristy, now the Cathedral Museum, are many works of art, including objects in gold and silver, ancient manuscripts, medieval icons and vestments. Of particular importance are the *Historia Saloniana* written by Archdeacon Toma in the 13th century, the *Supetar cartulary* – a 12th-century cartulary – and the *Book of Gospels* from the 6th century.

---

⑪
Braće Radić Square

In the southwest corner of the Palace of Diocletian is this medieval square, better known by locals as Voćni trg (Fruit Square). The tall Marina Tower (Hrvojeva kula) is the only evidence of the imposing castle built by the Venetians in the second half of the 15th century after the final defeat of Split. Built on an octagonal ground-plan, it stands on the southern side of the square.

On the northern side is the Baroque Milesi Palace, which dates from the 17th century. There is also a work by Ivan Meštrović in the centre of the square: the great monument to Marko Marulić, the writer and scholar (1450–1524) who was the founder of literature in the Croatian language. The imposing bronze statue has an inscription with some verses by the Croatian poet Tin Ujević.

←

Early evening in Split's Narodni trg, the People's Square

⑫
Prokurative

 Trg Republike

Named after the 17th-century Procuratie buildings on St Mark's Square in Venice, Split's Prokurative are an ensemble of arcaded neo-Renaissance buildings bordering Trg Republike. Built in stages between 1863 and 1928, they were initiated by 19th-century mayor Antonio Bajamonti. He wanted to turn Split into a modern Mediterranean metropolis, with shaded areas where people could socialise. Now housing offices and ground-floor cafés, the Prokurative form the back drop to many outdoor events, including the Split Song Festival held each June

EAT

Konoba Varoš

Varoš has an extensive menu of traditional local seafood and grilled meat dishes, best washed down with a house wine. Try the *pašticada* (beef stew cooked with prunes).

 Ban Mladenova 7
 konobavaros.com

Ⓚ Ⓚ Ⓚ

Hvaranin

Run by a family from Hvar, this restaurant is known for its seafood risottos and fresh grilled fish. It's long been a favourite of writers, both local and international.

 Ban Mladenova 9
☎ (099) 667 5891

Ⓚ Ⓚ Ⓚ

⑬ ⟨🛆⟩ ⟨🍴⟩ ⟨🛍⟩

PALACE OF DIOCLETIAN

🏛 Dioklecijanova ul 1 🕐 24 hours

After governing for 20 years, Emperor Diocletian retired from public life and moved to this grand palace. Fast forward 1,700 years, and these beautifully preserved ruins are now the beating heart of Split, home to shops, bars and restaurants.

Diocletian was probably a native of Salona (p106) and became emperor in 284. He made Maximian joint Augustus, senior co-emperor, in 285, and then appointed Galerius and Constantius as Caesars, junior co-emperors (the Tetrarchy), in 293. During his reign, Diocletian commissioned the architects Filotas and Zotikos to build a palace in the bay of Split and he retired here in 305, ten years after construction began. The palace was like a typical Roman military camp. It was 215 m (705 ft) long and 180 m (590 ft) wide and was enclosed by strong walls, in places 28 m (92 ft) high. After Diocletian's death in 316, the palace was used as clerical offices. Later, in 615, refugees from Salona found shelter here after their city was destroyed by the Avars. The richest settled in the emperor's apartments, the poorer in the towers.

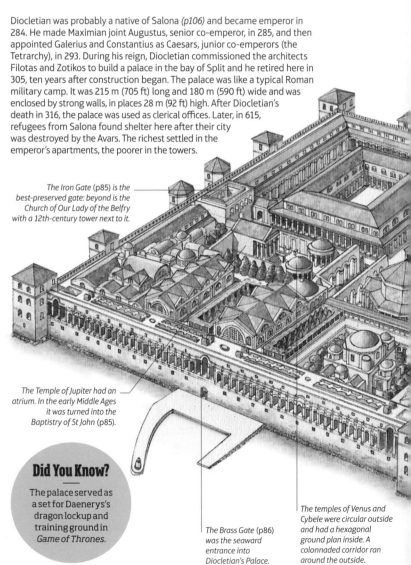

The Iron Gate (p85) is the best-preserved gate: beyond is the Church of Our Lady of the Belfry with a 12th-century tower next to it.

The Temple of Jupiter had an atrium. In the early Middle Ages it was turned into the Baptistry of St John (p85).

Did You Know?

The palace served as a set for Daenerys's dragon lockup and training ground in Game of Thrones.

The Brass Gate (p86) was the seaward entrance into Diocletian's Palace.

The temples of Venus and Cybele were circular outside and had a hexagonal ground plan inside. A colonnaded corridor ran around the outside.

The Golden Gate (p84), facing Salona, was the main entrance to the palace. This was the most imposing of the gates, with two towers and many decorations.

The Silver Gate (p85), or eastern gate, was a simpler copy of the Golden Gate.

① This bas relief can be seen in the Baptistry of St John, formerly the Roman Temple of Jupiter.

② The Silver Gate was the palace's eastern entrance during Emperor Diocletian's reign.

③ The Church of Our Lady of the Belfry and a 12th-century-tower beside the Iron Gate, show how the palace has evolved.

↑ Reconstruction of the Palace of Diocletian

THE MYSTERY EMPEROR

Why Emperor Diocletian retired, or why he was allowed to retire, remains a mystery. All of his predecessors ruled until they died (sometimes murdered by a rival). It's quite possible that Diocletian aimed to make retirement compulsory for Roman emperors, thereby weakening the potential for violent regime change. Diocletian remained politically active after retiring to his palace. He still casts an ambiguous shadow over Split: celebrated as the city's founder and yet condemned for the execution of the city's first Christian martyrs.

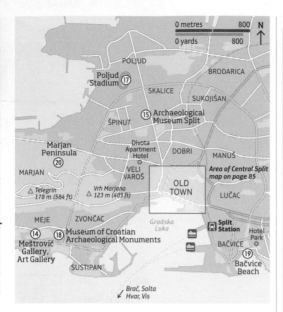

Area of Central Split map on page 85

Brač, Solta Hvar, Vis

KAŠTELA COASTAL PROMENADE

Northwest of Split, en route to Trogir, the Kaštela are a string of seven neighbouring coastal villages, each with a small waterside fortress. These were built in the 15th-century under Venetian-rule to protect against attack by the Ottoman Turks. The seven are: Kaštel Štafilić, Kaštel Novi, Kaštel Stari, Kaštel Lukšić, Kaštel Kambelovac, Kaštel Gomilica and Kaštel Sućurac. They are all connected by a pretty coastal promenade – the most pleasant stretch to walk lies between Kaštel Lukšić and Kaštel Gomilica (*www.kastela-info.hr*).

BEYOND THE OLD TOWN

Meštrović Gallery, Art Gallery

Galerija Meštrović

🏠 Šetalište Ivana Meštrovića 46 🕓 May-Sep: 9am-7pm Tue-Sun; Oct-Apr: 9am-5pm Tue-Sat 🌐 mestrovic.hr

This gallery was Ivan Meštrović's home in the early 1930s. Sculptures, including *Distant Accords* and *Persephone*, decorate the garden and interior. Among the statues are *The Contemplation* and *Psyche*. The Kaštilac, down the road at No 39, can be visited with the same ticket. This 16th-century residence was bought by Meštrović in 1939 as a place for prayer. The adjoining chapel displays a cycle of wood reliefs depicting scenes from the life of Christ, also by Meštrović.

Archaeological Museum Split

Arheološki muzej u Splitu

🏠 Zrinsko Frankopanska 25 🕓 Jun-Sep: 9am-2pm, 4-8pm Mon-Sat; Oct-May: 9am-2pm, 4-8pm Mon-Fri, 9am-2pm Sat 🌐 armus.hr

Founded in 1820, this museum has been on its present site since 1914 and contains a considerable number of finds from the Roman, early Christian and medieval periods. Of great interest are the finds from Roman Salona, including sculptures, capitals, sarcophagi, jewellery, coins and ceramics. There are also finds from the Roman town of Narona (*p77*).

Museum of Fine Arts

Galeria Umjetnina

🏠 Kralja Tomislava 15 🕓 10am-6pm Tue-Fri (to 2pm Sat & Sun) 🌐 galum.hr

Situated just a five-minute walk from Diocletian's Palace (*p88*), this museum displays art from the 14th century up to the present day. Founded in 1931 and now housed in a modern space, its permanent exhibition of paintings and sculptures includes works by prominent figures in the Adriatic art scene. It also hosts temporary exhibitions.

→ A carved sarcophagus from Roman Salona, Archaeological Museum

Enjoying the turquoise waters of Bačvice Beach in summertime

 (17)
Poljud Stadium

Built in 1979 to host the Mediterranean Games, Poljud Stadium is the home of Hajduk Split football team, and is used for sporting and music events. Croatian Architect Boris Magaš gave the stadium a bowl-like form, its gracefully curving roof inspired by half-open seashells. Considered a classic of its kind, it has had a profound influence on modern stadium design since 2015 has been a protected monument of culture.

(18)
Museum of Croatian Archaeological Monuments

Muzej hrvatskih arheoloških spomenika

⌂ Šetalište Ivana Meštrovića 18 🕐 Mid-Jun-mid-Sep: 9am-1pm, 5-8pm Mon-Fri, 9am-2pm Sat; mid-Sep-mid-Jun: 9am-4pm Mon-Fri, 9am-2pm Sat 🌐 mhas-split.hr

This museum displays finds from around Split dating from the early Middle Ages. The collection also includes the works of early Croat sculptors, dating from 800. The stone fragments, salvaged from churches and castles, consist mainly of tombs, capitals, altar fronts, ciboria and windows. Highlights here include the sarcophagus of Queen Jelena (10th century), discovered in Salona *(p106)*.

(19)
Bačvice Beach

Split's most popular urban beach is a glorious curve of shingle and sand separated from the harbour area by a rocky headland. The bay is sandy-floored and shallow, making it perfect for paddling. Bačvice is famous as the home of *picigin*, a local game that looks a bit like water volleyball. Just above the eastern curve of Bačvice Beach is a modern pavilion with a choice of eateries.

(20)
Marjan Peninsula

This protected nature reserve on the west side of town is closed to cars and can only be accessed by a network of footpaths leading through dense pinewoods. There are fine views out to sea here, with the islands of Šolta, Brač and Hvar clearly visible. You can also find lovely beaches in this pleasant area – perfect for escaping the city.

 2

HVAR

 E6 🚢 Split–Stari Grad/Hvar Town: www.jadrolinija.hr; www.krilo.hr ℹ️ www.visithvar.hr

Art treasures, a mild climate, good beaches and fields of scented lavender make this island one of the jewels of the Adriatic. Hvar's story begins in the 4th century BC when the Greeks founded Pharos (present-day Stari Grad) and Dimos (Hvar Town). Traces have been left by the Romans, Byzantines, medieval Croatian kings and Venetians. Hvar was an important centre of Croatian culture during the Renaissance, when local poets Hanibal Lucić and Petar Hektorović both wrote about the people and the landscape. In 1886, the Hvar Hygienic Society promoted the island as a health resort.

① Stari Grad

🚢 From Split 🚌 Hvar Town, Jelsa, Sućuraj, Vrboska
🌐 visit-stari-grad.com

Founded by the Syracusans in the 4th century BC and originally called Pharos, Stari Grad (literally, the Old Town) is Hvar's main ferry port. It lies at the end of a long bay and the main sights are scattered throughout a picturesque old quarter of low stone houses and tiny streets. The 17th-century parish Church of St Stephen (Sv. Stjepan) is the principal landmark. At the western end of the old quarter is the **Tvrdalj**, the fortified residence of Renaissance poet Petar Hektorović. Nearby is **Stari Grad Museum**, housed in the Renaissance Biankini Palace, which contains a stunning collection of Greek amphorae. On the edge of the old quarter is the **Dominican Monastery** (Dominikanski samostan), founded by Brother Germano of Piacenza in 1482. It was rebuilt and fortified after destruction by Uluz Ali, the Ottoman corsair who raided the Adriatic islands in 1571. Much feared, Uluz Ali was driven away by stubborn defenders of Korčula, and came to pillage the less well-defended island of Hvar instead. As well as a beautiful cloister, the monastery has a library rich in medieval incunabula, and a collection of paintings including a *Deposition* by Tintoretto. The monastery church contains the grave of Petar Hektorović.

East of Stari Grad, the Ager is a fertile plain that still preserves the field plan established by the island's ancient Greek inhabitants who cultivated wine, figs and olives, much as their modern counterparts do today. Added to the UNESCO World Heritage list in 2008, the Ager can be explored on foot or by bike.

 INSIDER TIP
Reliable Wine

You're unlikely to have a bad wine on Hvar, thanks to this island's fertile terroir. The house wine at any eatery is guaranteed to be good, and you can buy decent, affordable wines at any local supermarket.

↑ Stari Grad's sweeping coastline, studded with moored boats

Tvrdalj

🏛 Priko bb ⏰ May, Jun & Sep: 10am–1pm daily; Jul & Aug: 10am–1pm, 5pm–8pm daily

Stari Grad Museum

🏛 Braće Biankini 4 ⏰ May–Oct: 10am–1pm Mon–Sat (Jul & Aug: also 7–9pm daily); Nov–Apr: by appointment 🌐 msg.hr

Dominican Monastery

🏛 Trg sv. Petra bb 📞 (021) 765 442 ⏰ Jun–Sep: 10am–noon, 6–8pm daily; Oct–May: by appointment

Vrboska

🚌 Stari Grad, Jelsa

Vrboska is a pretty village huddled around a succession of stone bridges spanning a narrow canal connected to the open sea. At the heart of the village is the 16th-century Church of St Mary (Sv. Marija), fortified with huge buttresses to provide shelter for villagers in times of siege. A short walk north is the Glavica peninsula, with rocky beaches and pebbly coves. The seaside path from Vrboska to Jelsa is perfect for a relaxed stroll.

Zavala

🚌 Jelsa

Zavala is the principal village of Hvar's peaceful southern coast, where quiet hamlets lie below slopes covered with vineyards. The road here from Jelsa runs through a famously low and narrow single-lane tunnel. There is a long stretch of pebbly beach running along Zavala's shoreline. Boat captains here offer trips to the Islet of Šćedro just to the south, with even quieter beaches, pine trees and maquis vegetation.

④

Sućuraj

🚌 Drvenik

Lying in a sheltered bay at the eastern tip of the island, Sućuraj is where the ferry from the mainland arrives. Its pretty harbour has the remains of a fortress built by the Venetians in 1630. Nearby, Mlaska Bay and Perna Bay are two of Hvar's best beaches, with clear shallow water over fine sand.

Jelsa

🚌 Stari Grad, Vrboska 🌐 tzjelsa.hr

A traditional Dalmatian stone-built settlement around a small harbour, Jelsa is a popular base for family holidays, with several beaches on the outer fringes of town. Jelsa was a prosperous port, exporting the wines produced in the villages. Steps from Jelsa's café-filled main square ascend to the Gothic parish Church of St Mary (Sv. Marija). The park behind Jelsa's harbour contains a statue of 19th-century sea captain Nika Duboković by the prominent Dalmatian sculptor Ivan Rendić.

↑ Morning in Jelsa's main square, bounded by pavement cafés

TOP 4 BEACH AREAS AROUND HVAR TOWN

Sveti Klement, Pakleni Islands
The largest of the Pakleni Islands, just off the coast from Hvar Town, has a wealth of pebble beaches, walking trails and restaurants.

Marinkovac, Pakleni Islands
Two pleasant beaches can be found here: Ždrilca to the north and Uvala Stipanska to the south.

Jerolim, Pakleni Islands
This naturist spot is known for its same-sex couples beach on the far side of the island.

Milna and Mala Milna
Around 3 km (2 miles) from Hvar Town, Milna is a pebbly beach, with smaller and quieter Mala Milna beach just a 5-minute walk away.

Hvar Town

A D6 **=** Stari Grad
i Trg svetog Stjepana 42; www.visithvar.hr

Thanks to its wonderfully preserved Renaissance centre, Hvar Town is one of the most visited on the Dalmatian coast, and Hvar island's main settlement. It has long been popular with Croatian artists and celebrities, lending it a chic ambience reflected in the ever-growing number of stylish restaurants, bars and hotels. Much frequented by luxury yachts and boats in summer, Hvar's harbourside is one of the most glamorous in the Adriatic.

Hvar Town did not become the main town on the island until the 15th century, when Venetian governors decided that the harbour was easier to defend than the one at Stari Grad, and ordered all the island's noble families to move here. Hvar Town became one of the most important ports for Venetian fleets going to and from the Orient, bringing an upsurge in trade and wealth. Cultural life and monastic orders also flourished.

Dominating Hvar's harbourside main square (Trg svetog Stjepana) the Renaissance **Cathedral of St Stephen** (Katedrala sv Stjepana) has a trefoil pediment and a 17th-century bell tower standing to one side. The interior houses works of art, and the cathedral treasury has reliquaries and silverware.

On the south side of the square, the **Arsenal** (Trg svetog Stjepana) was built in the late 16th century as a dry dock for Venetian war galleys. A theatre built on the first floor in 1612 is one of the oldest in Europe. The theatre was open to all classes in a deliberate attempt to lessen social conflict between aristocrats and the working classes. The plush interior has been well preserved and there are great views of town from the balustraded terrace.

North of the main square is the ancient quarter of Groda, consisting of stone houses and narrow alleys. Here you'll find the **Hektorović Palace**,

an unfinished and strangely
alluring project by 15th-
century poet Petar Hektorović,
and a **Benedictine Convent**
(Benediktini samostan),
founded in 1664. It houses a
secluded community of nuns
who still make, display and
sell traditional Hvar lace.

Paths ascend from the
Groda district to the 16th-
century **Citadel** on the hill
above town, known locally as
Španjola. Superb views of the
surrounding coast are offered
by the citadel's ramparts.

Visible all over town is the
belfry of the former Dominican
monastery's **Church of St
Mark** (Crkva svetog Marka),
west of the main square. The
monastery was an important
centre of culture during the
Renaissance. The **Franciscan
Monastery** (Franjevacki

↑ Hvar's historic arsenal building beside
the waterfront

samostan), meanwhile, dates
from 1461 and is located
along the coastal path south
of the Old Town. The grave
of Renaissance poet Hanibal
Lucić can be seen on the floor
of the nave. There are also
many works of art in the
rooms facing the cloister.

Cathedral of St Stephen
⌖ Trg svetog Stjepana
☏ (021) 743 126 ⏰ Summer:
9am-noon, 5-7pm daily;
winter: by appointment

Arsenal
⌖ Trg svetog Stjepana
☏ (021) 741 009 ⏰ Summer:
9am-1pm, 5-11pm daily;
winter: 11am-noon daily

Hektorović Palace
⌖ Petra Keto

Benedictine Convent
⌖ Groda bb ☏ (021) 741
052 ⏰ 10am-noon, 5-7pm
Mon-Sat

Citadel
⌖ Tvrđava Španjola ⏰ Apr &
May: 10am-4pm daily; Jun-
Sep: 10am-10pm daily

Church of St Mark
⌖ Fabrika 17 ⏰ To the public

Franciscan Monastery
⌖ Križa bb ☏ (021) 741 193
⏰ May-Oct: 9am-noon daily;
Nov-Apr: 11am-noon daily

↑ Cathedral of St Stephen
overlooking Hvar Town's
central square

↑ Stone buildings and verdant cliffs along Komiža's waterfront

VIS

Ⓐ D6 🚢 From Split and Hvar; Jadrolinija, www.jadrolinija. hr 🛈 Šetalište stare Isse 5, Vis Town; www.tz-vis.hr

The island of Vis was occupied by the Greeks, who founded the town of Issa – now Vis Town. The island was later ruled by the Romans, Byzantines and Venetians. Vis went on to play a key role during World War II, when Marshal Tito used it for co-ordinating military operations. It was a closed military base until 1989 and has since been rediscovered by intrepid travellers, drawn to its jagged coastline of beaches.

①
Vis Town

🚌 From Komiža

The main town and original settlement of Vis is ranged along the shores of a broad bay. Scattered around the town are reminders of past inhabitants. On one hillside the ruins of an ancient Greek cemetery can be found, where you can see tombstones left by the town's earliest occupants. Further along the north side of the bay are remnants of Roman mosaics, once part of a 2nd-century baths complex. Just beyond, the Franciscan

Monastery Church sits on a small peninsula. Also found on the peninsula is the town's graveyard, where a monument in the form of a lion recalls the great 1866 sea battle that took place near here between the Austrian and Italian navies.

On the southern side of Vis Town's bay is the Renaissance **Church of Our Lady of Spilice** (Gospa od Spilica), with a painting by Girolamo di Santacroce. Occupying a former Austrian gun battery is the **Town Museum**, with a rich collection of Greek and Roman vases and amphorae. Beyond the town, there is a

British Cemetery that honours the servicemen who died while stationed here during both the Napoleonic Wars and World War II. There are also reminders of the early 19th-century British occupation of Vis, with the King George III Fortress and the Bentich Tower. Both are in ruins today, but are set in beautiful countryside with lovely views.

Church of Our Lady of Spilice
🏛 Ul Viški Boj 2

Town Museum
🏛 Šetalište Viškog boja 12
☎ (021) 711 729 🕐 Jun–Sep: 10am–1pm, 5–8pm daily; Oct–May: by appointment for groups only

②
Komiža

🚌 From Vis Town 🛈 Riva Svetog Mikule 2; www.tz-komiza.hr

On the western side of the island lies Komiža, a quaint port long associated with the anchovy-fishing industry. Lined with handsome stone houses and swaying palm trees, Komiža harbour is one

> **Lined with handsome stone houses and swaying palm trees, Komiža harbour is one of the most attractive in the Adriatic.**

of the most attractive in the Adriatic. A defensive tower, built by the Venetians and known as the Kaštel, can be found right on the quayside. It now houses the **Fishing Museum**, which commemorates the swift Falkuša sailing boats unique to this town that were once used to bring in the local catch. On the north side of the bay is the 16th-century **Church of Our Lady of the Pirates** (Gospa Gusarica), so-called because, legend has it, a band of pirates stole its wooden image of the Madonna before dying at sea while the statue floated safely back to shore. It has an unusual triple-nave layout. Just inland from the town centre, the Benedictine Monastery sits on a small hill, fortified by defensive bastions and flanked by vineyards. Komiža's best beaches lie south, where there is a series of coves.

Fishing Museum

Riva svetog Mikule, 4 ☎ (021) 713 019 🕒 Jun & Sep: 9–10am, 7–10pm daily; Jul & Aug: 10am–noon, 7–10pm daily

Church of Our Lady of the Pirates

🏠 Gusarica beach

---

③
Mount Hum

Looming above Komiža is Vis's highest point, Mount Hum (587 m/1,925 ft), which can be reached either by road or by a hiking path from Komiža. Superb views await at the summit, and adventure-sport enthusiasts use it as a base for hang-gliding. On the eastern side of the summit is Tito's Cave (Titova špilja), where the World War II partisan leader Josip Broz Tito based his HQ for several months in mid-1944. It was here that Tito's army planned the re-conquest of German-occupied Dalmatia. The cave is frequently open to visitors over the summer, but check with Komiža tourist office to make sure.

---

④
Plisko Polje

Plisko Polje is the main inland village on the south side of the island, where fertile fields yield some of the Adriatic's best Plavat wine, a dry red. The fields outside Plisko Polje were used to create a landing strip during World War II so that Allied planes could supply Tito's partisans, although the site is now largely covered by vineyards. One part of the former landing strip is occupied by Croatia's only cricket pitch – built by locals who emigrated to Australia and returned home with a love of the sport. South of Plisko Polje, tracks lead to the enchanting coves of Stiniva and Mala Travna, both popular with bathers despite being quite hard to reach – many trippers come on excursion boats from Vis Town or Komiža.

EAT

Pojoda

In a walled garden shaded by orange trees, Pojoda enjoys a country-wide reputation for its seafood. There are also a wealth of barley, lentil and chickpea dishes.

🏠 Don Cvijetka Marasovića 8, Vis Town
☎ (021) 711 575

Dako

Dako has one of Vis island's best terraces, with tables set out beside a pebbly beach. The menu revolves around white fish, either grilled or stewed in wine.

🏠 Gundulićeva bb Komiža
🌐 konobabako.hr

Jastožera

Local lobster is the focus here. In a pavilion mounted above the shoreline pens, there's also a strong wine list.

🏠 Gundulićeva bb Komiža 🌐 jastozera.eu

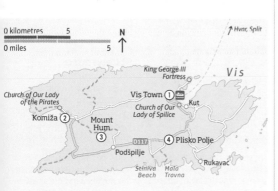

↑ Sun setting over the Dalmatian island of Trogir

4

TROGIR

D6 ✈ Split Airport, 7 km (5 miles) 🚌 (021) 881 405
🚌 (021) 881 508 🛈 Trg Ivana Pavla II 1; www.visittrogir.hr

Set on a small island just off the mainland, Trogir is one of the highlights of the Dalmatian coast. The Greeks of Issa (now Vis) settled here in the 3rd century BC, when they founded the fortified town of Tragyrion (island of goats). In the Middle Ages Trogir was protected by the Byzantine fleet, but in 1123 it was attacked by the Saracens, and abandoned. It revived 70 years later and a period of artistic growth ensued, first under the kings of Hungary and, from 1420, under Venetian rule.

Land Gate
Sjeverna vrata

Rebuilt in the 17th century, this gate once supported a drawbridge. A statue of the Blessed John of Trogir (Sv. Ivan Trogirski), a patron saint of the town, stands atop the gate.

Sea Gate
Južna vrata

🏠 Obala bana Berislavića

The Sea Gate was built at the end of the 16th century and has two beautiful columns made of blocks of light-coloured stone which frame the opening and support a projecting block on which stands the lion of St Mark.

Civic Museum
Muzej grada Trogira

🏠 Gradska vrata 📞 (021) 881 406 🕐 Jun & Sep: 10am-1pm, 5-8pm Mon-Sat; Jul & Aug: 10am-1pm, 6-9pm daily; Oct-May: 9am-2pm Mon-Fri

On the other side of the Land Gate is the Garagnin Fanfogna Palace, now the Civic Museum, with 18th-century furnishings.

There are archaeological collections, documents and antique clothes linked to the town's history.

Stafileo Palace
Palača Stafileo

🏠 Matije Gupca 20
🚫 To the public

Stafileo Palace was built in the late 15th century. A series of five windows in Venetian Gothic style punctuates each of the two floors, the openings framed by pillars, capitals and carved arches. Around the arches are reliefs of flowers and leaves. The design is attributed to the school of Juraj Dalmatinac, who worked for many years in Trogir.

Cathedral of St Lawrence
Sv. Lovre

🏠 Trg Ivana Pavla II
📞 (021) 881 426 🕐 May & Oct: 8am-6pm daily; Jun & Sep: 8am-7pm daily; Jul-Aug: 8am-8pm daily; Nov-Apr: by appointment

The cathedral stands on the site of an ancient church destroyed by the Saracens.

Construction started in around 1200, but was prolonged for decades and involved dozens of artists. The building has three semicircular apses: the central nave is higher than the side aisles, from which it is divided by eight columns.

The side door, dating from 1213, is very simple, while the cathedral's other entrance is a magnificent Romanesque door carved in around 1240 by the Dalmatian sculptor Master Radovan. It is the finest expression of Romanesque sculpture in Dalmatia. Stone lions support statues of Adam and Eve either side of the door. The church interior contains an octagonal stone pulpit from the 13th century, built and sculpted by local Dalmatian artists, a choir with wooden stalls inlaid by Ivan Budislavić towards the mid-15th century, and a ciborium on the main altar with sculptures depicting the Annunciation.

The tall bell tower was built in the 14th century, but was partly destroyed during the wars early in the following century and only the ground floor remains of the original building. When Trogir became part of Venetian territory, the bell tower was rebuilt. The first floor, with a balustrade by Matej Gojković (1422), is in the Gothic style. The third storey, from the late 16th century, was built by the sculptor Trifun Bokanić and has large arched openings

↑ Ornately carved portal of Trogir's Cathedral of St Lawrence

⑥
Town Hall
Gradska vijećnica

📍 **Trg Ivana Pavla II**

On the eastern side of the square is the Town Hall. This building was constructed in the 15th century and has three storeys with open arches. A monumental gothic staircase leads to a beautiful mullioned window with a balustrade on the upper floor, which was restored in the 19th century.

Numerous coats of arms decorate the façade, which has three Renaissance doors framed by projecting stones. The pretty porticoed court-yard is open to the public and worth taking a look at. However, the interior is arguably not the most interesting as decor goes.

EAT

Kamerlengo
In the heart of the Old Town, and with a lovely walled garden, this spot mostly serves local sea-food, with pasta dishes and steaks filling out the menu. The grilled squid is unmissable.

📍 **Vukovarska 2**
🌐 **kamerlengo.hr**

Ⓚ Ⓚ Ⓚ

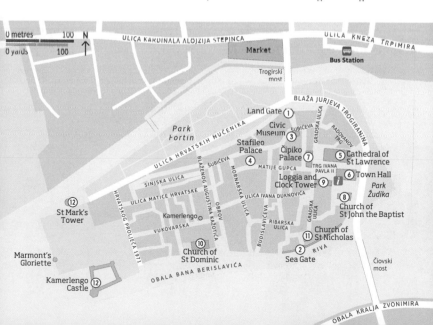

⑦ Čipiko Palace
Palača Čipiko

🏛 **Gradska ulica**
🚫 **To the public, except courtyard**

An inscription indicates 1457 as the year that the beautiful Čipiko Palace was completed. It was built for Trogir's most illustrious family, who essentially ruled here for more than 300 years and are greatly revered for their contribution to the town. Koriolan Čipiko (1425–93) was the family patriarch and gained his fortune as an admiral in the Venetian Navy. He built a string of castles on mainland Croatia.

Although the palace isn't open to the public, it is worth stopping in the town square to admire its façade, which is beautifully detailed and showcases the craftsmanship of the time. Look out for the Renaissance doorway, distinguished by its columns with capitals, and the attractive window and balcony, worthy of a *Romeo and Juliet* performance. You might be able to enter the palace's courtyard.

BORIS BURIĆ GENA

Trogir can boast a unique present-day success story: Boris Burić Gena, a tailor who specializes in making traditional, quality Croatian suits. His signature jackets are made without lapels and have antique-style brocade buttonholes. They are often worn in national ceremonies and local parades. The careful choice of fabrics, meticulous design and matching of accessories have made this talented craftsman's name. His workshop, the Burić Palace, now draws wealthy and famous clients from all over Europe *(www.gena.hr)*.

---

⑧ Church of St John the Baptist
Sv. Ivan Krstitelj

🕐 **Ask at tourist office for timings**

This small Romanesque church, built in the 13th century, is the pantheon of the powerful Čipiko family, who built the Čipiko Palace. The church once housed an impressive Art Gallery (Pinacoteca) with collections of medieval illuminated manuscripts, ornaments, paintings and precious gold pieces from various churches. This is now housed in the Museum of Sacred Art near the Cathedral of St Lawrence.

The collection also includes a sculpture (*Deposition*) by Nikola Firentinac, organ panels by Gentile Bellini (*St Jerome and St John the Baptist*) and two polyptychs by Blaise of Trogir.

---

⑨ Loggia and Clock Tower
Gradska loža

🏛 **Trg Ivana Pavla II**
🕐 **Daily**

The Loggia and the Clock Tower face John Paul II Square (Trg Ivana Pavla II). The Loggia has a roof supported by six columns with Roman capitals and dates from the 14th century. On the wall are two

reliefs, one from 1471 sculpted by Nikola Firentinac (*Justice*), and one from 1950 by Ivan Meštrović (*Ban Berislavić*). The Clock Tower stands to the left of the Loggia. It supports a pavilion dome, salvaged in 1447 from the Chapel of the Oratory of St Sebastian. The saint's statue on the façade was sculpted by Nikola Firentinac.

↑ Relief depicting Kairos, Church of St Nicholas

Church of St Dominic
Sv. Dominik

🏠 **Obala bana Berislavića**
🕐 **Summer: 8am-noon, 4-7pm daily**

Another of Trogir's churches is the Church and Monastery of St Dominic are Roman-esque-Gothic buildings con-structed in the 14th century. They were later renovated by Nikola Firentinac in the Renaissance style. The single nave church contains the tomb of Giovanni Sobota, a lawyer, attributed to Nikola Firentinac (1469),

and a very fine painting by Palma il Giovane (*Circumcision of Christ*).

Church of St Nicholas
Sv. Nikola

🏠 **Gradska ulica 2**
📞 **(021) 881 631**

The church and Benedictine convent date from the 11th century, but were rebuilt in the 16th century. The convent rooms now house the Zbirka Umjetnina Kairos, an art collection which includes the Kairos, a relief of Greek origin (1st century BC) depicting the god of opportunity, a Gothic Crucifix, and a Romanesque statue (*The Virgin with Child*)

Kamerlengo Castle and St Mark's Tower
Kaštel Kamerlengo

🏠 **Obala bana Berislavića**
🕐 **Summer: 8am-noon, 4-7pm daily**

In the southwest corner of the island stands Kamerlengo Castle, which was at one time the residence of the Venetian governor (the *kamerling* was responsible for the town's finances). It's worth taking an atmospheric walk here. The castle was built by the Venetians in about 1430, and is a four-sided structure with a hexagonal base. Facing the sea, its high walls connect the three towers and the bastion. This imposing struc-ture was once connected to St Mark's Tower (Kula svetog Marka). The large open space inside the castle is used for outdoor theatre performances and concerts during the summer months.

The bustling central square, overlooked by the Loggia and Clock Tower

St Mark's Tower (Kula svetog Marka) was built by the Venetians after the construc-tion of the castle and has the typical structure of defences created in the Renaissance period. A circular tower stands on a truncated cone base and there is a long series of embrasures on the roof. Artillery was installed on the top level to defend the strip of water that separates the island from the mainland.

What was once the parade ground, between the castle and St Mark's Tower, is now the town's sports field, often used for games of football. Look out for Marmont's Gloriette, which isn't far from the tower. This pillared gazebo, overlooking the shipyard, is often covered in graffiti but attractive nonetheless, particularly as the sun sets.

 INSIDER TIP
Spring vs Fall

A good time to visit Trogir is in the late spring or early autumn, when the narrow streets, flanked by ancient stone houses, aren't so busy. This allows space to stop and admire the carved doorways and hidden courtyards.

Sun setting dramatically over Korčula Town and island

5

KORČULA

E7 From Orebić, Split and Rijeka (060) 888 628 Korčula Town, www.jadrolinija.hr, www.krilo.hr Obala 3 br 19, Vela Luka; www.visitkorcula.eu

Dense forests of Aleppo pine, cypress and oak are found all over this island, one of the largest in the Adriatic at 47 km (29 miles) long. Mountains run the length of it, reaching 560 m (1,837 ft) at their peak. Inhabited since prehistoric times,the island was named Korkyra Melaina (Black Corfu) by the Greeks. After 1000 AD, it was fought over by Venice and the Croat kings and later by the Genoese and the Turks (in the 1298 naval battle between Genoa and Venice, the Genoese captured Marco Polo, said to have been a native of the island). Today Korčula is a popular holiday spot thanks to its cliffs and sandy beaches, its villages and Korčula, its main town *(p104)*.

1

Zrnovo

From Vela Luka and Korčula Town

Just inland from Korčula Town, Zrnovo is a sprawling area that comprises four neighbouring villages: Prvo Selo, Brdo, Kampus and Postrana. The last is the most interesting, with ancient stone houses above narrow, stepped alleys.

2

Blato

Trg dr Franje Tuđmana 4; www.tzo-blato.hr

The town of Blato has a wonderfully old-world feel. A good place to get a sense of this is the central square, with its Renaissance Arneri Castle (home to the Civic Museum) and All Saints' Church (Svi Sveti).

3

Vela Luka

Obale 3 br 19; www.tzvelaluka.hr

The island's main port and the starting point for ferries to Lastovo *(p115)*, Vela Luka was the chief harbour for exporting the wine and olive oil of Blato. On a hillside above the town is the partially open cave of **Vela spila**. It was inhabited from around 18,000 BC. Its finds are displayed in the **Vela Luka Museum**.

Vela spila

2.5km (1.5 miles) from town 5–8pm daily

Vela Luka Museum

Ulica 26/2 9am-1pm & 8-11pm Mon-Fri, 10am-1pm Sat czkvl.hr

INSIDER TIP
Olive Oil

Western Korčula is covered in olive trees, with the town of Blato at the centre of the oil industry. Head to Blato 1902 *(www.blato1902.hr)* or, in Vela Luka, Torkul *(www.fanito.hr)* for prize-winning oils.

Badija

📻 **From Korčula** 🌐 **badija. com**

Largest of the small islands surrounding Korčula, Badija is covered with fragrant pines and cypress trees. The island takes its name from the Franciscan Monastery built here in 1392 for monks who had fled from Bosnia. Island hoppers visit Badija for its blissful, secluded beaches.

Pupnat

📻 **From Vela Luka and Korčula Town**

Pupnat is situated on a ridge overlooking some of the island's most fertile land. It is here (and in the village of Čara) that the grapes for white Pošip wine are cultivated.

④

Lumbarda

📻 **From Korčula Town** 📋 **Lumbarda Tourist Board; www.tz-lumbarda.hr**

Lumbarda is a village 6 km (4 miles) southeast of the town of Korčula that is thought to have been founded by Greeks from Vis. Today the village is one of the centres of production for the liqueur-like white wine called Grk, which is made from grapes of the same name grown in the sand. There are many small beaches nearby, all havens of tranquillity (except in peak summer) that offer a number of dining options.

Pupnat is also the jumping off-point for two of Korčula's prettiest beaches: Bačva Bay and Pupnatska Luka.

EAT

Konoba Mate
This family-run establishment has become something of a legend on Korčula thanks to its creative approach to pasta. Hand-rolled *makaruni* (a Croatian pasta) is teamed with inventive ingredients, all locally grown or reared.

🏠 **Pupnat 20**
🌐 **konobamate.hr**

↑ Azure blue waters of the Pupnatska Bay near Pupnat

Did You Know?

According to myth, warrior Antenor founded Korčula Town after fleeing the Trojan horse.

↑ Steps ascending to the Land Gate, the gateway to the Old Town

HIDDEN GEM
Marco Polo House

Some say Marco Polo was from Korčula (not Venice), and this house, tucked behind St Mark's, is claimed to be his birthplace. Although doubtful, it's worth visiting for its views alone.

---

⑦

Korčula Town

🛈 Trg Travanj 1921 br 40; www.visitkorcula.eu

The whole town of Korčula is enchanting. This walled settlement hugs the coast and is steeped in history, but a modern way of life exists behind its weathered defences. From the selection of excellent restaurants and attractive palm-lined streets to the popular beaches within walking distance, Korčula Town makes for a lovely getaway.

The island's main town sits atop a peninsula, surrounded by strong 13th-century walls. These were reinforced with towers and bastions by the Venetians in the 15th century, after the town fell under their control – the first in the Adriatic. The gateway to the Old Town, the 14th-century Land Gate (Kopnena vrata), was fortified by a huge tower, the **Revelin**, which still offers brilliant views. A moat once surrounded this, with an impressive, sweeping staircase replacing it in the 19th century. Narrow, curved streets branching off the main road here were designed to lessen the impact of the bora wind.

Facing Trg sv. Marka, the central square, is the town's main monument: **St Mark's Cathedral** (Katedrala Sv. Marka), built in pale, honey-coloured stone. Most of it dates from the end of the 15th century. The skill of Korčula's sculptors and stone masons is evident in the door, where two lions guard the entrance, decorated with spiral columns and a lunette with the figure of St Mark, attributed to Bonino of Milan. On the left stands an imposing bell tower, which visitors can climb.

Next to the cathedral, in the Bishop's Palace, is the **Abbey Treasury** (Opatska riznica), known for its Dalmatian and Venetian art. The 16th-century Gabriellis Palace houses the **Town Museum** (Gradski muzej). This modest collection includes documents on Korčula's seafaring history and an archaeological section covering the period from prehistoric to Roman times.

On the seafront is **All Saints' Church** (Svi Sveti), belonging to the oldest confraternity on the island. It was built in 1301 and later remodelled in the Baroque style. In the nearby quarters is the **All Saints' Church Icon Collection** (Kolekcija Ikona), which is known for its collection of Byzantine icons from the 13th to 15th centuries.

Revelin
♿ 🚪 Land Gate ⏰ 9am–9pm daily

St Mark's Cathedral
🚪 Trg sv Marka bb ☎ (020) 715 701 ⏰ Times vary, call ahead

Abbey Treasury
🚪 Trg sv Marka ☎ (020) 711 049 ⏰ Call for times

Town Museum
🚪 Trg sv Marka ⏰ Apr–Jun: 10am–2pm Mon–Sat; Jul–Sep: 9am–9pm Mon–Sat; Oct–Mar: 10am–1pm Mon–Sat; by appt Sun 🌐 gm-korcula.com

All Saints' Church
🚪 Trg sv svetih

All Saints' Church Icon Collection
🚪 Trg Svih Svetih ⏰ Summer: 8am–3pm; winter: by appointment 🌐 bssko.com

---

ANCIENT DANCES AND FESTIVALS

The Moreška and the Kumpanija are Korčula's two most noted folk festivals. Officially, the Moreška sword dance takes place in Korčula on 29 July, the patron saint's day (St Theodore) but it is repeated on Mondays and Thursdays during the summer for tourists. It commemorates the clash between Christians and Moors in the attempt to free a girl kidnapped by the infidels. In Blato, the Kumpanija dance is dedicated to the patron saint, St Vincenca, and is celebrated with drum music. At the end, girls in bright costumes appear, accompanied by music. The dance takes place in front of the church on 28 April and is performed once a week for tourists.

Crystal blue waters off the shore of Brela, in the Makarska Riviera

EXPERIENCE MORE

⑥
Brela

▲ E6 **🛈 Trg Alojzija Stepinca bb; www.brela.hr**

The northernmost resort of the Makarska Riviera is Brela, a small seaside town of neat white houses. Brela's main advantage is its fine shingle beaches, which run along the seafront in an unbroken wave. The resort is backed by pine forest and the steep mountain wall of the Biokovo massif, which rises just inland.

⑦
Salona

▲ D6 **🚌 From Split** **🕐 Times vary, check** **🌐 solin-info.com**

The ancient town of Salona, 5 km (3 miles) from Split, is famed for its Roman ruins. Salona did not become an important centre until the Romans built a town next to the Greek city. During the rule of Augustus it became a Roman colony called Martia Iulia Salona, and later it was the capital of the province of Dalmatia. In the 1st and 2nd centuries AD the Romans built a Forum, an amphitheatre, baths and town walls reinforced with towers, and Salona became the richest, most populated city in the mid-Adriatic. In the 7th century, the Avars and the Slavs destroyed it and the city fell into disuse.

Today visitors can explore the impressive number of ancient ruins, peppered throughout olive groves and vineyards. The Manastirine area formed a burial spot and has a number of sarcophagi, as well as an early basilica.

⑧
Sinj

▲ D5 **🚗 🚌 Split** **🛈 Put Petrovca 12; www.visit sinj.com**

On the Cetina plateau the Romans founded Aequum, the present-day Čitluk, on the road to Bosnia, but the Avars and Slavs forced the inhabitants to abandon the town and move to a nearby hill called Castrum Zyn which, once fortified, was safer and easier to defend.

In the 14th century, some Franciscan monks fleeing Bosnia came here and built a **Franciscan Monastery** (Franjevački samostan) and a church. The church, which has been rebuilt several times, houses a miraculous icon of the Virgin and is a popular pilgrimage site. The monastery has been renovated and some of the rooms house archaeological finds from ancient Aequum. In 1513 the town, now called Sinj, was captured by the Turks and remained in their possession until 1686 when it was liberated by the Venetians. The Kamičak Fort's tall observation tower, allowed Sinj horsemen to ambush Ottoman troops attempting to recapture the town in 1715. In gratitude to the Miraculous Madonna for their victory, the townspeople gave her image a golden crown. This event is commemorated every August with a jousting tournament (Sinjska alka), in which expert riders compete to capture a shield. The **Museum of Sinjska alka** tells the story of this tradition, held since the 1700s.

Franciscan Monastery
🏛 A Stepinca 1 **🕐 7am–noon & 5–7pm daily** **🌐 gospa-sinjska.hr**

Museum of Sinjska alka
🏛 Put Petrovca 12 **🕐 Jun–Sep: 9am–7pm Tue–Sun; Oct–May: 8am–4pm Mon–Fri** **🌐 alka.hr**

⑨ Imotski

 🅰E6 ⓘ Ante Starčevića 3; www.visitimota.com

Stretching inland from the coastal mountains is a plateau of arid rocky terrain, covered in Mediterranean scrub and dotted with stone-built market towns that once served as frontier posts on the Venetian-Ottoman border. Imotski is typical of these: a medieval Croatian fortress that developed into a handsome ridge-top town of stone mansions. Set in a limestone landscape, Imotski is famous for the dramatic karst features on its own doorstep. The first of these is the Blue Lake (Modro jezero), a huge chasm with a lake at the bottom. A steep path winds down to the water's edge, where the level of the lake fluctuates according to rainfall – almost drying up

entirely during exceptionally hot summers. About 1.5 km (1 mile) west of town is the Red Lake (Crveno jezero), an even deeper fissure that gets its name from the ruddy tones of the surrounding rock.

⑩ Klis

🅰D6 🚉🚌 Split ⓘ Megdan 57; www.tvrdavaklis.com

This little village is dominated by the imposing **Klis Fortress** that consists of three concentric walls. Klis was founded by the Romans on a hill above a mountain pass. The Venetians strengthened the fort and enlisted the Uskoks to help fight off the Turks. The latter finally captured the fort, however, in 1537, and enlarged it, further building a mosque and a minaret. From here they menaced Split until 1648, when Venetian troops drove them off. The fort was in use until the Austrians took over, when the mosque was turned into a church and the minaret was demolished.

Klis Fortress

⏰ Summer: 8am–8pm daily; winter: 10am–5pm daily

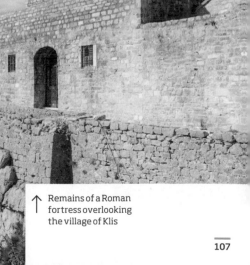

↑ Remains of a Roman fortress overlooking the village of Klis

Sun setting over the Roman ruins of Salona

Stunning landscape of
Gradac's coastline
in summertime ↑

DRINK

Bolero

Set beneath towering
pine trees on the
seaside promenade
leading to Zlatni rat,
Bolero is a cool place
to stop for coffee or
cocktails, either before
or after an excursion
to the beach. Relax on
wicker sofas with music
playing in the back-
ground and flickering
lamps as darkness
sets in.

🄰D6 🄾Put Zlatnog
rata bb, Bol, Brač
🄲(021) 306 200

Buba

Right on the beach,
Buba serves cold drinks
and hires out sun beds
and parasols by day. In
the late-afternoon,
a party mood sets in
as DJs play music.

🄰D6 🄾Biloševac bb,
Makarska 🅦beach
barbuba.com

⑪ Marina

🄰D6 Ante Rudana 47;
www.tz-marina.hr

Situated in the bay of the same
name, Marina is a small, picturesque Dalmatian town with
a marina and a pretty beach.
The town, surrounded by
top-quality olive groves, has
been inhabited since the 15th
century. Nearby, in a naturally
protected inlet, is the Yachting
Sport Agana marina. Also
located in the Riviera Marina
region are the small towns of
Vinišće, Poljica and Sevid,
which are all rich in sites of
archaeological interest.

⑫ Gradac

🄰E6 🄸Stjepan Radića 1
(May-Oct); www.gradac.hr

This town's popularity is due
to the fact that it has one of
the longest beaches in the
eastern Adriatic. Over 6 km
(4 miles) long, the beach is
lined with hotels and camp-
sites. In Gradac itself there are
two large 17th-century towers,
while in nearby Crkvine the
remains of a Roman staging
post have been found. Gradac
gets its name from the fort
(grad) built in the 17th century
to defend against the Turks.

West of Gradac is a
Franciscan Monastery, founded in the 16th century and
completed a century later. In
the rooms around the cloister
there is a fascinating folklore
collection, an art gallery and a
library. The Dalmatian scholar
Andrija Kačić Miošić (1704–60)
lived and died here.

Around 20 km (12 miles)
from Gradac is Živogošće, one
of the oldest settlements on
the Makarska coast and today
a busy tourist resort.

⑬ Brač

🄰D6 (021) 559 711
🖭(060) 393 060
🕾To Supetar from Split

The third largest island in the
Adriatic at 40 km (25 miles)
long and 15 km (9 miles) wide,
Brač has an interesting geological structure. The terrain
varies between limestone hills
and olive groves. Although

Ferries from mainland Split dock at the Old Town of Supetar on Brač, which has pebble beaches and shallow bays popular with families.

Brač has been inhabited for centuries, it was first subject to Salona (the rich Salonians built villas and sought refuge here when their town was attacked by the Avars), and later to Split. Both Split and Brač fell under Byzantine and then Venetian rule. Under the Venetians (1420–1797), villages were established but no defences were built to prevent pirates and Turks landing.

Ferries from mainland Split dock at the Old Town of **Supetar** on Brač, which has pebble beaches and shallow bays popular with families. Supetar's graveyard is the site of the Petrinović Mausoleum, a richly decorated rotunda designed by sculptor Toma Rosandić.

The village of **Pučišća** lies east of Supetar, inside a deep winding bay. Since Roman times its wealth has come from its quarries,

stone from which has been used in many grand buildings, including the Palace of Diocletian (*p88*) in Split. Pučišća is also home to the Klesarska Škola, where pupils learn to carve and sculpt the highly esteemed local stone – it's open to visitors in summer.

The major attraction at **Bol**, on the southern coast, is the long beach on the western side of town (Zlatni rat, meaning Golden Horn), a triangular spit of shingle that reaches into the sea and changes shape with the seasonal tides. It gets extremely busy in summer, with excursion boats bringing tourists here from Brač and from nearby Hvar island. It is also Croatia's top destination for windsurfing.

Bol itself is an attractive town with a pretty harbour. The Branislav Dešković Gallery sits on the waterfront and displays works by some of Croatia's leading 20th-century artists. A Dominican monastery, dating from 1475, is at Bol's edge and is decorated with paintings, including one attributed to Tintoretto.

From Bol you can climb Mount St Vitus (Vidova Gora), one of the highest peaks in the Dalmatian islands, at 778 m (2,552 ft). Hidden in a nearby ravine is Blaca Hermitage, a 16th-century monastery that's now a museum.

Supetar
📍 Porat 1; www.supetar.hr

Pučišća
📍 Trg Hrvatskoga skupa 1; www.tzo-pucisca.hr

Bol
📍 Porat bolskih pomoraca bb; www.bol.hr

BEACHES ON BRAČ

Lovrečina Bay
Just east of Supetar, Lovrečina is sandier than the other beaches on the island and comes with dramatic views of the mainland mountains. Lying below the coastal road, it is also relatively secluded.

Supetar
Situated west of the harbour, the pebble beach at Supetar curves around a shallow bay that's perfect for kids. Cafés and restaurants are close to hand and you can watch the Split ferry sailing in and out of port.

Zlatni rat
A long, pebbly spit just west of Bol, this is the most photographed beach in the whole of Croatia. It's a popular choice, and offers all the activities and refreshment facilities you would expect from a major resort.

→ Bronze sculpture depicting fishermen dragging nets, Bol harbour

 Tourists on the famous horseshoe-shaped Biokovo Skywalk in Makarska

⑭ Makarska

🅰 E6 🚌 Ulica Ante Starčevića 30; (021) 612 333 🚢 Obala kralja Tomislava 1a; (021) 611 977 🅸 Obala kralja Tomislava 1; www.makarska-info.hr

The Makarska Riviera extends from Brela to Gradac, and includes a long stretch of shore with lush vegetation sheltered by the Biokovo massif. Makarska is one of Dalmatia's most popular and sometime raucous mainland resorts, frequented by Bosnians from across the border in particular. It lies within a bay sheltered by the peninsula of St Peter's. The town was the site of the Roman Mucurum, which was destroyed by the Goths in 548 and rebuilt at a later date. It belonged to the Kingdom of Croatia until 1499, when it was conquered by the Turks, who used it as a port and trading centre until 1646, when Venetian rule began.

There are two ancient monasteries in Makarska. St Philip Neri (Sv. Filipa Nerija) was built in 1757, and has medieval and Roman-era fragments in the cloister.

The Franciscan Monastery (Franjevački samostan), built in 1614 on the foundations of a 15th-century monastery, now houses the **Malacological Museum** (Malakološki muzej), a collection of curiosities concentrated around underwater life and mollusc shells.

Opened in July 2020, the **Biokovo Skywalk** is a horseshoe-shaped walkway, cantilevered over Biokovo's rocky south-facing slopes at an altitude of 1228 m (4029 ft). With a glass floor and balustrades, it offers dizzying views over the Makarska Riviera. To reach it, hike up the old Napoleonic Road, a serpentine route built in 1810, intended to connect the coast to the mountainous hinterland.

Malacological Museum
🏠 Franjevački put 1 📞 (021) 611 256

Biokovo Skywalk
🏠 Biokovska cesta 21325, Makarska 🕐 7am–6pm daily 🌐 pp-biokovo.hr

→
The picturesque coastal town of Omiš, a popular holiday resort

Šolta

🅰 D6 🚢 From Split 🅸 Rogač; www.visitsolta.com

This long island, indented with bays and coves, covers an area of 52 sq km (20 sq miles). The economy is heavily based on agriculture thanks to reasonably fertile soil and, in recent years, tourism has also become important. The Romans called the island Solenta, and it was a holiday resort for the nobility of Salona. The ruins of many villas can be found in lovely locations across the island.

After the attack on Salona in 614, some of the refugees fled here and villages were built. Some still have small churches dating from the early Middle Ages. The island was later largely abandoned

> 💬 **INSIDER TIP**
> **Biokovo Hiking**
>
> Looming high above the resorts of the Makarska Riviera, the Biokovo massif offers limitless opportunities for the adventurous hiker. Do be aware that paths are steep, and weather conditions change quickly.

in favour of Split, due to constant Turkish raids.

Today, many people from Split have holiday homes on Šolta. The fishing ports of Stomorska, at the eastern end of the island, and Maslinica, in the west, both lie in beautiful bays. There are many pretty inlets near Maslinica that make ideal moorings for yachts and motorboats. But it is worth venturing inland, too: the main village of Grohote is an Adriatic settlement of well-preserved stone houses and narrow streets.

Omiš

ⓐD6 ☎(021) 864 210
☎(021) 861 025 **ⓕ**Fošal 1a;
www.visitomis.hr

In the late Middle Ages Omiš was known as the residence of the terrifying corsairs who fought fiercely against Venetian rule from the 12th century until 1444, when the town fell to Venice. Today it is a peaceful holiday resort, and the starting point for visits to the valley of the River Cetina.

In July, the Dalmatinksa Klapa festival attracts visitors who come to hear Klapa, a kind of plainsong traditional to Dalmatia. It is still very popular, even among the young.

Only a few traces of the Roman *municipium* of Onaeum remain but many of the medieval defences built by the counts of Kačić and Bribir are still visible on a hill, once the site of Stari grad ("Old Town"). These consist of the walls going down to the River Cetina and also the ruins of a large fort (Fortica) with its distinctive high tower. From the fort there is a splendid view of Omiš and the central Dalmatian islands.

There are three interesting religious buildings in the town. The Renaissance church of St Michael (Sv. Mihovil), has a pointed bell tower and was originally a defensive structure. Inside is a 16th-century wooden altar, a large 13th-century wooden cross and two paintings by Matteo Ingoli of Ravenna (1587–1631). At the end of the main road is the 16th-century Oratory of the Holy Spirit (Sv. Duh) with the painting *Descent of the Holy Spirit* by Palma il Giovane (1544–1628). The most fascinating monument here, however, is in Priko, on the opposite bank of the River Cetina. The 10th-century church of St Peter (Sv. Petar) is one of Dalmatia's most appealing pre-Romanesque churches. It has a single nave, a dome, and remains from the early Christian period incorporated into the walls.

Cetina Gorge, immediately behind Omiš, is a beautiful natural environment, and a fantastic place for rafting, canoeing and adventure sports. Many tour providers arrange one-day and half-day trips here.

 Sun-seekers enjoying
Tučepi's tree-lined
shingle beach

 17

Zaostrog

E6 **Fra A Kačića
Miošića; (021) 629 050**

Zaostrog is a peaceful beach-side village, particularly popular with campers. Its most important monument is the 15th-century Franciscan **Zaostrog samostan** (monastery), home to a beautiful cloister and garden. The monastery's most famous resident was Andrija Kačić Miošić (1704-60), author of *Pleasant Conversation of the Slav Peoples* (Razgovor ugodni naroda slovinskog), an influential history of the Croatian nation and its struggles against outside rule. The monastery now houses a museum, which contains rare manuscripts, an ethno-graphic collection, and a gallery of religious paintings by Mladen Veža (1916-2010). The monastery also displays a Mannerist painting of the *Last Supper*, in which a Dalmatian dog sits beneath the table. This is often taken as visual evidence that the spotted breed really did originate on the Croatian coast.

Zaostrog samostan
Obala hrvatskih domoljuba 36 Jun-Sep: 10am-noon, 7-9pm daily samostan-zaostrog.com

 18

Tučepi

E6 **From Makarska
Donji ratac; www.
tucepi.com**

Southeast of Makarska, Tučepi is another coastal resort that offers a glorious shingle beach. It is also a good base for exploring Mount Biokovo, whose stark grey slopes tower above the resort to the east. On the lower slopes of the mountain is Gornje Tučepi ("Upper Tučepi"), a half-abandoned settlement of grey stone houses that was once a centre of vine- and olive-growing. It is a prime example of the once thriving mountainside villages that became depopulated once the growth of tourism encouraged people to move down to the coast.

 19

Podgora

E6 **Kačića-Miošića 2;
ww.tz-podgora.hr**

Podgora is a relatively new settlement, formed when the inhabitants of Gornja Podgora, just inland, moved to the coast to take advantage of the booming tourism industry. Primarily visited for its attractive pebble beach, Podgora also harbours an unusual piece of modern architecture in the shape of the **Church of the Assumption** (Crkva Uznesenja). This concrete structure was built in 1962, and takes the form of a round-roofed tent. Its architect, Ante Rožić, left the exterior deliberately unadorned in order to give it a raw, newly built appearance. Uphill from the centre is a towering abstract monument known as Galebova Krila ("Wings of the Seagull"), built in 1962 to commemorate the exploits of the Partisan navy – founded at Podgora in 1942 – during World War II.

Church of the Assumption
Ivana Meštrovića 18
(021) 625 011

20

Vrgorac

E6 **From Split and
Trogir** tzvrgorac.hr

Inland from the Makarska Riviera, on the eastern flanks of the Biokovo massif, the town of Vrgorac nestles beneath the medieval Gradina Fortress. It was of crucial strategic importance during the 15th–17th-century period of Ottoman rule, when the circular Avala tower was built just beneath the summit of the hill. Due to Vrgorac's position on the Venetian-Ottoman frontier, its wealthier families built houses in the form of defensive towers, many of which can still be seen around the town centre. The Dizdarević Tower was the birthplace of Tin Ujević (1891–1955), the poet and Bohemian who is depicted in plaques and statues all over Central Dalmatia.

㉑

Živogošće

🗺 E6 ℹ Porat 87; www. zivogosce.hr

Živogošće is a long sprawling settlement with three main hubs, the most important of which is Porat (or "Port") to the northwest. As well as being the site of a pristine stretch of pebble beach, it is one of the few harbours on the Makarska Riviera where you can still see working fishing boats alongside tourist-excursion crafts. Rising above the eastern end of the beach is the Monastery of the Holy Cross (Samostan sv. Križa), founded in 1620 by Franciscans fleeing Ottoman rule in Herzegovina. Further southeast are Živogošće's remaining settlements: Mala Duba and Dlato, smaller and quieter places that both have popular beaches.

㉒

Lastovo

🗺 E7 🚢 From Korčula, Split and Dubrovnik during summer ℹ Pjevor 7; www. tz-lastovo.hr

The island of Lastovo, which is surrounded by about 40 small islands and rocky outcrops, was once a military area and thus closed to tourists. The lack of tourism has helped to preserve the old buildings. It is 9 km (5 miles) long and about 6 km (4 miles) wide. Although the terrain is mostly mountainous (Mount Hum reaches a height of 417 m/ 1,368 ft), vines, olives and fruit are cultivated on the terraced slopes. The vast majority of the coast is rocky, apart from the bay close to the town of Lastovo.

Traces of the long period of rule by Dubrovnik (1252–1808) are visible in the upper part of the town and in the fort, which was built by the French in 1819 on the site of an earlier castle, destroyed in 1606.

A church from the 14th century and a 16th-century loggia stand in the main square. Religious festivals – which are very popular on the island – are celebrated here. The locals wear brightly coloured traditional costumes, and celebrate with traditional dances accompanied by antique musical instruments.

Mention of the small Church of St Blaise (Sv. Vlaho), situated at the entrance to the village, is found in 12th-century documents. Also of ancient origin, in the cemetery, is the Romanesque Oratory of Our Lady in the Field (Gospa od Polja), which dates from the 15th century. Remnants of buildings and rustic villas testify to the presence of the Romans on the island.

→

Typical chimneys in Lastovo Town on the island of Lastovo

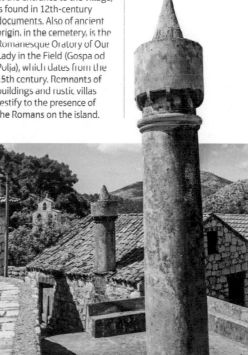

TOP 4 WATERSPORTS ACTIVITIES

Windsurfing
Bol on Brač is Croatia's top windsurfing destination, with Big Blue offering tuition and equipment *(www. bigbluesport.com)*.

Sea Kayaking
Paddle round the islets of the Korčula archipelago with Korčula Outdoor, which offers guided trips *(www.korcula-outdoor.com)*.

SUP
Explore Brač's north coast aboard a stand-up paddle (SUP) board with Aldura Sport *(www.aldura-sport.hr)*.

Scuba Diving
Discover some of Croatia's top dive sites with Aqualis Dive Centre *(www.hvardiving.com)*.

ZADAR AND NORTHERN DALMATIA

Northern Dalmatia is centered around two of Croatia's most seductive cities: Zadar, a vibrant blend of ancient, medieval and contemporary, and Šibenik, famous for its stunning collection of fortresses. Some of Croatia's most celebrated national attractions are within striking distance, with the waterfalls of the Krka National Park just inland from Šibenik, and the offshore wonderlands of Telašćica Bay and the islands of Kornati National Park a short boat trip away.

Zadar was settled by Liburnians although it was the Romans who gave the city its grid-plan layout that still survives today. Šibenik was founded by Croats in the early Middle Ages, although the whole region fell to Venice in 1408. Expansion of the Ottoman Empire in the 15th and 16th centuries caused huge population changes, with Orthodox Christian stockbreeders fleeing Ottoman rule to take up residence in the Dalmatian hinterland. The Venetians and Ottomans fought repeatedly for control of the seaboard; the imposing fortifications in both Zadar and Šibenik were the result. During the Homeland War of 1991–5 the front line ran just inland from Zadar and Šibenik, both of which were subject to enemy bombardment.

ZADAR AND NORTHERN DALMATIA

Must Sees

1. Zadar
2. Šibenik
3. Kornati National Park
4. Krka National Park

Experience More

5. Dugi otok
6. Pašman
7. Premuda
8. Ugljan
9. Molat
10. Olib
11. Drniš
12. Silba
13. Primošten
14. Pag
15. Nin
16. Paklenica National Park
17. Knin
18. Rogoznica
19. Vrlika
20. Lake Vrana
21. Murter
22. Zrmanja Canyon
23. Tisno
24. Biograd na Moru
25. Vodice

↑ The majestic Romanesque Cathedral of St Anastasia

①

ZADAR

🗺 C5 ✈ Zemunik 8 km (5 miles), www.zadar-airport.hr
🚍 (023) 212 555 🚌 Starčevića 6, www.liburnija-zadar.hr
⛴ Jadrolinija, (023) 254 800 ℹ Jurja Barakovića 5;
www.zadar.travel

This ancient city has been reborn and is arguably Croatia's coolest metropolis. Inhabited by the Illyrians and then the Romans, it became an important centre and port. The city saw conflict between Venice and Hungary, in the 12th–13th centuries, before being sold to Venice and named Zara. Churches and palaces were built, and suffered much damage in World War II. Today, creative bars and art installations sit alongside ancient ruins and stunning coastal vistas.

①
Land Gate and Walls
Kopnena vrata

The Land Gate was built in 1543 by the great Veronese architect Michele Sanmicheli and formed the entrance to the city. The gate has a large central aperture and two smaller openings at the sides, divided by four white stone pilasters supporting four half-columns. Above the main gate is a relief of St Chrysogonus on horseback and the lion of St Mark, a symbol of Venetian rule. Beyond the gate are a few remains of the ancient walls and the former Venetian arsenal. The walls were added to the UNESCO World Heritage List in 2017.

---

②
Church of St Simeon
Sv. Šime

🏛 Trg Petra Zoranića 7
📞 (023) 211 705 🕐 8:30am–noon, 5–7pm Mon–Sat

First constructed in Romanesque style, the church was rebuilt after 1632 to house the remains of the saint, which are kept in a silver reliquary. This work, nearly 2 m (6 ft) long, was made between 1377 and 1380 by Francesco da Milano. It was commissioned by Louis's wife, Elizabeth of Hungary, in atonement for stealing a finger of St Simeon when she entered the city. The reliquary is opened once a year on St Simeon's Day (8th Oct). A life-size relief of the saint appears on its lid.

EAT

Pet Bunara
Turning out traditional food with an experimental edge, Pet Bunara specializes in fresh seafood and home-grown organic produce. The menu changes constantly, depending on what's in season and the chef's own mood.

🏛 Stratico 1
🌐 petbunara.hr

 Ⓚⓝ Ⓚⓝ Ⓚⓝ

---

③
Cathedral of St Anastasia
Katedrala sv. Stošije

🏛 **Forum** ☎ **(023) 251 708**
🕐 **8am-noon, 5-7pm daily**

The magnificent Cathedral of St Anastasia stands on the site of the Forum *(p122)*. Founded by the Byzantines in the 9th century, it was rebuilt in the Romanesque style in the 12th–13th centuries. It has a rectangular ground plan with a large semicircular apse. The harmonious façade with three doors, completed in 1324, is divided in half horizontally with the upper part character-ized by arches and columns and two rose windows.

The three-aisle interior is divided by two rows of columns and pilasters which support the high arcades. At the sides of the raised presbytery are engraved wooden choir stalls, the work of the Venetian Matteo Moronzoni (early 15th century). The ciborium with four Corinthian columns is decorated with different motifs (1332). Underneath is a small sarcophagus containing the remains of St Anastasia, dating from the 9th century.

The altars are mostly Baroque and very impressive, with various adornments.

④
Sea Gate
Vrata sv. Krševana

Sometimes referred to as St Chrysogonus' Gate, this complex construction is the result of rebuilding work carried out by architect Michele Sanmicheli in 1573 on a Roman arch dedicated to the Sergi family. On the seaward side is the Venetian lion of St Mark and a memorial stone recalling the Battle of Lepanto (1571). On the inner side of the gate is a stone commemorating Pope Alexander III's visit in 1177.

⑤
Museum of Ancient Glass
Muzej antičkog stakla

🏛 **Poljana Zemaljskog odbora 1** 🕐 **Summer: 9am-9pm daily; winter: 9am-4pm Mon-Fri**
🌐 **mas-zadar.hr**

Housed in the restored Cosmacendi Palace, this gem of a museum displays an impressive number of ancient Roman glass objects found on archaeological sites in Zadar and its surroundings. Everything from perfume vials to funerary urns are displayed. Glass-blowing demonstrations are held during the summer (9am–2pm Mon–Sat) and there is a lovely gift shop containing all manner of glass souvenirs.

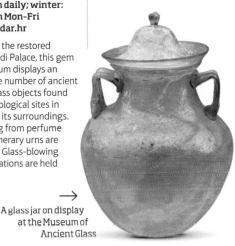

→ A glass jar on display at the Museum of Ancient Glass

⑥
Forum

This gathering place was the centre of public life in ancient times, though now it is a hotch-potch of ruins. The main square of the ancient Roman city of Jadera was built between the 1st century BC and the 3rd century. The Forum, which is around 90 m (295 ft) long and 45 m (147 ft) wide, was bordered on three sides by porticoes with marble columns. In the present-day square, Poljana pape Ivana Pavla II, are the foundations of public buildings, including a meeting hall, some of the original paving, several *tabernae* (rectangular-shaped trading areas) and a monumental pillar. This was used in the Middle Ages as a "pillar of shame", to which wrongdoers were chained. You can still see some metalwork embedded in the stone.

⑦
People's Square
Narodni trg

In the heart of Zadar's Old Town is Narodni trg, otherwise referred to as the People's Square. In better condition

Did You Know?

Alfred Hitchcock said that "Zadar has the most beautiful sunset in the world."

than the Roman Forum, this Renaissance square has also been a hub of public life in Zadar for centuries; it's still a bustling place, surrounded by numerous cafés.

The Town Hall, which was built in 1934, faces People's Square, as does the Renaissance City Loggia (Gradska loža) built by Michele Sanmicheli in 1565 as the city courts. Public announcements and court rulings were shouted from the Loggia. This building is now used for exhibitions of mainly contemporary art.

Also nearby is the 16th-century Town Guard Palace, which has a handsome clock tower over-looking the square. The building today houses the Ethnographic Museum, displaying fascinating collections of costumes and objects from across the county.

⑧
Church of St Chrysogonus
Sv. Krševan

🏛 Poljana pape Aleksandra III 🔒 For restoration

Prior to AD 1000 a church and monastery were built by Benedictines on the site of the Roman market. While the church, rebuilt in 1175, has survived with few alterations, the monastery was destroyed in World War II, when the city as a whole experienced heavy bombing. At the height of its splendour, the monastery possessed a rich library and a scriptorium, famous for its transcribed and illuminated manuscripts.

The three-aisle Church of St Chrysogonus is divided by columns that were salvaged from a previous building and has a simple Romanesque appearance. The main altar, however, is Baroque and has statues of Zadar's four patron saints: Chrysogonus, Zoilus, Simeon and Anastasia. The apse is the best-preserved part of the Church of St Chrysogonus, with a few 13th-century frescoes and a Romanesque crucifix on the altar.

Remains of the Roman Forum, flanked by the Church of St Donatus ↑

Church of St Mary
Sv. Marija i Zlato i srebro Zadra

🏠 Trg opatice Čike 1
📞 (023) 250 496
🕐 Summer: 10am–1pm, 5–7pm Mon–Sat, 10am–1pm Sun; winter: 10am–12:30pm, 5–6:30pm Mon–Sat

On one side of Poljana pape Ivana Pavla II square stands a tall Romanesque bell tower, built for King Koloman in 1105, and the Church of St Mary. The church, built in 1066, has undergone various alterations and now has a Renaissance façade. The three-aisle interior has a large women's gallery; the stuccowork is from 1744.

The former monastery next door is now the **Gold and Silver of Zadar** (Zlato i srebro Zadra). This museum is, quite literally, the jewel in Zadar's crown. On the ground floor are gold pieces; on the upper floor are paintings and statues, including a fine polyptych by Vittore Carpaccio (1487).

Gold and Silver of Zadar
🏠 Trg opatice Čike 1
📞 (023) 250 496 🕐 10am–1pm Mon–Sat, 10am–noon Sun

↑ Roman silver fibula, found at a grave outside of Zadar, Archeological Museum

Archeological Museum
Arheološki muzej

🏠 Trg opatice Čike 1
🕐 Jan–Mar: 9am–2pm Mon–Sat; Apr, May & Oct: 9am–3pm Mon–Sat; Jun–Sep: 9am–9pm daily; Nov & Dec: 9am–2pm Mon–Sat
🌐 amzd.hr

This brilliant museum is housed in a modern concrete building a stone's throw from the Roman Forum, offering an architectural contrast to the ancient ruins. The museum's trove of treasures includes objects that date from pre-history all the way to more recent times, and which originate from the entire Zadar area, including the Zadar archipelago. Of particular interest is glass from the Roman period and the early Christian and medieval liturgical objects; not forgetting the 2.5-m- (8-ft-) high statue of Emperor Augustus, who greets visitors in the entrance. The museum also has a model of the Forum, to help visitors better visualize the Roman meeting place. The museum does offer tours but note that these are by appointment only.

DRINK

Garden Lounge
Founded in 2004, this open-air lounge bar is located on top of Zadar's city walls and it remains the pick of the local bars. Mellow during the day, with board games and newspapers to hand, the bar transforms at night. Expect full DJ-driven energy and decent cocktails.

🏠 Bedemi zadarskih pobuna
🌐 thegarden.hr

↑ Gathering on the unique Sea Organ while the sun sets

⑪ Sea Organ and Greeting to the Sun

📍 Obala kralja Petra Krešimira IV

Not many cities can boast a public musical instrument controlled by the power of nature. Designed by Croatian architect Nikola Bašić (1946–), the Sea Organ is built into Zadar's quayside. Under white stone steps are a set of pipes which produce musical chords naturally as waves push air up through the pipes. To sit on the steps and listen to the organ's murmurs is a calming and meditative experience, and has proven massively popular. The site is particularly busy on mild summer evenings, when locals and visitors gather to enjoy Zadar's famous sunsets.

Near the organ is another installation by the same architect, called *Greeting to the Sun* (Pozdrav suncu). This circle set on the seafront is intended to be a companion to the Sea Organ. It consists of 300 glass plates with sensors, which absorb sunlight by day. Then, at night, these release light patterns and create a multicoloured, hypnotic display. You can walk acoss the installation, bathed in light, and become part of the spectacle, while also listening to the Sea Organ's haunting tunes drift across from the water's edge.

⑫ Museum of Illusions

📍 Poljana Zemaljskog odbora 2 🕐 Jun–Sep: 9am–10pm daily; Apr & May, Oct & Nov: 10am–8pm daily; Dec–Mar: 10am–4pm daily 🌐 zadar.muzejiluzija.com

This may not be a museum in the traditional sense but it does contain an entertaining collection of optical tricks and visual games. Rooms with sloping floors or furniture on the walls challenge the brain's ideas of perspective and proportion, while providing plenty of photo opportunities.

⑬ Rector's Palace
Kneževa palača

📍 Poljana Šime Budinića 🕐 Jun–Sep: 9am–8pm Mon–Fri, 10am–2pm Sat & Sun 🌐 kneziva.hr

Originating in the 13th century but reconstructed many times since, the Rector's Palace served as the heart of the

Austrian administration until World War I. The building was severely damaged during the Homeland War of 1991–5 and was painstakingly restored to provide a home for seasonal art exhibitions and some of the collections of the Zadar National Museum. Occupying the first-floor function rooms, the *Six Salon Stories* exhibition (Šest salonskih priča) covers six crucial periods in the cultural history of Zadar by juxtaposing the furnishings and artworks of the time. The star exhibit is the anonymous 18th-century canvas *The Sacrifice of Iphigenia*, which was damaged in World War II and fully restored in 2012. Exhibitions of contemporary art are held in adjoining galleries.

→ Captain's Tower overlooking the Square of the Five Wells

> The park is named after Croatia's 10th-century Queen Jelena, Zadar-born wife of King Mihajlo Krešimir II. Her epitaph called her "Helen the Glorious".

Square of the Five Wells

Trg pet bunara

Laid out in 1594, the Square of the Five Wells features a row of five hexagonal well-heads topped by cast-iron pulleys. The well-heads cover a vast underground water cistern, built at a time when the city was in danger of Ottoman siege. Repaved in and atmospherically lit at night, the square is now one of Zadar's most attractive public spaces. The pentagonal Captain's Tower was built at the same time and holds a small gallery open in the tourist season.

Queen Jelena Madijevka Park

Perivoj kraljice Jelene Madijevke

Rising above the Square of the Five Wells is the Queen Jelena Madijevka Park, laid out in 1829 on top of the 16th-century Grimani Bastion. Above the city moat, the bastion was a key component in the wave of fortification-building carried out by Venetian military engineer Michele Sanmicheli. The park is named after Croatia's 10th-century Queen Jelena, Zadar-born wife of King Mihajlo Krešimir II. Her epitaph called her "Helen the Glorious".

Vladimir Nazor Park

Perivoj Vladimira Nazora

Zadar's biggest green space fills the interior of the citadel known as the Forte, built in 1567 on the orders of Venetian commander Sforza Pallavicino. The park was opened to the public by Dragutin Blažeković, the Austrian governor of Dalmatia, in 1890. Its barracks now serve as a high school. The Forte was then bounded by a moat and became known as the "green island".

STAY

Bastion

This restored 19th-century mansion found beside the city walls exudes an intimate, boutique feel. Rooms are plush and the staff are attentive. There is a small spa on site, perfect for winding down after a busy day of sightseeing, and a superb spread at breakfast.

🏠 Bedemi zadarskih pobuna 13
🌐 hotel-bastion.hr

Forum

Offering vibrant and modern interiors and several private double rooms, this is one of Croatia's super design hostels. The downstairs Forum Café is a social hub for residents and non-residents alike. Some bedrooms have wonderful views.

🏠 Široka 20
🌐 hostelforum zadar.com

Club Funimation Borik

Located in a beachside suburb 4 km (2 miles) west of the city centre, this is one of the best family hotels in Croatia. As well as creche facilities there are play areas for kids, sports grounds, plenty of green space and a pebble beach.

🏠 Majstora Radovana 7, Borik
🌐 falkensteiner.com

⑰ ⊘

CHURCH OF ST DONAT

🏛 Forum 📞 (023) 250 613 🕐 Apr, May & Oct: 9am–5pm daily; Jun & Sep: 9am–7pm daily; Jul–Aug: 9am–9pm daily; Nov–Mar: by appointment 🌐 amzd.hr

This cylindrical church is unique. It was built in the early 9th century on the paving stones of the former Roman Forum, and remains one of the finest examples of Byzantine architecture in Dalmatia.

The Church of the Holy Trinity, which later took the name of its founder, Bishop Donat, is an important Croatian relic. It has a circular ground plan with three circular apses plus a Women's Gallery that circles the interior and creates an upper storey. St Donat has not been used as a church for several centuries, having since served as a storehouse and museum. Today it is a much-loved city landmark, and, thanks to its atmospheric space and excellent acoustics, is a venue for the St Donat Music Evenings in July and August (*www.donat-festival.com*).

↑ The circular interior of the church, seen from the Women's Gallery

Stones from the Roman Forum were used for the paving; other Roman material is visible in the walls, entrance and gallery.

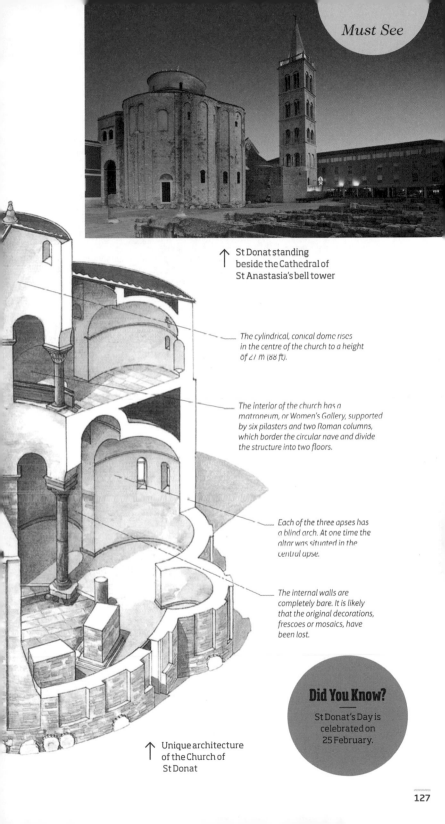

↑ St Donat standing beside the Cathedral of St Anastasia's bell tower

The cylindrical, conical dome rises in the centre of the church to a height of 27 m (88 ft).

The interior of the church has a matroneum, or Women's Gallery, supported by six pilasters and two Roman columns, which border the circular nave and divide the structure into two floors.

Each of the three apses has a blind arch. At one time the altar was situated in the central apse.

The internal walls are completely bare. It is likely that the original decorations, frescoes or mosaics, have been lost.

↑ Unique architecture of the Church of St Donat

Did You Know?

St Donat's Day is celebrated on 25 February.

↑ Šibenik's Old Town pressed up against the mouth of the River Krka

②
ŠIBENIK

🗺️C5 ✈️Split, 97 km (60 miles) 🚌Fra J. Milete 24 🚐Draga 44 🚢Dr. F. Tuđmana 7 ℹ️Local: Obala palih omladinaca 3; Regional: Fra N. Ružića bb 🌐visitsibenik.hr

This picturesque city, with its steep streets and arched passages, is a joy to explore. Between 1412 and 1797 it was ruled by the Venetians, becoming one of the liveliest cultural centres in Renaissance Croatia. This gave way to French then Austrian occupation until 1917. The war during the 1990s brought about the collapse of local industry, but the situation today is much improved.

①
Civic Museum
Muzej grada Šibenika

🏛️Gradska vrata 3 🕙10am-9pm Tue-Sat 🌐muzej-sibenik.hr

Otherwise known as the Count's Palace (Kneževa palača), the building takes its name from the Count Niccolò Marcello, who built it in the 12th–13th centuries. It was the Venetian governor's residence and now serves to uphold the cultural-historical heritage of Šibenik.

The Civic Museum houses coin collections, archaeological finds from the Neolithic to Roman periods, tomb finds, early Croatian sculptures (7th–9th centuries) and a rich archive of historical documents about the city and its territory, many of which are from the medieval period.

②
Church of St Francis
Sv. Frane

🏛️Trg Nikole Tomaszea 1 🕙7:30am-7:30pm daily 🌐muzejsvetogfrane.hr

Along the busy seafront, on the southern edge of the Old Town centre, once stood the Monastery and Church of St Francis, founded in 1229 and destroyed during a raid in 1321. Some capitals, a few statues, and parts of the arches in the cloister remain of the original structure. Towards the middle of the 15th century several new chapels were added on.

In the middle of the 18th century the church underwent top-to-bottom renovation: the buildings were completely rebuilt in the Baroque style, the wooden ceiling and the sumptuous gilded carved wooden altars were remade, and every wall was decorated with paintings.

Inside, in the first chapel on the left, is a great organ from 1762, made by the famous Croation organ-builder Petar

← An ancient cast-iron bell housed in the Civic Museum of Šibenik

Nakić. The large cloister has kept its 14th-century structure and the monastery is home to a library with manuscripts and liturgical material.

---

③

Church of St Barbara
Sv. Barbara

🏛 Kralja Tomislava 📞 (022) 214 899 🕐 Museum: May–Oct: 9am–1pm, 5–7pm; Nov–Apr: by appt

The small Church of St Barbara, hidden behind the Cathedral of St James, was built around the middle of the 15th century, and conserves parts of an older building. Irregular openings make the façade unusual: the lunette on the main door has a statue of St Nicholas from the workshop of Bonino of Milan (1430). Inside is an altar made by a youthful pupil of Juraj Dalmatinac, Giovanni da Pribislao, who was obliged to painstakingly recreate another altar which had been saved from the previous church.

The church also houses a modest museum featuring a rich and interesting collection of religious art, with paintings, sculptures and illuminated texts dating from the 14th to the 16th centuries.

↑ The arches of the Town Hall opening onto the square in front of the cathedral

④

Town Hall
Gradska vijećnica

🏛 Trg Republike Hrvatske

In front of the cathedral's Door of Lions stands Šibenik's old Town Hall, formerly the seat of the city council, built by Michele Sanmicheli between 1532 and 1543 and restored after it was damaged during World War II.

This two-storey structure has an open portico with nine arches on the ground floor, while the upper floor consists of a loggia with a balustrade.

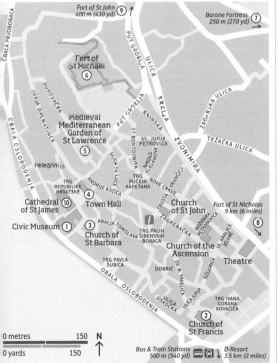

EAT

Pelegrini
This Michelin-starred restaurant has been consistently voted number one by Croatian foodies, so you'll need to book ahead. The three-to six-course menus bring out the best of local meat and fish. Enjoy the views of the cathedral from the outdoor terrace.

🏛 Jurja Dalmatinca 1
🌐 pelegrini.hr

Ⓚ Ⓚ Ⓚ

↑ The crossed pathway and central fountain of the Medieval Mediterranean Garden

⑤
Medieval Mediterranean Garden of St Lawrence

Srednjovjekovni samostanski mediteranski vrt sv. Lovre (SSMV)

⬜ Trg Republike Hrvatske 📞 (022) 212 515 ⏰ Summer: 8am–11pm daily; winter: 9am–4pm daily

Maintained by the children of a local high school, the MMG is one of Šibenek's most popular attractions. This monastery garden, which fans out from a central fountain into four sections separated by a cross-shaped pathway, follows a medieval design – the only one of its kind in Croatia. It has a varied assortment of flowers, herbs and plants. Capers have been planted in the gaps of the stone walls as a homage to renowned Venetian sculptor and architect Juraj Dalmatinac, who is believed to have been the first to bring them back to Šibenek from Venice. It also hosts a pleasant open-air café through summer.

⑥
Fort of St Michael

Tvrđava sv. Mihovila

⏰ Winter: 10am–5pm Tue–Sun 🌐 tvrdava-kulture.hr

The first historical records of this restored medieval fort date it to around early 12th century, when it was used as a base for Adriatic pirates and suffered attacks from Venetian forces. Later it was destroyed by rebellious locals, and once again when the powder magazine was struck by lightning. When it was rebuilt in the 16th–17th centuries, the city's changing defence needs were taken into account and the towers were omitted.

The fortress's keep offers a superb panorama of Šibenik's Old Town and has the best possible vantage point from which to admire the dome and roof of the cathedral. The fortress is used for rock and pop concerts in the summer. The maritime views from the raked seating are amazing.

↑ A cannon inside Barone Fortress with a mural behind

TOP 3
ISLANDS OFF ŠIBENIK

Zlarin
A 30-minute boat ride away is sleepy Zlarin, which excels at charm without mass tourism. The beaches here are rocky and backed by pine trees.

Prvić
A 15-minute ride brings you to Prvić Luka, the main settlement, which has a variety of beach and dining options. Prvić Luka is also home to the Faust Vrančić Memorial Centre, dedicated to the Da Vinci-esque scientist and inventor who drew diagrams of incredible devices such as wind turbines and parachutes.

Krapanj
Just 300 m (980 ft) across the water, this peaceful island is distinguished by its traditional stone dwellings fronted by delightful beaches.

⑦
Barone Fortress

Tvrđava Barone

Barone Fortress, also called Šubićevac, was constructed concurrently with its near neighbour the Fort of St John, and withstood a long siege by Ottoman forces. It now houses a museum in which visitors can use augmented reality spectacles in order to see how the fortress might have looked in the 17th century and get a taste of fortress life. There is also a gastro-cultural centre devoted to the traditional food and wine of the central Dalmatian region, and the opportunity to buy delicatessen products in the fortress shop. The views from the battlements are superb.

⑧ Fort of St Nicholas
Tvrđava sv. Nikola

🚌 🕐 May–Oct daily 🌐 kanal-
svetog-ante.com

The Fort of St Nicholas is a UNESCO-listed masterpiece of military architecture and a monumental triangular structure jutting out into St Anthony's Channel, commanding seaborne approaches to the city. It was built by Venetian engineer Michele Sanmicheli in 1540–1547 to shield Šibenik from Ottoman naval attacks and was one of the strongest and most unusual fortifications in the Adriatic Sea.

You can visit the fort by boat between May and October. Boats depart from Šibenik waterfront – the ride takes 20 minutes and is followed by a 50-minute tour of the fort.

Did You Know?
The Fort of St John is sometimes called "Tanaja", meaning "pliers", referring to its pincer shape.

⑨ Fort of St John
Tvrđava sv. Ivan

🔒 For restoration
🌐 tvrdava-kulture.hr

Highest of all the fortresses above the city, the Fort of St John was built rapidly in 1646 in response to the growing danger of Turkish invasion. With the help of the citizens of Šibenik, it was completed in a matter of weeks. Built on a star-shaped plan to provide a variety of defensive angles, it helped protect the city from the Ottomans for many years, including an attack by 20,000 troops in 1647.

The fort is now empty, although visitors are free to enter and explore the walled compound – albeit at their own risk. There are plans to turn it into a major tourist attraction in the coming years. For now, you can enjoy the stunning views over the Old Town below, taking in St Michael's Fortress further down the hill and St Anthony's Channel beyond, and out onto the Adriatic Sea.

STAY

D-Resort
With its winding, asymmetrical form, this is one of those skyline-changing buildings that gives a city a whole new image. D-Resort was designed by Nikol Bašić, the man behind Zadar's Sea Organ *(p124)*, to complement the shape of the peninsula on which the hotel sits. This award-winning resort is replete with smart contemporary interiors, curving facades, several plush bars and restaurants and a roof garden with superb maritime views.

🏠 Obala Jerka Šizgorića 1, Šibenik
🌐 dresortsibenik.com

Ⓚ Ⓚ Ⓚ

↑ A visitor looking out over Šibenik from the ruins of the Fort of St John

⑩ ✍

CATHEDRAL OF ST JAMES

📍 Trg Republike Hrvatske 1 📞 (022) 214 418 🕐 Apr-May 8:30am-7:30pm daily; Jun-Nov: 8:30am-8:30pm; Dec-Mar: for Mass

The Cathedral of St James is the city's most famous landmark. Built of local stone, it includes stunning artistic details, such as 71 stone heads depicting locals who refused to contribute to the building's cost.

It took Croatian and international experts several years to restore Šibenik's cathedral after its shelling in 1991. Its original construction by renowned Dalmatian and Italian artists began in 1432 and was completed in 1555. The original project was entrusted to the Venetian Antonio Dalle Masegne, who built the lower Gothic level. His successor, Juraj Dalmatinac, designed much of the cathedral, including the 71 faces on the apse, and, along with Andrija Aleši, the beautiful baptistry. On Dalmatinac's death in 1475, the work was continued by Nikola Firentinac.

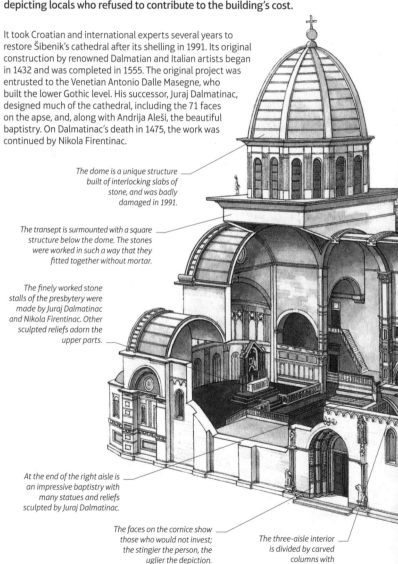

The dome is a unique structure built of interlocking slabs of stone, and was badly damaged in 1991.

The transept is surmounted with a square structure below the dome. The stones were worked in such a way that they fitted together without mortar.

The finely worked stone stalls of the presbytery were made by Juraj Dalmatinac and Nikola Firentinac. Other sculpted reliefs adorn the upper parts.

At the end of the right aisle is an impressive baptistry with many statues and reliefs sculpted by Juraj Dalmatinac.

The faces on the cornice show those who would not invest; the stingier the person, the uglier the depiction.

The three-aisle interior is divided by carved columns with carved capitals.

1 The cathedral was started in 1432. Its incredible craftsmanship continues to astound art historians today; it's now on the UNESCO World Heritage list.

2 The intricate baptistry and its lovely font include sculptures by a number of Croatian artists.

3 The cathedral's tall central nave includes a frieze and a women's gallery.

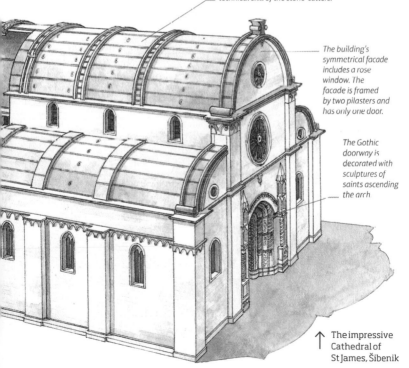

The barrelled roof, built, like the rest of the cathedral, in local stone, is a tribute to the technical skill of the stone-cutters.

The building's symmetrical facade includes a rose window. The facade is framed by two pilasters and has only one door.

The Gothic doorway is decorated with sculptures of saints ascending the arch

↑ The impressive Cathedral of St James, Šibenik

③

KORNATI NATIONAL PARK

C5 🚢Booked trips from Biograd, Murter, Primošten, Zadar, Rogoznica, Vodice 🛈Butina 2, Murter 🌐np-kornati.hr

This part of the Zadar Archipelago forms an idyllic national park, set up in 1980s to protect the waters and their marine life. It measures 36 km (22 miles) in length and 6 km (4 miles) in width and comprises 89 islands. There are no permanent human inhabitants, and vegetation appears to be sparse, but flora and fauna are rich here. The islands are hemmed temptingly by clear blue sea, jagged coastlines, hidden coves and underwater caves. The best way to explore the area is by a private sailing boat.

Kornat

The island of Kornat is the largest in the park. There is a small medieval church dedicated to the Virgin Mary here. There is also a look-out tower with the Venetian name of Toreta dating from the 6th century, an example of Byzantine military architecture. Near the old village of Vrulje, the main settlement in the archipelago, is Vela Ploča, where there is a spectacular chalk cliff leaning at a 40-degree angle over the sea, measuring 200 m (656 ft) long and 150 m (492 ft) high.

Mana

The island of Mana is famous for its cliffs. Spray from the waves breaking on the cliffs can reach up to a height of 40 m (131 ft). On top of the cliffs are the ruins of a Greek-style fishing village, built for the film *The Raging Sea* in 1961.

---

③
Levrnaka

The island of Levrnaka is one of the largest and highest islands of Kornati National Park, with two peaks, Veli Vrh and Svirac, which, at 117 m (380 ft) and 94 m (310 ft) respectively, afford stunning views of almost the entire Kornati archipelago. Also on Levrnaka is Lojena, the only sandy beach of the Kornati park, located in a lovely sheltered bay.

Lavsa

This island, with its pretty bays and coves, is a popular tourist destination. The ruins of a partly submerged wall are all that remain of an ancient Roman salt works. Today, no one lives here.

> 💬 **INSIDER TIP**
> **The Kornati Islands by Boat**
>
> These islands are a paradise for sailors; stunning views are paired with the sounds of lapping waves and whistling winds. There is just one small marina, Piškera, which is open from Easter (Mar or Apr) to October. Fresh water and electricity are rationed.

↑ Structures on Mana island, frequently used as a movie set

↑ Rocky terrain and azure waters in Kornati National Park

⑤
Piškera

As on Lavsa, there are traces of Roman presence on the island of Piškera. It is understood there was a village here encompassing around 50 houses, a warehouse for storing fish and a tower used by a tax collector. The houses and tower are now almost all in ruins. However, a church from 1560 is still standing. On Piškera you'll also find a well equipped yachting marina at the island's port.

⑥
Svršata

On the small island of Svršata there are two walls that lead down to the sea and continue into the water, where they join with a further wall. It is thought that this square structure was a Roman construction, used as a tank for keeping fish fresh. Like its sister islands, Svršata lies almost totally abandoned today and its coastline and beaches are wonderfully secluded.

THE LANDSCAPE OF KORNATI

These bare, arid islands are characterized by steep cliffs, stony ground and sinkholes typical of a limestone landscape. The vegetation disappeared when shepherds cut down the trees and burned the scrub in order to grow grass for their livestock. Dry-stone walls were built between plots of land to form animal pens. On some of the islands near the coast are small cottages with stables and an outdoor hearth. Many also have a small jetty.

The Kornati Islands have become a popular destination for scuba divers and sailors. The marine life is varied, with around 350 plant species and 300 animals. Fishing is prohibited throughout the entire Kornati National Park, and scuba diving is limited to a few sites.

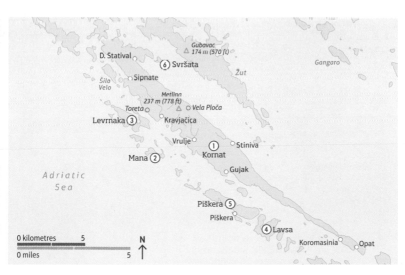

Did You Know?

It is estimated that the park is home to 222 kinds of birds and 860 species of plants.

Exploring the boardwalk trail in Krka National Park *(inset)* and the cascading waters of Skradinski buk ↑

KRKA NATIONAL PARK

🅐D5 🚩 Trg Ivana Pavla II br 5, Šibenik 🕐 May & Sep: 8am-7pm daily; Jun-Aug: 8am-8pm daily 🌐 np-krka.hr

Tumbling waterfalls and winding walkways, emerald lakes and lush greenery – Krka National Park is spectacular. It covers a whopping 109 sq km (42 sq miles) and further comprises scenic monasteries and rugged Roman ruins.

Now a huge attraction, the park was established in 1985 to protect the middle and lower stretches of the River Krka, which flow into the bay of Šibenik. The source of the river is near Knin, and the river begins its journey of 75 km (47 miles) inside a canyon on the limestone plateau behind Šibenik. It finally spills over into the spectacular Roški slap and Skradinski buk waterfalls, forming a series of lakes and rapids popular with those looking to take a dip.

Visiting the Park

The protected area begins at the Knin valley and continues to the bridge of Skradin. Road signs mark the entrances to the park; each has a parking area, a tourist information centre, and a ticket office. Cars can enter from Lozovac, while the Roški slap waterfalls can be reached from Miljevci or Skradin. About 15 km (9 miles) from Burnum, other road signs indicate the entrance to the area of the Roški slap waterfalls. Boats leave from Skradin for trips to the Skradinski buk waterfalls and from here it is possible to take a short cruise to the Roški slap falls, crossing the lake of Visovac and visiting the monastery on the island.

TOP 4 PARK HIGHLIGHTS

Lake Visovac
This is at the heart of the park. Cast at its centre is a tiny island, home to a monastery.

Skradinski buk
One of Croatia's most impressive natural displays, this waterfall cascades from a height of 45 m (147 ft).

Roški slap
At 25 m (82 ft), these waterfalls can be enjoyed from a wooden walkway. Nearby are traditional water mills, open April-October.

Burnum
The ruins of this Roman military camp include an amphiteatre set in scrubland.

↑ A boat gliding along a river in Skradin, part of Krka National Park

EXPERIENCE MORE

 Dugi Otok

🄰 B5 🚢 From Zadar
ℹ️ Obala P. Lorinija bb, Sali;
www.dugiotok.hr

Covering an area of 124 sq km (48 sq miles), Dugi Otok is the largest island in the Zadar archipelago. The southern, hillier terrain of the island is given over to sheep farming, while fishing and farming are prevalent in the north. The western coast is steep and desolate, but beaches and bays punctuate the eastern coast. The island's close proximity to Zadar meant that from Roman times it was a popular place for the city nobles to build holiday villas. In the Renaissance period, more summer residences were built here, particularly in Sali. This is the largest town and port on the island, and there are some houses in the flamboyant Gothic style.

The fishing village of Božava, at the island's northernmost point, is also a popular yacht marina. Almost 4 km (2.5 miles) from Božava, Sakarun is a spectacular white pebble beach. South of Sali is the long, spectacularly indented Telašćica Bay, dotted with small, bare islets. Most of the bay now falls under the protection of **Telašćica Nature Park**. Visitors can follow a trail from the western edge of the bay along its southern shore towards Uvala Mira ("Bay of Peace"), site of a café-restaurant. Trails head uphill to the south where dramatic cliffs descend to the open sea, or east to Jezero Mira ("Lake of Peace"), famed for its therapeutic mud. At the far end of Jezero Mira is a desolate, rocky strip of land that separates the lake from the Adriatic Sea. The place has an eerie, almost unearthly appearance thanks to numerous teetering piles of stone, the construction of which became a tradition among visitors.

Telašćica Nature Park

🏠 Sali X 1 🌐 telascica.hr

 Pašman

🄰 C5 🚢 From Zadar
🌐 pasman.hr

Wild and unspoiled, this island has a population of 3,500 living in villages on the coast facing the mainland. The western side is given over to vineyards, the eastern to thick maquis right down to the coastline, where there are also some pebble beaches. On Mount Čokovac is the Benedictine Monastery of SS Cosmas and Damian (Sv. Kuzma i Damjan). Built in 1125,

🔍 HIDDEN GEM
Iž

Tucked behind the southern coast of Dugi otok, Iž is one of Croatia's least visited islands. With its enchanting small port, a clutch of secluded coves and lots of wild Mediterranean scrub, it's a great place for a relaxing getaway.

← Terracotta rooftops
on the verdant island
of Ugljan

main ferry port, Brgulje, and
Molat. There are no hotels on
the island but private guest-
houses can be found in the
port towns.

Adventure sports provider
Malik Adventures *(www.
malikadventures.com)* offers
one-day sea-kayaking, kayak
and cycle combination trips,
and SUP (stand-up paddle)
board rental.

the church and monastery
were rebuilt in the Gothic
style when taken over by
the Franciscan order in the
15th century.

❼ Premuda

 B4 From Zadar

Covering an area of 9 sq km
(3 sq miles), Premuda has
fewer than 100 inhabitants, all
living in the village of Premuda.
It is the most isolated island in
the archipelago, with thick pine
woods and peaceful beaches.
There are no hotels but visitors
can find rooms in private
houses. There are several
weekly connections to Zadar.

❽ Ugljan

C5 From Zadar
Šimuna Kožičića Benje 17;
www.uglijan.hr

This lush, green island covers
an area of 50 sq km (19 sq
miles), and its small villages lie
along the eastern coast. Ugljan,
the main village, is home to
the Franciscan Monastery of
St Jerome, built in the 15th
century. Its library contains
numerous works written in
Glagolitic script. A more
modern village is Preko, where
the wealthier citizens of Zadar
own villas. It is dominated by
the large Venetian fortress of
St Michael. The island is linked
to Pašman by a bridge.

❾ Molat

B4 From Zadar

The three villages on Molat
support several hundred
people, who depend on fishing and farming. There are
three ports: Zapuntel, the

❿ Olib

D4 From Zadar

About 700 people live here
in the village of Olib. The
16th-century Church of
St Anastasia was once part of
a monastery. In the parsonage
are manuscripts and sacred
books in Glagolitic script, as
well as many stone remains,
which confirm the presence
of a community here in Roman
times. The sea is delightful,
and rocky cliffs alternate with
coves and sandy beaches.

> **LIGHTHOUSES**
>
> As befits a shoreline
> studded with islands
> and peninsulas, light-
> houses are a major
> feature of the Croatian
> coast. Many were built
> by Austrian engineers
> in the 19th century,
> when the country was
> part of the Habsburg
> Empire. Famously
> iconic lighthouses
> include those at the
> uninhabited island of
> Palagruža, and the one
> at Veli Rat on Dugi otok,
> which is the tallest in
> the Adriatic. Visit
> www.lighthouses-
> croatia.com for further
> tourist information.

 Sunbathers and
swimmers relaxing
on a Dugi otok beach

↑ The crumbling remains of an abandoned fort on the island of Pag

Did You Know?

Croatian lace-making was added to UNESCO's "intangible cultural heritage" list in 2009.

Drniš

🅰D5 🚂 Šibenik, 25 km (15 miles); (022) 333 699 🚌 Šibenik; (022) 216 066 ℹ Domovinskog rata 5; www.tz-drnis.hr

The town of Drniš first appears in official documents towards the end of the 15th century, as the site of a fort built to prevent a Turkish invasion at the point where the River Čikola cuts into the valley and flows down towards Šibenik.

In 1526, the fort was captured and enlarged by the Turks, who made it one of their outposts. A village with a mosque and baths developed around the fort, but both fort and village were almost destroyed by the Venetians during the 1640–50 wars between Venice and the Ottoman Empire. In the reconstruction that followed, the mosque was remodelled and became the Church of St Anthony. The minaret became the bell tower of the Church of St Roch. Serbs populated the town and it became part of the Krajina territory.

Along the road from Drniš to Šibenik, the ruins of walled defence structures can be seen. Drniš is also known for its *pršut*, a type of prosciutto that is popular in Croatia. The rich flavour of the meat produced in this area is attributed to the region's specific micro-climate. Every year in August, Drniš hosts the International Pršut Festival.

Some 9 km (5 miles) east of Drniš is the village of Otavice, the birthplace of Ivan Meštrović's parents. The great sculptor (*p204*) built the Church of the Most Holy Redeemer here for himself and his family. It is simply designed in the form of a stone cube with a shallow dome.

Silba

🅰B4 🚢 ℹ Silba 412; www.tzsilba.hr

The island of Silba, not far from Pag, is as idyllic as they come. Just 8 km (5 miles) in length and 1 km (0.5 miles) wide, this unspoiled island is unique for the absence of hotels or cars. Bikes are further banned in July and August, allowing the local population (of just 300) and island-hoppers to enjoy Silba in relative peace.

Silba town is situated at the narrowest point of the island and is the main settlement, where a clutch of restaurants and souvenir shops can be found. At the heart of the town is Marinić Tower, a striking stone structure bounded by a spiral staircase. Legend says this was built by a sea captain for the daughter of a woman who jilted him. The town's tangle of streets lead down to pebble bays, where sun worshippers watch boats ferrying visitors to and from the island. Šotorišće Beach is a popular spot, particularly in summer when a café and bar opens here. A short walk from the town is Dobre Vode, a rocky and more secluded bay.

Primošten

🅰C6 🚂 Split 🚌 Split; (021) 329 180 ℹ Trg biskupa Josipa Arnerića 2; www.tz-primosten.hr

Originally an isolated island, Primošten is now connected to the mainland by a bridge and a causeway. Indeed, the name Primošten means "brought closer by a bridge". The island was inhabited in prehistoric times, and was settled by Bosnian refugees

 INSIDER TIP
Cheese Please!

Pag cheese is one of the culinary treasures of Croatia: a tangy delicacy made from the milk of sheep that graze on sage and other local herbs. The best place to stock up on it is the village of Kolan, where renowned producer Gligora offers tours (www.gligora.com).

fleeing from the Turks. Under Venetian rule, walls were built around the town. The top of the town is dominated by the Church of St George, built in the late 15th century and enlarged around 1760. Inside is a silver icon of the Virgin, and a Baroque altar.

A resort with pebbly beaches and bike trails, Primošten is famous for its vineyards (p112) and a red wine called Babić.

facing the mainland, rocky and jagged and white in colour, is exposed to the bora wind and bears little vegetation. The typical dry-stone walls that dot the landscape were built to protect the land from the wind and to separate the flocks of sheep belonging to different farmers. The south-west coast is a little flatter with some small beaches. Here the land is covered in maquis, olive groves and aromatic herbs, particularly sage. As well as the production of olive oil and a distinctive wine called Žutica, sheep farming remains one of the main occupations on the island.

Pag town is the island's main settlement, with a number of ruins acting as reminders of its history. In 1443, Venetian rulers entrusted the design of the new town to the sculptor Juraj Dalmatinac. It took several decades to build the town seen today.

 14

Pag

C4 **Prizna-Žigljen, Pag** **Od špitala 2; www.tzgpag.hr**

The island is 68 km (42 miles) long and has two mountain chains running parallel to the coast. The Slavs settled in Pag in the 6th century and became sheep farmers. After 1000 AD Zadar and Rab fought over the island to gain control of the salt pans (p142), and in the 12th century Pag fell under Venetian rule, which brought a long period of peace and prosperity.

The island, connected by a bridge to the Magistrala coast road (E65) at its eastern tip, near Miškovići, is dry and barren, with only a few areas cultivated with vines and olive trees. The coastline

PAG'S TRADITIONAL LACE

Pag is known for its clean waters and sheep's cheese, but it is also famed for its lace. For centuries this lace has been hand-sewn by the women of the island who, in warm weather, sit by their doorsteps intent on creating the intricate material. Made using a special stitch, the finished lace decorates blouses, bedlinen, table centrepieces and altar cloths. There is even a school in Pag to train new lacemakers, which also has a lace shop and a small museum in some of the rooms.

Nin

C4 🛫🚌🚌 **ℹ** Trg braće Radić 3; www.nin.hr

The ancient core of Nin lies in a natural lagoon, a sheltered position that made it an attractive choice for settlement. The town's many archaeological sites have enabled its past to be traced from prehistory through the Liburnian, Roman and early Christian times to its period of greatest glory, in the 9th–12th centuries, when it was both a bishopric and a royal Croatian town. Nin's finest monuments date from this time.

Within the town walls is the 9th-century **Church of the Holy Cross** (Sv. Križ), a pre-Romanesque building of great beauty. Its windows are positioned to act as a kind of calendar by which, according to the sun's rays, the exact date of the equinox and solstice can be determined.

Nearby is the former **Cathedral of St Anselm** (Sv. Anselm), where the kings of Croatia were crowned. The first cathedral in Croatia, it has a rich treasury with silver reliquaries from the 9th to 15th centuries. Near the church is a copy of Ivan Meštrović's statue of Bishop Gregory of Nin, the original of which stands in Split.

At the head of Nin's small square is the modest **Museum of Nin Antiquities** (Muzej Ninskih Starina), which has Liburnian and Roman artefacts as well as a reconstructed 11th-century ship.

One of Nin's oldest sources of income was salt-harvesting, and salt pans still stretch to the southeast of town. The Nin Salt Works (Solana Nin) has a vistor's centre displaying a history of the industry and offers guided tours of the pans themselves.

Nin's other main claim to fame is its sandy beaches, which stretch northwest of town. The main Queen's Beach or Kraljičina Plaža is backed by reedy wetland that yields therapeutic mud. It gives onto a shallow lagoon, popular for kite-surfing.

A short way southwest of Nin stands the **Church of St Nicholas** (Sv. Nikola) atop a mound in Prahulje. This unusual building, a fine example of Croatian primitive art, once held inscriptions and tombs of members of the court of Princes Višeslav and Branimir, now in the fascinating archaeological museum in Zadar.

Church of the Holy Cross
🏠 Ul Petra Zoranića 8 🕐 Daily

Cathedral of St Anselm
🏠 Ul Župana Godečaja 2
🕐 For Mass only

Museum of Nin Antiquities
🏠 Trg Kraljevac 8 🕐 Times vary, see website 🌐 amzd.hr

Church of St Nicholas
🏠 Prahulje 🕐 St Nicholas's Day and St Mark's Day only

A LAND OF SALT WORKS

Salt trading was a very lucrative business in the Middle Ages. Three areas were suitable for its production in the upper Adriatic: the mouth of the River Dragonja, the lowlands around Nin and the bay of Pag. The latter were the largest and most profitable, and were once owned by Nin. The possession of these still-profitable flats has sparked various wars throughout history.

16
Paklenica National Park

🅰C4 🕒Apr–Oct: 6am–8:30pm daily; Nov–Mar: 7am–3pm daily
ℹ️ Starigrad Paklenica; www.paklenica.hr

Situated in the imposing Velebit massif, Paklenica National Park (Nacionalni park Paklenica) was founded in 1949. It covers an area of 95 sq km (41 sq miles), and is formed by two gorges, Velika Paklenica (Big Paklenica) and Mala Paklenica (Small Paklenica).

Deep in the Velika Paklenica Canyon, there is an extensive system of tunnels, built by the Yugoslav army in the 20th century. These are currently being renovated to create a multi-purpose visitor centre. The bare rock faces of Velika Paklenica are popular with rock climbers, as well as making an ideal breeding habitat for birds of prey.

The park's Velebit mountain chain stretches nearly 150 km (93 miles). In 1978 UNESCO listed Velebit as a biological reserve for humanity. The *kukovi* – strange rock formations sculpted by wind and water – are also protected.

Hiking and mountain biking are popular in the park too, and in summer visitors can stay overnight in the mountain hut on the banks of Velika Paklenica creek, or in the villages of Ramići and Parići.

Paklenica National Park's dramatic gorges, popular with rock-climbers *(inset)*

played an important role in Dalmatia's history. It occupies a strategic position on the plateau, and there have been defences here since prehistoric times – such as the 10th century Fort of Knin, built on Mount Spas and first used by Croat monarchs.

In 1991, the Serbian army used the fort, which became a focus for the Serb rebellion, and the Republic of the Serb Krajina – of which Knin was the capital – was created. In August 1995 the territory was returned to the Croats.

18
Rogoznica

🅰D6 ℹ️ Obala Kneza Domagoja; www.loverogoznica.eu

Set in a broad bay, Rogoznica is a charming resort with a beautiful shingle beach. The oldest part of town occupies an offshore islet joined to the mainland by a causeway. On the western side of the bay is Marina Frapa, one of Dalmatia's biggest yachting marinas and almost a town in its own right, with plentiful restaurants and

17
Knin

🅰D5 📞(022) 663 722
ℹ️ Dr Franje Tuđmana 24; www.tz-knin.hr

A town on the main road from Zagreb to Split, Knin has long

 ←

The bleached stone exterior of the Church of the Holy Cross in Nin

shops. Nearby Lake Galešnica (Dragon's Eye) is an elliptical lake surrounded by sheer cliffs, and connected to the sea by underground passages.

19
Vrlika

🅰D5 🚌From Split
ℹ️ Put Česme 4; www.visitvrlika.com

A small market town, Vrlika spreads beneath the ruined 14th-century castle of Prozor. It is renowned as the home of one of Croatia's most colourful regional costumes. The Vrličko kolo also originated here – a circle dance that is conducted silently. Just north of the town, the 10th-century Church of Holy Salvation (Crkva svetog Spasa) is a unique example of Romanesque architecture. East of Vrlika is the Serbian Orthodox Dragović Monastery, entirely rebuilt in 1959 when the original site was submerged beneath Peruća Reservoir.

Wooden boardwalk winding through Lake Vrana's nature park

20
Lake Vrana

C5 **pp-vransko-jezero.hr**

Lying just inland from the coast, Lake Vrana (Vransko jezero) is the largest lake in Croatia, with a surface area of just over 30 sq km (12 sq miles). It is an important haven for migrating birds, and attracts over 100 nesting species in spring and late summer, including numerous types of heron. The area has been a protected nature park (Park prirode) since 1999. Much of the shore is marshy and inaccessible, although visitors can use the boardwalk trail and observation tower at Crikvine on the western shore of the lake. The Information Centre at Kamenjak has displays related to the wildlife in the park.

Sprawling above the northern shoulder of the lake, the town of Vrana was ruled by the Ottomans from 1527 until 1683. Evidence of their presence is provided by the Maškovića Han, a fortified roadside inn that is one of the few surviving examples of Ottoman architecture in western Croatia. It was built in 1644 for Jusuf Mašković, a local man who rose to become grand admiral of the Ottoman fleet, and is now a hotel with a beautiful garden courtyard.

21
Murter

C5 **From Sibenik** **Rudina bb; www.tzo-murter.hr**

The economy of this town, on the north coast of the island of the same name, was traditionally focused on the Kornati islands, where most Murterians owned land or flocks of sheep. The locals were constantly going to and fro in their boats, and the town's seafront is characterized by a row of jetties where they moored their crafts. The most atmospheric part of the settlement is the Old Town perched on a

hill 1 km (0.5 miles) inland. Murter is also a key departure point for boat trips to the Kornati National Park (p134).

Immediately north of Murter, the village of Betina was once famous for its traditional ship-building industry. Exhibits in the Betina Museum of Wooden Shipbuilding (Muzej betinske drvene brodogradnje) present the history of the trade.

22
Zrmanja Canyon

C5

South of Mount Velebit, the River Zrmanja flows through the rocky Zrmanja Canyon and down to the Adriatic Sea. It's a great area for adventure sports, such as river rafting. Guided trips start from the bridge in Kaštel Žegarski, 64 km (40 miles) east of Zadar, and

Did You Know?

Shakespeare's *Twelfth Night* is set in Illyria, which was the western part of the Balkan Peninsula.

Sun setting over the waterside village of Betina, just north of Murter

go as far as Muskovci. Most trips last 3–4 hours depending on conditions – the river runs fuller and swifter in spring and autumn, following seasonal rain.

 23

Tisno

 C5 **𝒊** Istočna gomilica 1a; www.tz-tisno.hr

Tisno stretches along both sides of the channel that divides Murter from the mainland, with a small bridge connecting the two shores. Beneath the soaring 17th-century belfry of the Church of the Holy Spirit (Crkva svetog Duha) sits the Old Town and pleasant waterfront promenades. Tisno's reputation among younger tourists has been boosted in recent years by the music festivals held at the Garden Resort in nearby Rastovac bay.

 24

Biograd na Moru

C5 **🚌** From Zadar **𝒊** Trg hrvatskih velikana 2: www.tzg-biograd.hr; Solina 4: www.discover-biograd.com

Founded by Croats in the 10th century, Biograd was a fortified cathedral city throughout the Middle Ages, and witnessed the coronation of Croatian-Hungarian king Koloman in 1102. Destroyed by the Venetians in 1125, it rose again to become an important military base in Venice's wars with the Ottoman Empire. Since the 1920s, the town has been a family-oriented tourist resort. A local Museum (Zavičajni muzej) has an absorbing collection of naval guns and model boats. Stretching east from town is a sequence of attractive beaches with sandy sea floors and a wealth of facilities. Crvena Luka, 3 km (2 miles) along the coastal path, is a particularly beautiful bay for swimming.

25

Vodice

C5 **𝒊** Obala Vladimira Nazora bb; www.vodice.hr

Just north of Šibenik, Vodice is northern Dalmatia's most successful package-holiday destination. There are several high-rise hotels, and a succession of part-concrete, part-shingle beaches stretching around the shore. In the town centre are some quiet stone alleys and the 15th-century Čorić Tower (Čorićev toranj), built for a Šibenik landowning family. The nearby aquarium shows off the local marine life alongside an impressive display of model ships and ancient amphorae.

West of Vodice is the traditional fishing village of Tribunj, a picturesque huddle of Dalmatian houses occupying a small island reached by bridge.

EAT

Konoba Boba

A stylish but well-priced restaurant that serves freshly caught fish and traditional dishes that you don't see much of elsewhere.

 C5 **🏠** Dutina 22, Murter **🕐** Jan-Feb **🌐** konobaboba.hr

Ⓚ Ⓚ Ⓚ

Tic Tac

This cosy restaurant offers a wide menu but is best known for its fish, which can be stewed, roasted or grilled according to your preference.

 C5 **🏠** Ilrokešina 5, Murter **🕐** Jan-Feb **🌐** tictac-murter.com

Ⓚ Ⓚ Ⓚ

Marin

On the main coastal highway, Marin is an enduringly popular stop-off for travellers. The main speciality here is lamb, spit-roasted and garnished with spring onions.

 C5 **🏠** Kapela 61, Dubrava kod Tisna, Tisno **🌐** restoran-marin.hr

Ⓚ Ⓚ Ⓚ

ISTRIA

At the northern most point of Croatia's coastline, protruding into the Adriatic Sea, lies Istria. This peninsula is home to some of Croatia's most developed seaside resorts, with swish hotels clustering around historic towns like Novigrad, Poreč and Rovinj. Inland Istria couldn't be a bigger contrast, with hilltop villages looking out onto a green landscape of fruitful vineyards and rolling pastures. The amphitheatre at Pula and the Basilica of Euphrasius in Poreč are outstanding examples of Istria's importance during the Roman and Byzantine eras. Venetian rule followed, and the peninsula's coastal strip remained Italian-speaking well into the 20th century. The interior was predominantly Croat from the early Middle Ages onwards. An Italian minority remains in Pula, Rovinj and elsewhere, and most road signs are bilingual. Tourism possibly dates back to Roman times – although it wasn't until the emergence of resorts like Briuni and Rovinj just before World War I that Istria was transformed into one of the Mediterranean's most desirable destinations.

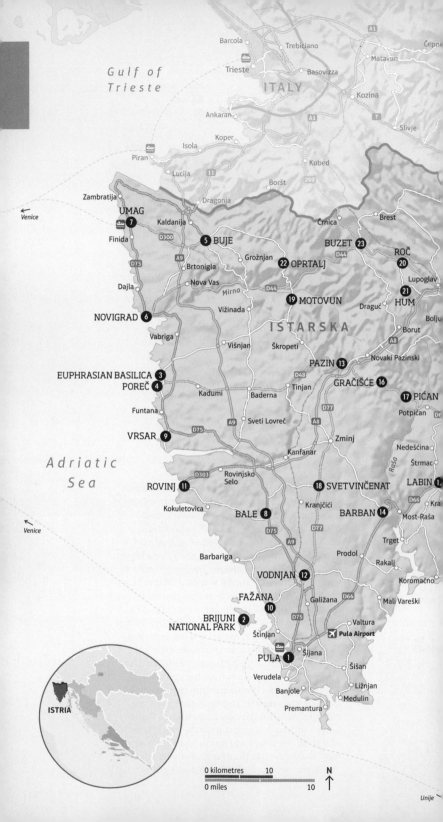

ISTRIA

Must Sees
1 Pula
2 Brijuni National Park
3 Euphrasian Basilica

Experience More
4 Poreč
5 Buje
6 Novigrad
7 Umag
8 Bale
9 Vrsar
10 Fažana
11 Rovinj
12 Vodnjan
13 Pazin
14 Barban
15 Labin
16 Gračišće
17 Pićan
18 Svetvinčenat
19 Motovun
20 Roč
21 Hum
22 Oprtalj
23 Buzet

KVARNER
AREA
p170

↑ Pula's Roman amphitheatre, dominating the city's attractive skyline

❶

PULA

🛬 A3 ✈ 8 km (5 miles), www.airport-pula.hr
⛴ Jadroagent, (052) 210 431 🚌 (052) 541 722 🚍 43 istarske divizije, (060) 304 090 🛈 Forum 3; www.pulainfo.hr

Pula is well known for its magnificent monuments from the Roman era, when it was a colony known as Pietas Julia. It became an episcopal seat in 425 and still has the foundations of some 5th-century religious buildings. It was destroyed by the Ostrogoths, but flourished again when it became the main base for the Byzantine fleet in the 6th and 7th centuries: the cathedral and Chapel of St Mary of Formosa date from this time. In 1150 it came under Venetian rule, but by the mid-17th century the population had declined to 300. It was revitalized in 1856 when Austria made it the base for its fleet. Today, Pula is buzzing coastal city with a handful of good restaurants and a gritty, untamed edge.

①

Chapel of St Mary of Formosa

Kapela Marije Formoze

🏛 Maksimilijanova ulica
🚫 To the public

This small Byzantine chapel was once part of the large Basilica of St Mary of Formosa. Inside are the remains of mosaics from the 6th century. The chapel is sometimes used as an art gallery in the summer.

②

Church of St Francis

Sv. Frane

🏛 Upson B Lupetine 5
🕐 Jun–Sep: 10am-1pm, 4-8pm daily; Oct-May: for Mass

Built in the late 13th century, along with the adjacent monastery, this church has a fine doorway with a Gothic rose window. The interior is a single nave with three apses; on the main altar is a splendid wooden 15th-century polyptych of the Emilian school. Various exhibits from the imperial Roman era can be seen in the monastery cloisters.

③

Temple of Augustus

Augustov hram

🏛 Forum 🕐 Apr & Oct: 9am-7pm daily; May-Sep: 9am-9pm (Jul & Aug: to 11pm); Nov- Mar: by appointment
🌐 ami-pula.hr

Built in the 1st century AD, this impressive temple stands in the square that was once the site of the city's Roman forum; today a charming, café-lined square. The Temple of Augustus is a splendid example of Roman architecture, and is one of the finest Roman temples outside of Italy. It is built on simple lines, with six plain columns and beautifully carved capitals. After Roman rule the temple was used as a church and a warehouse for storing grain. It was damaged by a bomb in 1944 and so underwent reconstruction. Today it houses a small museum showcasing a number of Roman antiquities found in Pula, including a couple of sculptures, such as the torso of a Roman commander that was found in Pula's amphiteatre.

Church of St Nicholas
Sv. Nikola

Castropola 39 **(052) 212 987 (tourist office)** **For Mass**

This modest church dates from the 6th century but it was partially rebuilt in the 10th century. Towards the end of the 15th century it was assigned to the Orthodox community. Inside are some fine icons from the 15th and 16th centuries.

Gate of Hercules
Herculova vrata

Carrarina

Somewhat overshadowed by other antiquities, the arched Gate of Hercules was built in the 1st century BC and is the oldest and best-preserved Roman monument in the city. At the top of the arch is a carving of the head of Hercules, holding his club; this motif is weathered but you can make out his curly hair and full beard. It is understood that the towers flanking the gate were built in the Middle Ages.

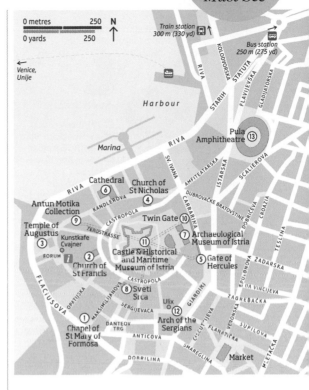

0 metres 250
0 yards 250
N

Train station
300 m (330 yd)

Bus station
250 m (275 yd)

Venice, Unije

Harbour

Marina

Cathedral ⑥
Church of St Nicholas ④

Antun Motika Collection ⑨
Temple of Augustus ③
Kunstkafe Cvajner
FORUM

Pula Amphitheatre ⑬

Twin Gate ⑩
Archaeological Museum of Istria ⑦
Castle & Historical and Maritime Museum of Istria ⑪
Gate of Hercules ⑤

Church of St Francis ②
Sveti Srca ⑧
Ulix ⑫
Arch of the Sergians
Chapel of St Mary of Formosa ①

Market

Cathedral
Katedrala

Trg sv Tome 2 **Jun–Sep: 10am–1pm, 4–6pm daily; Oct–May: for Mass**

The Cathedral, dedicated to the Blessed Virgin Mary, was founded in the 5th century after Pula became an episcopal seat. Its present, fairly modest appearance dates back only as far as the 17th century. However, parts of the walls, some of the capitals and the windows are from the original building. On the right is a doorway from 1456, while the bell tower, which was built by 1707, contains stone blocks from the amphitheatre. Holy relics await visitors inside.

> **HIDDEN GEM**
> **Zerostrasse**
>
> Numerous tunnels were built by the Austrians during World War I, both as air-raid shelters and ways of moving through the city unseen. The main, 400-m (1,312 ft) tunnel, Zerostrasse, is open to tourists (Jun–Sep). Head to Carrarina for the entrance point.

↑ Pula's cathedral and clocktower, standing beside the city harbour

←

Seated statue at the Archaeological Museum of Istria

 ⑦ 🖼 🏛

Archaeological Museum of Istria

Arheološki muzej Istre

📍 Carrarina 3 🕐 For restoration until 2022 🌐 ami-pula.hr

This encyclopedic museum is housed within a park reached from the Twin Gate. On display are all the moveable finds of Pula and outlying areas, with collections dating from the prehistoric era to the Middle Ages.

On the ground floor are architectural remains, mosaics, altars and other exhibits from antiquity to medieval times. The rooms on the first floor contain exhibits from the Neolithic to the Roman era, while three rooms on the second floor are dedicated to Roman treasures. Highlights of this collection include a headless female statue found at Nesactium, near Pula. Two rooms have exhibits from the late Classical to medieval periods. Of particular interest are pieces from Slavic tombs dating from the 7th to the 12th centuries.

The museum is regularly undergoing work to extends its space and better showcase its treasures. When it is open, tours are by appointment.

⑧ 🖼

Sveti Srca

📍 De Villeov uspon 🕐 May–Aug: 9am–9pm Tue–Sun (Jul & Aug: to 11pm); Sep–Apr: 11am–7pm Tue–Sun 🌐 ami-pula.hr

Built by the Jesuits in 1910, the former Church of Sveti Srca ("Sacred Hearts") is an imposing example of Neo-Romanesque architectural style. Disused after World War II, the building was transformed into a stunning modern exhibition space in 2011. It falls under the ownership of the Archaeological Museum of Istria and, like its sister museum, Sveti Srca displays fascinating archaeological, historical and art pieces. The exhibitions here are seasonal; it's worth speaking to the tourist office to find out what is on display when you visit. The space also hosts special one-off events, such as musical performances.

⑨

Antun Motika Collection

📍 Kandlerova 8 📞 (052) 544 178 🕐 10am–2pm & 5–8pm, Mon–Fri; noon–3pm Sat

Pula native Antun Motika (1902–92) was one of the most inventive and versatile figures in Croatian art. He moved from Post-Impressionist watercolours to expressionist portraits and avant-garde collages in the course of a long and illustrious career. This wonderful collection – which is free to visit – displays a cross-section of Motika's work. This includes some of his "luminokinetic" pieces in which sketches and designs were placed on film and lit from behind. There are also temporary exhibitions from current artists here, which offer a dynamic contrast to Motika's works.

PULA'S BEACHES

City-breakers might enjoy the lovely (if stony) beaches that lie just outside the centre of Pula. To the south of the city, beyond the suburbs, is Verudela, which has a number of beach options. If you scale the boundary of the peninsula you might stumble across a surprisingly secluded cove. North of here, the rocky coastlines of Valkane and Valsaline are also options, although a number of the hotels around this area means they can be over-subscribed with sun-soakers.

↑ Pedestrians passing under the Arch of the Sergians, one of Pula's key landmarks

Twin Gate

Dvojna vrata

🅰 Carrarina

This grand gate, built in the 2nd–3rd centuries, has two arches with an ornate frieze. Nearby are parts of the wall that once encircled Pula. It is thought that there were once ten gates allowing access into the city.

Castle and Historical and Maritime Museum of Istria

Povijesni i pomorski muzej Istre

🅰 Gradinski uspon 6
📞 (052) 211 566 ⏰ Castle: Jun–Sep: 8am–9pm daily; Oct–May: 9am–5pm daily 🔒 Museum: for restoration

This star-shaped castle was built by the Venetians in the 17th century on the ruins of the city's Roman Capitol. Today the fortress houses the Historical and Maritime Museum of Istria, a modest museum with a few exhibits.

The stellar attraction, are the walls, which link four towers. These ramparts offer wonderful views out over the city and down to the harbour, where the Lighting Giants installation can be seen. Near the castle are the remains of a small 2nd-century Roman theatre.

Arch of the Sergians

Slavoluk obitelji Sergijevaca

🅰 Ulica Sergijevaca

The arch was erected in the 1st century BC on the orders of Salvia Postuma Sergia, to honour three brothers who held important positions in the Roman Empire. It is small with fluted columns, a winged Victory and Corinthian capitals. Its frieze has a bas-relief depicting a chariot pulled by horses.

The arch remains a city landmark today, its ancient structure a contrast to the colourful buildings that flank it. Pedestrians pass underneath as they shop, dine and meet friends at the likes of the nearby Uliks bar.

DRINK

Uliks

One of Pula's most characterful places to drink is Uliks ("Ulysses"), located in the building where a 22-year-old James Joyce worked as an English-language teacher in 1904-5. There's a seated statue of Joyce outside, and charming historical memorabilia within.

🅰 Trg Portarata 1
🌐 caffeuliks.eatbu.hr

Galerija Cvajner

This bohemian hangout is based in a disused bank in the city's Old Forum. Vintage furniture and art by locals meets reliable coffee, craft beers and good cocktails.

🅰 Forum 2
📞 (052) 216 502

⑬ ⌖

PULA AMPHITEATRE

📍 Flavijevska ulica 📞 (052) 351 301 🕐 Jul–Aug: 8am–11pm daily; Jun & Sep: 8am–9pm daily; May & Oct: 8am–8pm daily; Nov–Apr: 9am–5pm daily

This magnificent amphitheatre is Pula's most iconic landmark and Croatia's best preserved ancient monument. Not only that, it's the world's sixth largest surviving Roman arena and the only remaining amphitheatre to have four side towers. Once a bloody gladitorial ground, today it's used as a music and film venue.

A small amphitheatre was built here by Claudius before it was enlarged by Vespasian in AD 79, specifically for gladiator fights. Why such a large arena was constructed for a Roman town with a population of around 5,000 remains somewhat of a mystery. It remained intact until the 15th century when some of the stone was used to construct the castle and other buildings in the city. The amphitheatre was restored in 1816 and again in 1932, when it was adapted for musical events. Today, it can seat 5,000 spectators and is used as a venue for concerts, as well as hosting an annual film festival. Visitors can climb its stone remains and visit the underground spaces, where wild animals and expectant gladiators once paced.

↑ Pula's Roman amphitheatre, today a performance venue

The towers had cisterns filled with scented water that was sprayed onto the stalls. It is also thought that awnings were used as protection from the sun and rain.

The external wall of the arena has three floors on the side facing the sea, and two on the opposite side, because it was built on an incline. At its highest point, the wall measures 29.4 m (96 ft).

Pula's spectacular Roman amphitheatre, an Istrian icon ↑

↑ Grand and dramatic, the amphitheatre is Pula's most famous landmark

When first built, the broad tiers could seat thousands and shows of every kind were performed. Today, during the summer season, operas, ballets and plays are put on here.

The first two floors have 72 arches and the third has 64 large rectangular openings. The arches lit the internal corridors which enabled spectators to move from one sector to another.

Many archaeological finds from the amphitheatre and other Roman buildings are kept in the underground passages, where there were once cages and prisons.

RECONSTRUCTION

The main floor of the arena, 67.75 m (222 ft) long and 41.05 m (135 ft) wide, was originally framed by iron railings to separate spectators from the performance. Between the tiers of seats and the railings there was a space, 3 m (10 ft) wide, reserved for staff. Along the main axis, under the arena, were underground corridors used by the gladiators and cages for animals. The animals were kept here before being sent into the stadium.

2

BRIJUNI NATIONAL PARK

🅰 A3 🚢 4 from Fažana ⏱ 24 hours, but access limited to crossing times
🌐 np-brijuni.hr

An excellent day trip from Pula is Brijuni National Park. This archipelago was the holiday home of Marshal Tito in the early 20th century before it was declared a national park in 1983. Today visitors can visit two of the islands: small Veli Brijun and larger Mali Brijun, which are home to lush vegetation, roaming wildlife and ancient ruins.

🔍 HIDDEN GEM
Roman Villa

Excavations on Veli Brijun have unearthed the foundations of a Roman villa, its *calidarium* (hot room) and a *frigidarium* (cold room). A large room where the family met for banquets and ceremonies is decorated with mosaics.

The park's main islands have been inhabited since the Palaeolithic era and the Romans later built villas and religious buildings here. An outbreak of malaria meant the islands were abandoned in 1630, with people returning in the following century to work the stone quarries. In the late 19th century, the islands were bought by industrialist Paul Kupelwieser. Remains of the archipelago's history are prevalent throughout the park. On Mali Brijun, there is an Austro-Hungarian fort built at the end of the 19th century. Over on Veli Brijun are the ruins of the Tegetthoff Fortress and the White Villa, which dates from the Venetian period and was used as Tito's summer residence. Around the harbour are a number of hotels and restaurants.

Note that individuals and groups must book on an excursion, which includes the boat crossing. Bicycles can also be hired.

↑ Verdant islands comprising Brijuni National Park, cast in the waters of the Adriatic

PAUL KUPELWIESER

Steel magnate Paul Kupelwieser (1843–1919) was one of the first people to spot the tourist potential of the Adriatic coast, buying the Brijuni islands in 1893 with the firm intention of turning them into an elite resort. He first rid the islands of malaria, with the help of Nobel-winning German bacteriologist Robert Koch. The Brijuni Islands soon became the resort of choice for Austrian aristocrats, civil servants and business-men. Kupelwieser's son retained the islands as an top resort during the 1920s, only to commit suicide due to mounting debts. The islands kept high society in the early 20th century, when Yugoslav President Tito hosted political meetings and inter-national movie stars here. Sophia Loren famously cooked up pasta dishes in Tito's kitchen.

↑ Leafy garden on Veli Brijun, Brijuni National Park

→
Wildlife, including birds, fly or roam freely in Brijuni National Park

③ ⑤

EUPHRASIAN BASILICA

⌂ Eufrazijeva ulica 22, Poreč █ (052) 451 784 ⊙ Daily (times vary, call ahead)

Poreč's Byzantine masterpiece was built in the 6th century and drips with intricate mosaics. Once a house of worship, today the building is a UNESCO World Heritage Site and plays host to classical concerts in summer.

The Euphrasian Basilica (Eufrazijeva bazilika) was built for Bishop Euphrasius between 539 and 553 by enlarging the existing 4th-century Oratory of St Maurus Martyr, so named after the saint who is believed to have lived on the site. The complex comprises an atrium, baptistry, belfry and bishop's palace, where some of the original floor mosaics still survive. However, it's the sumptuous 6th-century mosaics in the apse, made from semi-precious stones, that are the real attraction.

Did You Know?

When Christianity was an underground religion, this basilica was a place of worship.

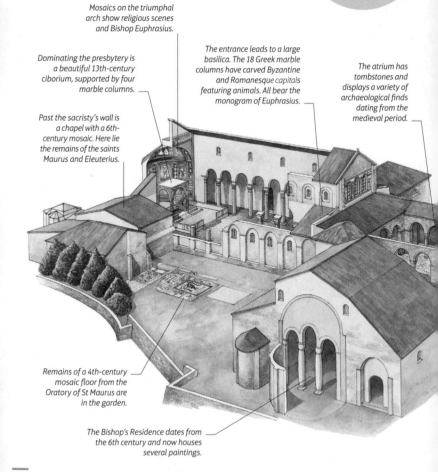

Mosaics on the triumphal arch show religious scenes and Bishop Euphrasius.

Dominating the presbytery is a beautiful 13th-century ciborium, supported by four marble columns.

The entrance leads to a large basilica. The 18 Greek marble columns have carved Byzantine and Romanesque capitals featuring animals. All bear the monogram of Euphrasius.

The atrium has tombstones and displays a variety of archaeological finds dating from the medieval period.

Past the sacristy's wall is a chapel with a 6th-century mosaic. Here lie the remains of the saints Maurus and Eleuterius.

Remains of a 4th-century mosaic floor from the Oratory of St Maurus are in the garden.

The Bishop's Residence dates from the 6th century and now houses several paintings.

 Looking up at the basilica from the atrium's portico

The baptistry dates from the 6th century and here there are fragments of mosaics. To the rear rises a 16th-century bell tower.

↑ The impressive Euphrasian Basilica in Poreč, Istria

EXPERIENCE MORE

4

Poreč
Parenzo

🄰A3 ✈Pula, 53 km (33 miles) 🚊Pazin, 32 km (20 miles) 🚌Karla Huguesa 2, (060) 333111 🛈Zagrebačka 9; www.myporec.com

Poreč was a Roman town (Colonia Julia Parentium) which, after centuries of splendour, was sacked by the Goths and fell into decline. In 539 it was conquered by the Byzantines, who founded a bishopric around the year 800. The town then became part of the kingdom of the Franks, who gave it to the Patriarchate of Aquileia. In 1267 it was the first Istrian town to choose Venetian rule, and the town acquired a Venetian look as palaces, squares and religious buildings were built. In 1354 it was destroyed by the Genoese and later, plague, pirates and a long war greatly reduced the population. During Austrian domination it became the seat of the Istrian parliament and an important shipyard.

The old centre shelters on a narrow peninsula protected by rocks and the island of St Nicholas. Despite being a popular base for visitors to Istria, the Old Town has remained intact and Poreč

invariably wins an annual award for "best-kept town". Having said this, it is a tourist town and is usually overrun with holiday-makers during the summer months, thanks to its resorts, party scenes and proximity to beaches.

Aside from the Euphrasian Basilica, the town has a handful of attractions, including typical Croatian churches. At the easternmost point is the Baroque Sinčić Palace (18th century), which houses the **Poreč Museum** (Zavičajni Muzej Poreštine), which is dedicated to Roman and early Christian archaeology; an ethnographic section illustrates daily life in the Poreč region.

A great day trip from the town is the **Baredine Cave**, which encompasses a number of incredible subterranean chambers. According to myth, two lovers called Gabriel and Milka died looking for one another here. Guided tours of the cave are compulsory.

Poreč Museum

📍Sinčić Palace, Dekumanska 9 🕐8am–4pm Mon–Fri 🌐muzejporec.hr

Baredine Cave

♿👁 📍7km (4 miles) north of town 🕐Times vary, check website 🌐baredine.com

↑ Vibrantly coloured buildings lining the water in Poreč

 Sunlight streaming through the stone archways of a building in Grožnjan

 Buje

Buie

A2 ✈ Pula 🚌 From Pula, Rijeka, Kopar, Trieste, Padova, Zagreb, Rovinj, Poreč 🛈 1 svibnja 2; (052) 773 353; www. coloursofistria.com

On an isolated hill, among flourishing vineyards, stands Buje, the ancient Roman settlement of Bullea. Once a Frankish feudal village, in 1102 it became part of the Patriarchate of Aquileia and in 1412 the town came under Venetian rule.

Buje still retains the outline of an ancient walled castle and has kept its original medieval layout, with narrow alleys and lanes leading to the main square. The Cathedral of St Servelus (Sv. Servol) stands here, built in the 16th century over the remains of a Roman temple, of which a few columns and pieces survive.

Inside the church are wooden statues from the 14th and 15th centuries (*Madonna with Child* and *St Barbara*), sculptures representing St Servelus and St Sebastian

(1737) by Giovanni Marchiori, and an organ by Gaetano Callido (1725–1813).

Outside the town walls is the Church of St Mary (Sv. Marija), erected in the 15th century; a wooden statue of the Virgin and a *Pietà* are from the same period. Some of the paintings of biblical scenes are by Gasparo della Vecchia (early 18th century).

The nearby Civic Museum houses some interesting handicrafts and pieces made by local craftsmen.

Perched on a hilltop, 8 km (5 miles) southeast of Buje, is the medieval town of Grožnjan (Grisignana). It was first documented in 1102 when the town became the property of the Patriarchate of Aquileia. In 1358 the Venetians bought Grožnjan from Baron Reiffenberg and since that time it has been the administrative and military centre of the surrounding area. A tower,

some parts of the walls and two doors are all that remain of the Old Town.

After World War II, the majority of the inhabitants, nearly all of them Italian, abandoned the town. In 1965, however, it was declared a "City of Artists". Contemporary artists work and exhibit their art in the various local galleries and workshops.

Novigrad

Cittanova

A3 ✈ Pula 🚉 Pazin 🛈 Mandrač 29a; (052) 757 075; www.colours ofistria.com

Originally a Greek colony and later a Roman one called Aemonia, Novigrad stands at the mouth of the River Mirna. In the Byzantine period (6th century), it was called "New

> **Buje still retains the outline of an ancient walled castle and has kept its original medieval layout, with narrow alleys and lanes leading to the main square.**

Town" (Neopolis). From the early Middle Ages until 1831 it was an episcopal seat. In 1277 it passed into Venetian hands and oak from the Motovun forests was shipped to Venetian dockyards.

In the 13th century Novigrad was walled for defence, but the town was unable to withstand a Turkish attack in 1687 and it was partially destroyed, along with many works of art.

Evidence of the Venetian period can be seen on the façades of the houses in the narrow lanes that lead to the main square (Veliki Trg). In the town's present-day Baroque church are paintings from the Venetian school of the 18th century. Artifacts from the Roman and medieval periods can be seen in the museum in the Urizzi Palace.

7

Umag
Umago

 A2 🚌 Pula 🚌 Joakima Rakovca bb, (060) 317 060 ℹ Trgovačka 6; (052) 741 363; www.coloursofistria.com

This town is located on a narrow peninsula that frames a small bay. It was founded by the Romans and given the name Humagum. In 1268, it passed into Venetian hands and became an important port.

Umag still has many 15th- and 16th-century stone houses. On the left outer wall of the 18th-century Church of the Assumption of the Blessed Virgin Mary (Crkva Uznesenia Blažene Djevice Marije) is a relief of St Pilgrim and the fortified

town of Umag, and inside the church is a 15th-century Venetian school polyptych. Today, Umag is a busy seaside resort with numerous hotels. It is known for its well-equipped sports centres, and major tennis tournaments are held here.

8

Bale
Valle

 A3 🚌 Pula 🚌 Pula 🚌 Trg palih boraca ℹ Rovinjska 1; www.bale-valle.hr

On a hill of limestone, the Illyrians constructed a fort that dominated the surrounding countryside. The Romans also built a *castrum* (Castrum Vallis) on the same site, which was renovated when the place became a feudal estate of the Patriarchate of Aquileia. During Venetian rule the town grew in size and acquired its present layout of an elliptical wall enclosing two parallel rows of houses. Interesting buildings include the Gothic-Venetian Magistrates' Court with coats of arms on the portico, the loggia, and the castle dating from the 15th century, a residence for the Soardo Bembo family. Under one of the two side towers is a gate leading to the Old Town.

The Romanesque Church of St Elizabeth (Pohođenje Blažene Djevice Marije) was reconstructed in the 16th

century and again in the 19th. It contains a splendid crucifix, a sarcophagus, a polyptych and a marble Renaissance altar.

There are also two other churches: a 14th-century one dedicated to St Anthony and a 15th-century one, dedicated to the Holy Spirit.

EAT

Čok
A family-run joint offering fresh seafood and handmade pasta.

 A3 🏠 Ul Sv. Antona 2, Novigrad 📞 (052) 757 643

ⓚ ⓚ ⓚ

Monte
Michelin-starred Monte offers three tasting menus of contemporary Mediterranean cuisine.

A2 🏠 Montaibano 75, Rovinj 🌐 monte.hr

ⓚ ⓚ ⓚ

La Grisa
Head here for seafood or the more meaty dishes of the Istrian interior.

A3 🏠 La Grisa 23, Bale 🌐 la-grisa.com 🕐 Oct–Apr: Mon

ⓚ ⓚ ⓚ

La Puntalina
This restaurant and wine bar is known for its Istrian seafood specialities.

A2 🏠 Sv Križ 38, Rovinj 🌐 puntulina.eu

ⓚ ⓚ ⓚ

 ←
Historic buildings in the main square of Roman-founded Umag

9

Vrsar
Orsera

🅰A3 ✈Pula 🚆Pazin
ℹRade Končara 46; www.
infovrsar.com

The remains of a villa, a quarry and further foundations all provide evidence that Romans once settled in this small port town. Previously the feudal territory of the bishop of Poreč, Vrsar came under Venetian rule in 1778.

The town is dominated by the 18th-century Vergottini Castle. Near the Romanesque gate in the medieval wall – which once surrounded the town – is the small Church of St Anthony. On the harbour sits the Church of St Mary (Sv. Marija), one of the most important Romanesque monuments in Istria.

Just outside Vrsar lies Koversada, one of the oldest naturist resorts in Europe. To the south of Vrsar is the Limski Channel, now a marine reserve. The channel is 9 km (5 miles) long and 600 m (1,970 ft) wide, with steep sides perforated by limestone caves. In the early 11th century, one of the caves was the home of the hermit St Romualdo, who founded a monastery near Kloštar.

12,000

The number of visitors that naturist resort Koversada can accommodate in one day.

10

Fažana
Fasana

🅰A3 ✈Pula 🚌Vodnjan
⛴Brijuni Islands ℹ43
istarske divizije 8; www.
infofazana.hr

This small fishing town is mainly known as the embarkation point for the islands of the Brijuni National Park (p156). Facing the sea is the Church of SS Cosmas and Damian (Sv. Kuzma i Damjan), which was founded in the 11th century. Inside is a *Last Supper* by Jurai Ventura (1578), and in the sacristy are remains of frescoes by Italian artists that date from the 15th–16th centuries.

Other churches in the area include Our Lady of Carmel, built in the 14th century and the 6th-century St Eliseus, which has a stone doorway and blind-arch windows.

Due to the rise in visitors heading for the Brijuni Islands, Fažana has grown and new facilities have been built.

11

Rovinj
Rovigno

🅰A3 ✈Pula 🚆Pula 🚌Trg
na lokvi, (060) 888 611
ℹObala Pina Budicina 12;
www.rovinj-tourism.com

Rovinj was originally an island port built by the Romans. In 1763, it was joined to the coast by filling in the channel. The city was initially ruled by the Byzantines and the Franks, from 1283 until 1797 it was under Venetian control.

The Califfi Palace, dating from 1680, is now the Rovinj-Rovigno City Museum, and houses 18th-century Venetian art and a variety of works by modern Croatian artists.

The cathedral, dedicated to St Euphemia, dominates the town. The saint's remains are preserved in a Roman sarcophagus in the apse. The adjacent bell tower was modelled on that of San Marco in Venice.

Along the waterfront is the Centre for Maritime Research which was founded in the 19th century and has an

aquarium. Nearby, Red Island is in fact two islands linked by an embankment.

Vodnjan

Dignano

A3 ☒ Pula ☐ Željeznička ulica; (052) 511 538 ☐ Narodni trg 3; www.vodnjan dignano.com

The town of Vodnjan stands on a hill among vineyards and olive groves. Once an Illyrian fort and later a Roman military post, it was under Venetian rule from 1331 until 1797.

The large People Square in the centre of the town is surrounded by notable buildings such as the Benussi House and the Neo-Gothic City Hall.

The old part of town still contains various buildings in Venetian Gothic style, including the Bettica Palace and the 18th-century **Church of St Blaise** (Sv. Blaž). The latter houses some splendid statues and paintings, including a *Last Supper* by G Contarini (1598). There are also six mummies of saints, which have miraculously survived without being embalmed. The most revered is that of St Nicolosia.

Church of St Blaise
☐ Župni trg ☐ (052) 511 420 or (052) 511 420 ☐ Collection of Religious Art: Jun–Sep: 9:30am–7pm Mon–Sat, noon–5pm Sun; Oct–May: by appt

Pazin

A3 ☐ (052) 624 310 ☐ (060) 306 040 ☐ Ulica Veli Jože 1; www.central-istria.com/pazin

Commonly known as the "Heart of Istria", the town of Pazin originated in the 9th century as a fort and stands on a cliff 130 m (426 ft) high. The huge abyss on one side of the cliff is said to have inspired Dante's description of the Gateway to Hell in *Inferno*, and Jules Verne's *Mathias Sandorf*.

The present layout of the medieval castle dates from the 16th century. The tower now houses the interactive Ethnographic Museum of Istria (Etnografski muzej Istre) and the Pazin Town Museum, where weaponry and finds from the medieval castle are on display.

←
A picturesque jumble of houses in coastal Rovinj

↑ The Neo-Gothic façade of Vodnjan's City Hall

Barban

A3 ☒ Pula ☐ Pula ☐ From Pula ☐ Barban 69; www.tz-barban.hr

A free town in the late Middle Ages, Barban came under the rule of the county of Pazin in the 13th century, and from 1516 until 1797 it was part of Venetian territory. During this period many buildings acquired their current Venetian look. The town still has some medieval fortifications that now incorporate several Renaissance buildings.

The **Church of St Nicholas** (Sv. Nikola) faces the square, which is reached through the Great Gate (Vela Vrata). The church has five marble Gothic altars and many Venetian paintings (16th–18th centuries), one attributed to the Italian artist Padovanino.

In the same square is the Loredan Palace from 1606 and, towards the Small Gate (Mala Vrata), the Town Hall, dating from 1555.

Outside the Great Gate is the 14th-century Church of St Anthony (Sv. Antun), with frescoes from the 15th century.

Church of St Nicholas
☐ (052) 567 173 ☐ By appt

Weather-beaten houses lining the water in Rovinj

The 14th-century Church of the Blessed Virgin Mary's Birth in Labin

16 Gračišće

 A3 Pazin, 7 km (4 miles) During school year only; contact Pazin (060) 306 040 Ulica Veli Jože 1, Pazin; www.central-istria. com/gracisce

This small village stands on a hill among woods and vineyards. It was once a military garrison, and the second line of defence for the Venetian Republic and the Habsburg Empire. The village has some interesting buildings, such as the 15th-century Salamon Palace and the Bishop's Chapel (both in Venetian-Gothic style) where the bishop of Pićan used to spend the summer.

The Church of St Mary (Sv. Marije) was consecrated in 1425 and has a barrel vault and many frescoes. The Romanesque Church of St Euphemia

15 Labin

A3 Ulica 2, marta; (060) 888 613 Aldo Negri 20; www.rabac-labin.com

The medieval town of Labin is situated on a hill above Rabac, a popular seaside resort. It is home to a 19th-century Town Hall, a 17th-century bastion, a loggia (1550) and the St Flora gate (1589) with a Lion of St Mark.

In the square named Stari Trg lies the Magistrates' Court (1555) and in a street leading off the square stands the Church of the Blessed Mary's Birth (Rođenje Marijino), built in the late 14th century. The church is decorated with six marble altars, one of which contains St Justin's relics

(brought here from Rome in 1664). The main altar and altarpiece features six figures – the Virgin, St Pauline and the saints – by Dalmatian artist Natale Schiavone. The altar of the Madonna of Carmel is much more valuable, with a 17th-century altarpiece thought to be the work of Palma il Giovane. Valentin Lukas, a young Labin painter from the 19th century, is responsible for the painting featuring the Stages of the Cross.

In the same street are the Scampicchio Palace and the early 18th-century Baroque Battiala Lazzarini Palace, also Venetian-influenced, and now the **Town Museum**. Here visitors can find Roman and medieval finds plus a lifelike reconstruction of a coal mine. Labin was Croatia's most important coal mining town until the mines were closed down in 1988. In 1921, in opposition to rising Fascism in Italy, about 1,000 coal miners set up the Labin Republic, a socialist mini-state that lasted for only 37 days.

Town Museum
Ulica 1 svibnja (052) 852 477 Apr-Oct: 10am-1pm Mon-Sat (Jun & Sep: also 5-8pm; Jul & Aug: 6-10pm)

 GREAT VIEW
Peak Scenery

Lovran is the best starting point for the hike up towering Mount Vojak, the peak that overlooks the Kvarner Gulf. The climb takes 3.5 hours on foot, although you can also drive to a point just under the summit.

(Sv. Eufemija) was built in 1383 and renovated in 1864. It still has a wooden crucifix from the 13th century. The loggia at the main gate dates from 1549.

Pićan

 A3 ⬛ During school year only; contact Pazin (060) 306 040 🚹 Ulica Veli Jože 1, Pazin: www.central-istria.com/en/pican

Known as Petina under the Romans, Pićan stands on a hilltop 350 m (1,150 ft) high. It was a bishop's seat from late antiquity to the end of the 18th century, and has some intriguing medieval buildings.

Inside the town walls is a cathedral dedicated to St Nicephorus; it was built in the 14th century and rebuilt in the early 18th century after an earthquake. The story of Christian martyr Nicephorus is shown in a painting by Valentin Metzinger (1699–1759) in the cathedral. The Romanesque Church of St Michael (Sv. Mihovil) in the cemetery has early 15th-century frescoes.

18

Svetvinčenat

🅰 A3 🚉 Pazin 🚌 From Pula 🚹 Svetvinčenat 20; www.tz-svetvincenat.hr

This walled, hilltop village was built in the 10th century around a much restructured fort. The main square is one of the most beautiful in Istria. Many of the village's key buildings are found here, including the 15th-century Church of the Annunciation, which contains two paintings by Palma il Giovane and an *Annunciation* by Giuseppe Porto-Salviati.

The castle dates from the 13th century and is one of the best preserved in the region. It belonged to the Venetian families of Castropola: the Morosini and the Grimani. In 1589, the Grimani commissioned the architect Scamozzi to convert one of the square towers into a residence for the Venetian governors, and the other into a prison. High walls connecting the two towers enclose a large courtyard. This is reached through the citadel's only gate, which at one time had a drawbridge. The village's coat of arms and that of the Grimani family can also be seen here.

The village's name derives from the Romanesque church and cemetery of St Vincent (Sv. Vinčenat), whose walls were frescoed by an unknown 15th-century artist.

About 10 km (6 miles) outside Svetvinčenat are the ruins of Dvigrad (Duecastelli), an atmospheric, abandoned walled village. Around 1000 AD, two castles were built on neighbouring hills and were later enclosed by an oval wall.

↑ Svetvinčenat's main square, lined by weathered historic buildings

Motovun

🄰A3 🚌From Pazin and Pula **ℹ️Trg Andrea Antico 1; www.tz-motovun.hr**

Motovun is the most celebrated of the Istrian hill-towns. Heaped upon a rounded hill, the knot of tall stone houses has preserved its medieval-Renaissance appearance almost unchanged. The town had a predominantly Italian-speaking population until 1945, when many of the inhabitants were forced to leave in the aftermath of World War II. Motovum remained depopulated until the 1970s, when artists and craftsmen were encouraged to set up studios in its vacant houses. Growing tourism also helped to revive the town, and the annual Motovun Film Festival (held every year in late July) has placed it firmly on the international culture map.

Visitors with cars usually have to park in Kanal, the modern suburb at the bottom of the hill. From here the town is entered via a steep street that passes through Gradiziol, a suburb of narrow, hillside-hugging alleys. At the top of the street is the medieval New Gate (Nova Vrata), decorated with the arms of patrician families. It leads to a long, narrow square overlooked by the 13th-century Communal Palace (Komunalna palača), an austere building that retains its Romanesque mullioned windows. The inner core of

the town is accessed through the Main Gate (Glavna Vrata). The centrepiece of the main square is St Stephen's Church (Crkva svetog Stjepana), a Renaissance building thought to have been designed by the Italian architect Andrea Palladio. Its 27-m (89-ft) tower acts as both the town's lookout post and as a belfry. An essential part of the Motovun experience is a stroll around the walls, savouring the expansive views over the Mirna Valley (famed for its oak forests where locals hunt for truffles). These thick fortifications were built by the Venetians in the 14th century.

PARENZANA CYCLE ROUTE

The Parenzana is the title of a narrow gauge railway built in 1902 to connect the port city of Trieste with Poreč on the Istrian coast. The line was closed in the 1930s and its tracks pulled up, but its viaducts, embankments and tunnels still survive. Large stretches of the Parenzana have since been transformed into a cycle path, running past the picturesque towns of the Istrian interior. It is a thrilling route to follow through the green, unspoiled countryside.

Roč

🄰A2 🚌From Rijeka and Buzet **ℹ️Roč bb; (092) 1694 598**

Settled since prehistoric times, the little town of Roč, eight hours drive from Buzet, nestles behind well-preserved town walls. Inside one of its two surviving gates is a lapidarium containing Roman tombstones. In the centre of town, St Anthony's Church (Crkva svetog Ante) still shows signs of its Romanesque origins, while the adjacent St Bartholomew's Church

(Crkva svetog Bartula) sports an unusual, chisel-shaped bell tower.

Just north of Roč and accessible by a minor road is the summit of the Ćićarija ridge, which offers wonderful views across the Buzet region.

Hum

 A3

Huddled on a slope overlooking the wooded Mirna Valley, the compact settlement of Hum is often described as the "smallest town in the world". It has walls, a church and a soaring 16th-century belfry, but only two tiny streets and a population that currently numbers less than 30. Proof that Hum used to be a prosperous market town is provided by the Church of the Assumption, which was

Did You Know?

Legend says giants built these Istrian towns and Hum is so small because they ran out of rocks.

rebuilt with a monumental Neo-Classical façade in 1802. Just outside the town walls, the graveyard Chapel of St Jerome preserves extraordinarily vivid 12th-century frescoes illustrating the lives of Jesus and the Virgin Mary.

To the southwest of Hum is the semi-deserted village of Kotli, a picturesque knot of stone houses set above a series of small cataracts in the Mirna River. There are popular bathing spots beside the river and numerous local walks.

You'll need your own car to reach Hum, as no public transport passes this way.

Oprtalj

 A3 🛈 **Matka Laginje bb; www.oprtalj.hr**

Located on a ridge on the opposite side of the Mirna Valley to Motovun, Oprtalj is a typical example of Istria's smaller hilltop settlements. Stone houses form an uneven circle around a parish church, while a freestanding tower functions as both belfry and lookout point. Just outside town, on the road to Buje, the Church of St Mary (Crkva svete Marije) contains spectacular 15th-century frescoes that depict the life of the Virgin.

↑ A rock climber clinging to a cliff face in the hilly region of Buzet

Buzet

A2 🚌 **From Pula** 🚌 **From Rijeka and Pula** 🛈 **Ul Vladimira Gortana 9; www.tz-buzet.hr**

The main commercial centre of northeastern Istria, Buzet comprises a quiet, atmospheric Old Town perched on a hill, and a modern town stretched out on the plain below. It is the truffle capital of Croatia, and is situated at the centre of the wooded, hilly area in which most truffle-hunting takes place. September's Buzetska Subotina ("Buzet Saturday") is one of the country's biggest food-related festivals.

Buzet's Old Town preserves its medieval walls, but otherwise lacks the grandeur of Motovun or Grožnjan. The Regional Museum (Zavičajni muzej) – open on weekdays during summer and by appointment throughout the rest of the year – displays local crafts and customs. There is a section devoted to the "Buzet Earring", an early-medieval accessory that consists of a decorated, delicate bronze arc.

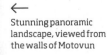

← Stunning panoramic landscape, viewed from the walls of Motovun

KVARNER AREA

Stretching southeast of the Istrian peninsula, the Kvarner is a deep, broad gulf scattered with some of Croatia's most popular islands. Dominating the gulf from the mainland is Rijeka, a busy port city and a vibrant hub of culture and cuisine. Just west of Rijeka is Opatija, the birthplace of Adriatic tourism and still retaining something of the Belle Epoque. While most of the Adriatic coast fell under the control of Venice in the Middle Ages, the Kvarner remained in the hands of Croatian-Hungarian kings. Local aristocratic families flourished, especially the Frankopans, whose castles still dominate the landscape in Rijeka, Krk, Bakar and Kraljevica. Rijeka emerged as a major manufacturing centre, although it is now a post-industrial city strong on culture and the arts. It was the Austrian-Habsburgs who saw the tourist potential of the Kvarner Gulf in the late 19th century, with one branch of the family patronizing Opatija, another adopting the resort of Crikvenica. The idyllic island of Lošinj emerged as a quieter alternative to both.

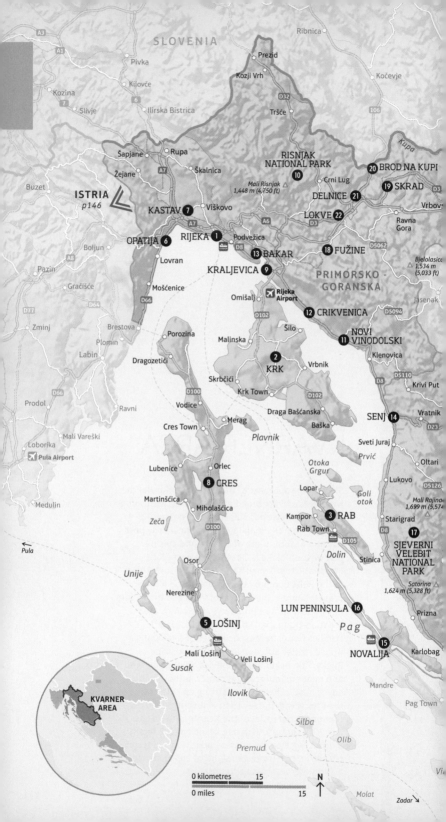

KVARNER AREA

Must Sees
1. Rijeka
2. Krk
3. Rab
4. Plitvice Lakes National Park
5. Lošinj

Experience More
6. Opatija
7. Kastav
8. Cres
9. Kraljevica
10. Risnjak National Park
11. Novi Vinodolski
12. Crikvenica
13. Bakar
14. Senj
15. Novalja
16. Lun Peninsula
17. Sjeverni Velebit National Park
18. Fužine
19. Skrad
20. Brod na Kupi
21. Delnice
22. Lokve

Semič

Črnomelj

Vinica

Ogulin

-tok
usulinski

**CENTRAL AND
NORTHERN CROATIA**
p216

Velika Kladuša

Vrnograč

Lubarda

Slunj

Jezerane

Križpolje

Brinje

Ličка Jesenica

Grabovac

Cažin

Bosanska
Otoka

Bosanska
Krupa

Plitvice

4

**PLITVICE LAKES
NATIONAL PARK**

**BOSNIA AND
HERZEGOVINA**

Otočac

Kuterevo

Ličko Lešće

Ramljani

Korenica

Bihać

Gola Plješevica
1,646 m (5,400 ft)

Nipaš

LIČKO - SENJSKA

Bjelopolje

Krnjeuša

Perušić

Bunić

Kruge

Ozeblin
1,657 m (5,436 ft)

Vrtoče

Lički Osik

Gospić

Metla
1,288 m (4,226 ft)

Donji
Lapac

Brušane

Siljevača
1,449 m (4,754 ft)

Počitelj

Mogorić

Udbina

Lukovo
Šugarje

Gornja Ploča

Donja Suvaja

Raduč

Lovinac

Bruvno

Vaganski vrh
1,757 m (5,764 ft)

Deringaj

Povljana

**ZADAR AND
NORTHERN
DALMATIA**
P116

 The attractive city of Rijeka cascading down a hillside

 RIJEKA

🅰B3 ✈Krk, www.rijeka-airport.hr 🚌Krešimirova ulica, (060) 333 444 🚆Trg Žabica 1, (060) 888 666 ⛴Senjsko pristanište 3, (051) 212 696; Jadrolinija, Riječki lukobran bb, (051) 211 444 🅸Korzo 14; www.visitrijeka.hr

Founded by the Liburnians and conquered by the Celts, this town then became the Roman city of Tarsatica before finally coming under the rule of the Habsburgs in 1466. In 1719, to develop its maritime role, Emperor Charles VI declared Rijeka a free port. The city became part of Hungary in 1870 and its economic importance continued to grow. Rijeka is now one of Croatia's main ports and a key rail and road junction. In February and March, it plays host to Croatia's largest carnival.

① City Tower
Gradski Toranj

📍Trg Ivana Koblera

About halfway along the Korzo is the City Tower, built in the Middle Ages and remodelled several times: the clock dates from the 1600s, the dome from 1890. An imposing building, it is decorated with coats of arms, including those of the city and the Habsburgs, and busts of Leopold I and Charles VI.

② Church of the Assumption of the Blessed Virgin Mary
Crkva Uznesenja Blažene Djevice Marije

📍Pavla Rittera Vitezovića 3 📞(051) 214 177 🕐8am–noon & 4–6:30pm daily

The Church of the Assumption, once a cathedral, preserves little of its original 13th-century aspect. It was renovated in the Baroque style in 1695 and with Rococo details in 1726. Inside, the altars, the chancel and some of the paintings are from the Baroque period. The part-Romanesque, part-Gothic bell tower outside the church dates back to the 14th century. Thanks to subsidence, the tower has developed a subtle slope and has come to be known as "The Leaning Tower".

TORPEDO

The world's first torpedo was launched in Rijeka on 20 December 1866. It was invented by Robert Whitehead, a Bolton-born engineer who had worked in the naval yards of the Habsburg Empire. Whitehead was inspired by the work of his colleague Blaž Lupis, who had tried to build a projectile that would travel on the surface of the sea. Whitehead's stroke of genius was to put it underwater. His factory went on to be one of Rijeka's main employers, exporting weapons all over the world until it ceased production in 1966.

③

St Vitus Cathedral
Katedrala sv. Vida

🏛 Grivica 11 📞 (051) 330 879 🕐 7am-noon, 4:30-7pm daily

What was once the Church of St Vitus, patron saint of the city, became a cathedral in the interwar period. This large rotunda was built between 1638 and 1742 by the Jesuits and is the only one of its kind in Croatia. Baroque altars and a 13th-century Gothic crucifix adorn the interior, and by appointment you can view a collection of rare books and religious works of art.

④

Capuchin Church of Our Lady of Lourdes
Kapucinska Crkva Gospe Lurdske

🏛 Kapucinske stube 5 📞 (051) 211 289 🕐 7am-noon, 4-8pm daily

North of Žabica Square (Trg Žabica), the church was built between 1904 and 1929 on the orders of Father Bernardin Škrivanić, the abbot of the neighbouring Capuchin monastery, to mark the 50th anniversary of the Virgin's apparition at Lourdes in France. The father had returned from a reportedly miraculous pilgrimage to the holy site and commissioned the new church in celebration. A faith healer was called on to help raise funds for the church's construction.

Her performance entailed falling into a trance and sweating blood – in reality she squeezed a pouch of calf's blood hidden under her cloak. The building is notable for its unique and imposing red-and-white Lombard-style Neo-Gothic façade and double staircases. Conceived with a large belltower, a white marble statue of Our Lady of Lourdes instead stands here.

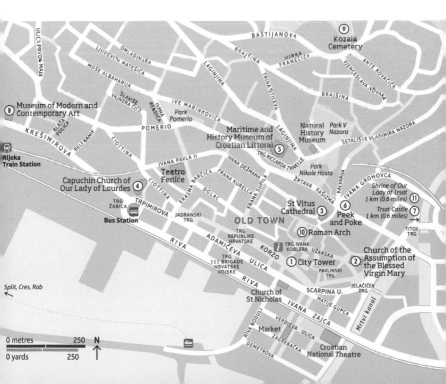

↑ The red-and-white façade and symmetrical staircases of the imposing Capuchin Church

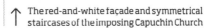

⑤ Maritime and History Museum of Croatian Littoral

Pomorski i povijesni muzej Hrvatskog primorja

📍 Trg Riccarda Zanelle 1
🕐 9am-4pm Mon, 9am-8pm Tue-Sat, 9am-1pm Sun 🌐 ppmhp.hr

The Maritime and History Museum is housed within the magnificent Governor's Palace. The history of navigation is told through the collections of model ships, weapons and seafaring equipment from the 17th and 18th centuries. There are also rich archaeological collections of items from prehistory to the Middle Ages, displays of prints, furniture, paintings and an ethnographic collection.

> At the heart of the cemetery are some beautiful examples of pre-World War I funerary sculpture, adorning the graves and chapels of 19th-century industrialists.

There is a room devoted to Gabriele D'Annunzio, the Italian poet, aviator and demagogue who occupied Rijeka illegally in 1919. The most valued exhibit is an original lifejacket from RMS *Titanic*, brought back to Rijeka by a seaman on RMS *Carpathia*, the only ship that went to pick up survivors of the wreck.

⑥ Peek and Poke

📍 Ivana Grahovca 2
🕐 May-Oct: 10am-6pm Mon-Fri, 11am-4pm Sat; Nov-Apr: 11am-4pm Sat
🌐 peekpoke.hr

A one-of-its-kind museum devoted to the age of the computer, Peek and Poke displays historical artifacts from the world of information technology. There are early Hewlett Packards, IBMs and Commodores, as well as all kinds of calculators and game consoles. Also on display are other innovations belonging to the world of consumer electronics, including the ill-fated Sinclair C5 electric tricycle, and a library of vintage books and magazines.

> ### INSIDER TIP
> **Market Food**
>
> Rijeka occupies a unique place in Croatian gastronomy, with the rich fishing grounds of the Kvarner Gulf bordered by a hilly hinterland of cheeses, hams, honeys and jams. All of these things can be found in profusion in the central market, held in the Art Nouveau pavilions just inland from the harbour.

⑦ Trsat Castle

Trsatski kaštel

Partizanski put 9a 📞 (051) 217 714 🕐 9am-9pm daily

On the opposite bank of the Rjecina, high above the centre of Rijeka, is Trsat, where you will find the ruins of a Roman castle. In the 13th century, the town was owned by the Frankopans, who built another castle on the same site. It has fine views over the Kvarner gulf and a popular open-air café.

↑ A winding path leading to the entrance to the modest but charming Trsat Castle

→
The remains of the Roman Arch, thought to be the old gateway to Roman Tarsatica

Museum of Modern and Contemporary Art

Muzej moderne i suvremene umjetnosti

📍 Krešimirova 26c
🕐 Hours vary, check website 🌐 mmsu.hr

Founded in 1948, this museum has one of the biggest avant-garde collections in Croatia, although only a fraction of the its holdings are on show at a time. Opened in 2017 and housed in a restored factory in the former industrial Benčić Complex, the building is an attraction in itself. Exhibitions by international artists are an important part of the pro-gramme. Ongoing renovations will eventually see the Rijeka City Museum, Rijeka City Library and the Childrens House opening here.

Kozala Cemetery

Groblje Kozala

📍 Ulica Petra Kobeka

Occupying a hillside just north of the centre, Kozala is one of the most evocative cemeteries in the Mediterranean. At its heart are beautiful examples of pre-World War I funerary sculpture, adorning the graves and chapels of 19th-century industrialists. The mausoleum of Robert Whitehead, inventor of the torpedo and resident of Rijecka, is the largest and most ornate of them all.

Poplars and palm trees give the cemetery a park-like feel. Overlooking the cemetery is the steeple of the Church of St Romuald and All Saints (Crkva svetog Romualda i Svih Svetih), built in the 1930s by the Futurism-influenced Italian architect Bruno Angheben.

Roman Arch

Stara vrata

📍 Trg Ivana Koblera

In an alley leading from the north side of the square are the remains of a Roman arch, which was probably a gate to the old city. Nearby, excava-tions have unearthed the foundations of a perimeter wall from the Roman period.

Shrine of Our Lady of Trsat

Svetište Majke Božje Trsatske

📍 Frankopanski trg 🕐 6am-8pm daily 🌐 trsat-svetiste.com.hr

At the top of the 561 steps from Tito Square (Titov trg) is the Shrine of Our Lady of Trsat. The church and Franciscan monastery were built in 1453 by Martin Frankopan. It was in this church, from 1291 to 1294, that parts of the Holy House of Mary of Nazareth were preserved before being transferred to Loreto in Italy. To compensate the town, in 1367 Pope Urban V donated a Virgin with Child, painted by St Luke, a copy of which now stands on the main altar.

The church was remodelled in 1864 but retained the trium-phal arch, the altar under the painting of the Virgin, and the Frankopan family tombs.

↑ The magnificent main altar inside the Shrine of Our Lady of Trsat

The popular resort of Baška, hugging the coast beneath Krk island's rolling hills

②

KRK

 B3 www.rijeka-airport.hr Valbiska: (051) 863170; Baška: (051) 856 821 Krk island: Trg sv. Kvirina 1, www. krk.hr; Krk town: Vela placa 1, www.tz-krk.hr; Baška: Kralja Zvonimira 114, (051) 856 817; Njivice: Ribarska obala 10, (051) 846 735; Punat: Pod topol 2, (051) 854 860

The largest of the Adriatic islands, Krk is linked to the mainland by a bridge, providing good connections to the international airport. Along the eastern coast the island looks almost ghostly, its white rocks swept by the bora wind. Inland and on the more protected western coast, there is rich, lush vegetation.

①

Košljun

Just offshore from Punat, this small islet is best known for its Franciscan Monastery, where for centuries the monks have collected all manner of sacred objects and valuable and curious items.

 Statue of Saint Francis petting a dog, from the Košljun Monastery

②

Krk Town

Krk developed in the Middle Ages on the site of the Roman town of Curicum. The wall and three Venetian city gates are still visible. Facing the main square are Renaissance-era buildings, and near the Roman baths you will find the bright façade of the Cathedral of Our Lady of the Assumption, dating from the 1100s. Inside is a fine Baroque pulpit.

In the adjacent Romanesque Church of St Quirinus is the Diocesan Museum, containing works from around the island, including the silver Frankopan altarpiece depicting the *Virgin Mary in Glory* and a polyptych (1350) by Paolo Veneziano.

Behind the cathedral stands Frankopan Castle, with four square towers from 1191 and a round Venetian tower. Inside are the churches of Our Lady of Health and St Francis.

③

Omišalj

W visit-omišalj-njivice.hr

Omišalj lies near the ancient Roman site of Fulfinum. Some of the enclosing walls survive. There is a square with a 17th-century Venetian loggia,

> Q HIDDEN GEM
> **Stara Baška**
>
> Krk's best beaches are at Stara Baška, a village at the bottom of steep hills on the southwestern coast of the island. There are several stretches of pebble, of which Oprna Bay, just north of the village, is the prettiest.

the Church of St Helen, with copies of Glagolitic script, and the Church of the Assumption of St Mary.

Baška

Not to be confused with Stara Baška (Old Baška), this is a popular tourist resort with a beautiful beach and clear sea. The Church of the Holy Trinity (1723) stands in a small square; nearby, in the Church of St Lucy in Jurandvor, is a copy of the Baška Tablet, the oldest document in Croatia, written in Glagolitic script in 1100.

Malinska

🛈 Obala 4G 🚍 Rijeka, Zagreb
🌐 visitmalinska.com

Malinska is a modern town huddled around a small bay on Krk's northern coast. It was discovered as a tourist resort by the Viennese aristocracy in the 1880s, when Crown Prince Rudolph came to hunt. The most popular beaches are on the coastal path that leads west of the centre; Rupa is the nearest, followed by the shingle coves of Vrtača and Rova.

Vrbnik

🏛 Placa vrbničkog statuta 4
🚌 Krk town 🌐 vrbnik.hr

The town of Vrbnik occupies a rocky headland on the eastern coast of the island, its cobbled alleys coiled around a hilltop parish church. Vrbnik is famous for its vineyards, which stretch across the fertile plateau just inland. The refreshing white Vrbnička Žlahtina wine is sold in shops and wine cellars throughout the town.

↑ Steps leading up to Frankopan Castle

⑦
Dobrinj

🚩 Stara cesta bb
🌐 visitdobrinj.hr

The village of Dobrinj is a colourful jumble of stone houses and narrow alleys. The main square and parish church are overlooked by a bell tower. A villa on the main square holds the Barbarić Collection, which covers the ethnography of the island with an array of domestic and agricultural objects. The **Infeld Gallery** (Galerija Infeld), in the house of 19th-century sea captain Franjo Vušković, holds exhibitions by contemporary artists.

Infeld Gallery

🏛 Dobrinj bb 🕐 Jul-Sep: 11am-2pm, 5-9pm daily
🌐 infeld.net

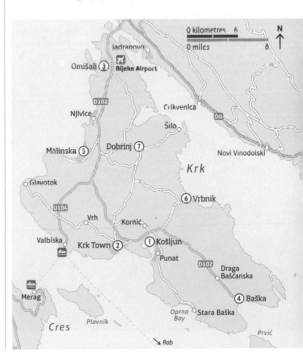

Vrbnik's pretty harbourfront, Krk island

↑ The rooftops and spires of Rab town, with the blue Adriatic beyond

③

RAB

🅰 B4 🚢 From Rijeka, Stinica, Pag, Valbiska (Krk); (051) 724 122 🚌 Palit, (060) 306 080 ℹ Trg Municipium Arba 8, Rab town; www.rab-visit.com

The island of Rab lies parallel to the Velebit massif, creating a channel that was dreaded by sailors because it forms a tunnel for the cold, dry bora wind. The opposite, western side of the island is protected from the wind and the climate is mild. Here the landscape is much greener and maquis alternates with woods of pine, oak and holm oak. The Romans knew the island by the name of Arba, or Scadurna, and, after its conquest, built a settlement on the site of the present-day town of Rab. This island is perhaps most famous for its part in the 1936 royal scandal, when British King Edward VIII and Wallis Simpson visited. Today Rab is popular for its sandy beaches and rocky coves.

①

Rab Town

The main town, Rab, which gives its name to the island, became a bishopric in the early Christian period and was inhabited by Slavic people in the 6th century. After it had been conquered by the Franks, it was administered by Venice and a treaty of mutual defence was agreed upon which lasted until 1000 AD. Rab was at times under the rule of the Hungarian kings until 1409, when it became Venetian territory. Venice ruled the island until 1797.

The town, famous for its four bell towers which make it look like a ship with four masts, has some lovely architecture. Ancient medieval walls once encircled the Old Town on the southern point of the peninsula and, in the 15th century, a wall was built to enclose the New Town, called Varoš. Part of this wall is well preserved. The town is beautiful, thanks in part to the various church towers and spires that pierce the sky, dotting the terracotta town-scape. These include the **Cathedral of St Mary the Great** (Katedrala Sv. Marija Velika), a majestic Roman-esque building with a 13th-century bell tower standing 70 m (230 ft) away from the cathedral. It is the tallest of all the bell towers on the island and arguably the most beautiful. Further churches of note include the Convent and **Church of St Justine** (Sv Justine), which has a lovely

↑ The Altar and polyptych of Kampor's Franciscan Convent of St Euphemia

bell tower and onion domes, and is found beside a stretch of shingle – perfect for a paddle to cool off while sightseeing.

Cathedral of St Mary the Great
⊛ 🏠 Ulica Ivana Rabljanina
🕒 Summer: 10am–noon, 6:30–9pm daily; winter: 4–6pm for Mass

Church of St Justine
🏠 Gornja ulica 📞 (051) 724 064 🕒 Times vary, call ahead

---

② Kampor

Kampor village lies at the end of a long bay (Kamporska Draga) and has preserved its stone houses and terraces of olives and vines. Not surprisingly, many holiday houses have sprung up around the charming village. The Franciscan Convent of St Euphemia, with a small adjacent Romanesque church, is near the Church of St Bernard and contains some beautiful artworks.

BEST BEACHES
Rab's most famous beach is Rajska plaža (Paradise Beach), a golden sand crescent east of Lopar. The bay here is shallow, making it possible to paddle a long distance from the shore. More secluded sandy beaches are found in the coves on the northern side of the Lopar peninsula and can be reached by taxi boat from Rajska plaža, or by walking through a pine forest from Lopar. One of the beaches, Sahara, is reserved for naturists. Best of the rocky beaches are at Frkanj, a wooded peninsula popular with naturists. It can be reached by taxi boat from Rab Town.

In sharp contrast, Kampor is also the site of a notorious World War II concentration camp, run by Fascist Italy from 1942 to 1943. An estimated 4,500 people died here due to the horrendous conditions, with malnutrition and disease rife. It is now a memorial park – **Graveyard of the Victims of Facism** (Groblje žrtava fašizma) – marked with symbolic graves and lined with poplar trees.

Graveyard of the Victims of Facism
🕒 24 hours daily

---

③ Lopar

The village of Lopar is at the end of a rocky peninsula. It is a popular holiday spot, particularly with Central Europeans, thanks to its sandy beaches fringed by luscious pinewoods and the leisure facilities on offer here – tennis, football and mini-golf to name a few.

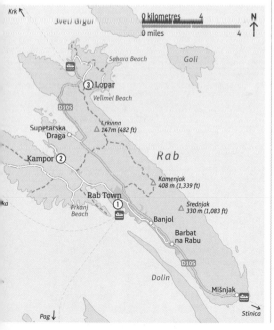

Did You Know?
One of the first naturist tourists on Rab was King Edward VIII; his trip even inspired a Croatian musical.

PLITVICE LAKES NATIONAL PARK

🅰C3 🚌🚤Shuttle buses and electric boats are included in the ticket price
🕐Times vary, check website 🆆np-plitvicka-jezera.hr

This national park is the jewel in Croatia's crown. Set in the heart of the country, Plitvice Lakes is famed for its bewitching landscape, which tells a new story with each season. Its emerald waters, flourishing foliage and spectacular waterfalls are best admired from the footbridges that wind endlessly around the park.

Plitvice's remarkable landscape was formed over several millennia. The flow of water across travertine – the soft rock found here – carried fragments downstream where they were deposited, creating the cataracts and water-falls that are characteristic of the park today.

Visiting the Park

The 16 labrynthine lakes that snake for 8 km (5 miles) are intertwined with lakeside paths and boardwalk trails, allowing visitors to get up close to the famous waterfalls. Allow plenty of time to get the most out of a trip here. The park is particularly busy in summer and progress along the trails can be slow. The lakes have a special magic in autumn, when deciduous leaves turn golden; in winter, waterfalls freeze and branches are covered in frost, giving the park a really mystical appeal.

Popular parts of the lake system include Lake Kozjak and Lake Galovac, which are nearest to the main entrance points. Lake Proščansko is slightly quieter; you'll find it at the southern end of the park, and it can be accessed by shuttle bus or shoreside path. Various hiking trails lead from the eastern shores of the lakes into woodland and away from the crowds.

Plitvice has a hotel complex within the park boundaries and a string of villages outside the park offering homestays and pensions.

1 Plitvice Lakes National Park is home to a wide variety of flora, including delicate marsh orchids that can be found in wild meadows.

2 This shuttle boat is one of several that ferry visitors around the lakes.

3 The national park tranforms with each season, so whatever time of year you visit you're guaranteed a spectacle. In winter the waterfalls freeze over.

> **INSIDER TIP**
> **Cave In and See More**
>
> It would be a shame to leave the Plitvice area without first exploring some of the outlying attractions. The Barać Cave, 10 km (6 miles) north of the lakes, offers the chance to see several chambers of dangling rock formations as part of a guided tour *(www. baraceve-spilje.hr)*. The village of Rakovica, 10 km (9 miles) north of the lakes, has a well-marked network of bike paths surrounding it, a wonderful way of exploring the area's rolling pastures and picturesque woodland.

←

Footbridge winding through Plitvice Lakes National Park in autumn

Looking out over Lošinj's sprawling main town, Mali Lošinj ↑

⑤
LOŠINJ

 B4 🚌 Mali Lošinj, (051) 231 765 ℹ Priko 42, Mali Lošinj; www.visitlosinj.hr

The island of Lošinj is rich in subtropical vegetation – pines, palms, oleanders and citrus trees galore – and is often associated with neighbouring Cres *(p188)*. The main town, Mali Lošinj, was founded in the 12th century, when 12 Croat families landed here. The most famous beach is at Čikat bay, southwest of Mali Lošinj. It is 30 km (19 miles) long and a popular place for water sports.

①
Mali Lošinj

This pretty port town, with its charmingly worn 18th- and 19th-century buildings, punctuated with swaying palms and towering cypress trees, was once advertised as a winter resort for consumptive Europeans. Times have changed since then. The oldest part of the town lies around the 18th-century Church of St Mary but Mali Lošinj's main visitor attraction is the stunning **Museum of the Apoxyomenos** (Muzej apoksiomena), built to house a spectacular Hellenic-era statue discovered on a nearby seabed in 1996.

Based inside a 19th-century palace, this informative museum uses multimedia exhibits to tell the story of the statue, which occupies a pod-like white room at the end of the display. The statue of an athlete is every bit as iconic as the museum build-up suggests and should not be missed.

The nearby **Lošinj Museum** (Muzej Lošinja), located in the 19th-century Fritzy Palace, contains a rich display of inter-national fine art, assembled by local collectors.

Occupying a hillside just south of the town centre is the **Fragrant Island Garden** (Miomirisni vrt), a beautifully landscaped and highly fragrant gathering of indigenous herbs and medicinal plants. The island garden is free to visit, and its fragrances are particularly prevalent after it has rained.

Museum of the Apoxyomenos

⊕ ⊙ 🏛 Riva lošinjksih kapetana 13 🕒 Apr-May: 10am-6pm Tue-Sun; Jun-Sep: 9am-10pm Tue-Sun; Oct-Mar: 9am-5pm Tue-Sun 🅦 muzejapoksiomena.hr

Lošinj Museum

⊕ 🏛 Vladimira Gortana 35 🕒 Mar-Dec: times vary, check website; Jan & Feb: call (051) 231 173 🅦 muzej.losinj.hr

Fragrant Island Garden

🏛 Bukovica 6 🕒 Mar-Jun & Sep-Dec: 8am-3pm daily; Jul & Aug: 8:30am-12:30pm & 6-9pm daily 🅦 miomi risni-vrt.hr

> ### Did You Know?
> Mali Lošinj's prized Apoxyomenos statue depicts an athlete wiping dust off his body.

②
Veli Lošinj

This lovely town is smaller and quieter than Mali Lošinj, in spite of *veli* meaning "big" and *mali* meaning "little". Villas are hidden in the vegetation here, and there is a harbourfront strung with cafés. In late spring, you might spot dolphins here; you can also join dolphin-watching tours.

The **Church of St Anthony Abbot** (Sv. Antun Pustinjak) was built in the 18th century on the site of a smaller 15th-century church. It has a rich store of paintings. The Baroque style is much in evidence on the seven altars. The **Lošinj Marine Education Centre** houses a brilliant compilation of conservation displays, and interactive exhibits and documentary films bring the cause to life.

Church of St Anthony Abbot
🏠 Obala Maršala Tita

Lošinj Marine Education Centre
🞉 🏠 Kaštel 24 🕐 May: 10am–2pm Mon–Sat; Jun–Aug: 10am–4pm Mon–Sat; Sep: 10am–3pm Mon–Fri; Oct: 10am–2pm Mon–Fri; Nov–Apr: 10am–3pm Mon–Fr; 🌐 blue-world.org

③
Čikat Peninsula

When Lošinj began to take off as a health resort at the end of the 19th century, locals embarked on the reforesta-tion of the Čikat Peninsula immediately west of the main towns. Shaded by tamarisks and Aleppo pines it became a favourite seaside strolling area, and many of Mali Lošinj's more opulent holiday villas were built along its shores. It is now the site of a well-equipped pebble beach, numerous cafés, and a trio of stylish hotels.

NEARBY ISLANDS

Susak is fruitful. Vines grow well in the island's soil and all the islanders have vineyards. Their traditional and brightly coloured women's costumes are famous. The island of Ilovik is home to about 170 people, and vines, olives, fruit and flowers grow here. Nearby is the uninhabited island of Sv. Petar, where there are the ruins of a fortress. Hilly and rocky Unije is the largest of the lesser islands. Locals here make their living from market gardening or fishing.

↑ Enjoying leafy surroundings and bay views on the Čikat Peninsula

EXPERIENCE MORE

EXPERIENCE Kvarner Area

6
Opatija

 B3 ✈ Rijeka, Krk island
🚆 Rijeka ⛴ Rijeka
ℹ Local: Maršala Tita 128;
www.visitopatija.com;
Regional: Nikole Tesle 2;
www.opatija-riviera.info

The resort of Opatija takes its name from a 14th-century Benedictine abbey, around which a village was built. On the site of the monastery now stands the Church of St James (Sv. Jakov), built in 1506.

Tourist interest began to grow around 1844 when a nobleman from Rijeka, Iginio Scarpa, built the grand Villa Angiolina here as a holiday villa (now home to the Croatian Tourism Museum). The Austrian Empress Maria Anna stayed here as one of Scarpa's guests, raising the profile of Opatija as a potential resort. Tourism was also boosted by the construction of a railway line that linked Austria with Rijeka, with a tram line to Opatija.

The area's mild climate made it a leading winter health resort, patronized by the Austrian royal family and the middle classes from all over the Habsburg Empire. Today the coast is still lined with luxury late 19th-century hotels and villas. The town's main attraction is the Franz Joseph Promenade (Šetalište Franza Jozefa), a scenic seaside pathway running from Lovran to Volosko, and the stunning Angiolina Park.

7
Kastav

 B2 ✈🚆⛴ Rijeka
ℹ Matka Mandića 11a;
www.kastav-touristinfo.hr

On a hill a short distance from Rijeka is the town of Kastav, which originated in the early Middle Ages. The castle was the residence of the local lord of the manor until the 16th century, and later the home of the Austrian governor. In Lokvina square stand the Church of St Anthony of the

> ### Did You Know?
>
> Opatija's "Maiden with a Seagull" statue originally had a fish in the gull's mouth, but this has vanished.

Desert, which dates from the 15th century, and a Loggia from 1571, restored in 1815. By the water trough a plaque recalls the drowning in 1666 of Captain Morelli, guilty of imposing excessive taxes.

8
Cres

 B3 ☎ (051) 211 444
ℹ Cres: Peškera 1;
www.tzg-cres.hr

The narrow island of Cres is 65 km (40 miles) long, and tourism here focuses on

villages such as Cres and Osor. In the north, a colony of native griffon vultures, protected by law since 1986, nests on a plateau swept by the dry bora wind. The south is milder and olives and vines are grown.

Cres Town nestles in a sheltered bay. It became important when the bishopric and governor's seat were transferred here from Osor. The town's walls and the three arched gates give it a Venetian feel, and the Church of Our Lady of the Snow has paintings by artists from the Venetian school. The 16th-century Town Hall is now a fruit and vegetable market and the old port bustles with fishermen and visitors. The Church of St Isidore (the patron saint) dates from the 12th century.

Until the mid-15th century, Osor was the main town on the island. It later declined, and today the entire town is a museum, with Bronze Age remains and monuments, making it a centre of great artistic interest. The beautiful Cathedral of the Assumption was completed in 1497 and is built of honey-coloured stone.

Aquamarine waters and fine white pebbles on Cres island ↑

Inside the church there is a painting of SS Nicholas and Gaudentius on the altar. The Cres Museum (Creski muzej) occupies the Arsan Palace and has stone inscriptions and interesting finds from the Illyrian and Roman periods, and the early Middle Ages. The façade of the Bishop's Palace bears coats of arms of the island's bishops and nobles and the interior is richly decorated. Some walls, foundations and mosaics are all that remain of the Church of St Peter.

9

Kraljevica

 B3 Rijeka (051) 282 078 Rovina 6; www.tzg-kraljevica.hr

A well-known tourist resort on the mainland, Kraljevica is linked to the island of Krk by a long bridge that also leads to Rijeka airport (on Krk). In the Old Town (Stari Grad) is a castle, built in the 16th century by the family of the counts of Šubić-Zrinski. Its walls also shelter the Church of St Nicholas.

A village inhabited by families from the fortress of

←

Colourful buildings hugging the harbour in Volosko, Opatija

Hreljin developed around the castle. In the new district (Novi Grad), on a promontory above the sea, is a castle built by the Frankopan family in 1650 in Late Renaissance style. It was turned into a magnificent palace in the mid-18th century.

In 1728, the Austrian emperor Charles VI began to create a sizeable port here, at the end of a road that went from Karlovac to the sea.

EAT

Plavi Podrum
Award winning Plavi Podrum sits by the harbour in pretty Volosko. Try the shrimps.

 B3 Obala F Supila 6, Opatija plavipodrum. com

Ⓚ Ⓚ Ⓚ

Draga di Lovrana
Set high on the coast, this hotel-restaurant offers a great view and serves Michelin-starred cuisine.

 B4 Lovranska Draga 1, Lovran dragadi lovrana.hr/restaurant

Ⓚ Ⓚ Ⓚ

Trekking through the
verdant forests of
Risnjak National Park

Novi Vinodolski

B3 ✈ **Rijeka, Krk island**
🚌 **Rijeka** 🛈 **Ulica kralja**
Tomislava 6; www.tz-novi-
vinodolski.hr

The Old Town of Novi
Vinodolski, built on a hill overlooking the Vinodol valley,
holds an important place in
Croatian history. In its castle
on 6 January 1288, the Vinodol
Codex, one of the oldest legis-
lative Croatian texts in the
ancient Glagolitic script, was
produced. The document is
now in the National Library in
Zagreb. It was signed by
representatives from nine
communes, and established
rules for the ownership and
use of local land.

In 1988, the 700th anni-
versary of the Vinodol Codex,
a fountain created by the
sculptor Dorijan Sokolić was
placed in the central square of
Novi. The fountain bears the
names of the places that parti-
cipated in drawing up the laws.

The town is also remem-
bered for the stratagem
used by Bishop Kristofor to
save the troops defeated
by the Turks: their horses'
shoes were put on backwards
so as to foil their pursuers.
Having reached the safety
of Vinodol Castle, the bishop
gave thanks by rebuilding
the Church of SS Philip and
James (Sv. Filip i Jakov), where
he was buried in 1499. The
church, decorated in the 17th
century in the Baroque style,
has a magnificent altar from
that period. The side altar
features a Gothic Virgin Mary
from the 15th century.

Risnjak National Park

B2 🛈 **Bijela Vodica 48,**
Crni Lug; (051) 836 133;
www.np-risnjak.hr

The vast Gorski Kotor plateau,
which separates Croatia from
Slovenia, begins north of
Rijeka. Part of the area has
been declared a national park
in order to protect the forests
and natural environment, and
the ecological balance of the
area. The park, set up in 1953,
originally covered an area of
32 sq km (12 sq miles), but it
is now double that size, most
of it comprising forests and
grasslands with many karst
(limestone) features.

Within the park are
examples of ancient beech,
spruce and silver fir trees, and
also some rarer trees, such as
the mountain elm and maple.

> **The trail winds
> through woodland,
> with colossal fir and
> beech trees and an
> undergrowth of
> hazlenut, bilberry
> and elder bushes.**

When strong winds blow
down old or sick trees, the
fallen trees y are left where
they fall as they provide
suitable growing conditions
for microorganisms such
as fungi. Fungi thrive in the
cracks of old tree trunks,
providing a source of food
for insects too.

The climatic conditions,
caused by the territory's
particular exposure and
altitude, are very varied and
about 30 different plant
communities have been
identified. The Leska trail was
set up in 1993, and information
panels inform visitors about
various aspects of this area.

The trail winds through
woodland, with colossal fir
and beech trees and an
undergrowth of hazelnut,
bilberry and elder bushes.
The areas that were once
deforested for agriculture or
grazing land for animals are
now mountain meadows. In
late spring they explode with
the varied colours of heather,
purple moor grass, fescue and
other grasses.

There is also a viewing
platform in the park, from
which you can spot wild
animals, such as bears,
boar and deer.

→

Crikvenica's historic
monastery-turned-hotel
on a sunny day

The 13th-century Frankopan Castle has been restored and is now a museum, with exhibits from the Roman and medieval periods and a varied collection of traditional folk costumes.

Crikvenica

 B3 ✕ Rijeka 🚌 Nike Veljačića 3, (060) 300 100 ℹ Trg Stjepana Radića 1c; www.rivieracrikvenica.com

In 1412 Nikola Frankopan (whose name derives from the noble Roman family of the Frangipani) built a castle here. It was later donated to the Pauline order, who set up a church, monastery and school. In the 16th century a wall and a round tower were built and, in 1659, the church was enlarged by adding a nave. The town, now a popular tourist resort, takes its name from the monastery. At the beginning of the 19th century, the Pauline order was dissolved and in 1893 the monastery was turned into a hotel.

Crikvenica town has a long pebble beach and is one of the most popular tourist resorts along this stretch of coast. Thanks to its position, protected from the winds by the Velebit mountains, it enjoys a mild climate with dry summers and warm winters.

⑬ Bakar

B3 ℹ Primorje 39; www. tz-bakar.hr

The demolition of a refinery and a coke plant has brought visitors back to this town, which was once a popular destination for people curious about the phenomena of the freshwater springs. These springs originate in underground sources and flow out to the coast.

The Frankopan Castle and surrounding fishing village are also worth a visit. The village stands on the site of the Roman Volcera. From the 13th century until 1577 it belonged to the Frankopans who, in the early 14th century, built a triangular-shaped castle. The castle is still well preserved, with high windows which were salvaged when it was transformed into a palace for the Šubić-Zrinski family, who lived in the property after the Frankopans.

The parish Church of St Andrew the Apostle has a 14th-century crucifix and a painting by Girolamo da Santacroce.

Situated close to the Church of St Andrew, the Turkish House – also known as "The House of Painters" – has long been a draw for visitors, who come to admire its exotic, Ottoman-style architecture.

Bakar keeps its naval traditions alive thanks to the prestigious Maritime Academy, which was founded in 1849.

14

Senj

A B3 **🚆** Rijeka, 52 km (32 miles); Krk island **🚌** Obala kralja Zvonimira 8, (060) 394 394 **ℹ** Stara cesta 2; www.visitsenj.com

The cold wind known as the bora of Senj blows through a pass in the Velebit chain of mountains, making town the chilliest place in the Adriatic. A strong bura can disrupt transport, close down ferry routes and send everyone scuttling indoors (although, more positively, it also brings fresh air and the scent of mountain plants). Despite the wind, Senj was inhabited first by the Illyrians, and then by the Romans, who created a port at Senia. This became a bishopric in 1169 and an important trading port for the transport of timber.

📷 PICTURE PERFECT
Zavratnica Cove

For that envy-inducing photograph of gorgeous Croatian coastline, head to Zavratnica cove, a 15-minute walk from Jablanac. There's a footpath and small secluded beach, so it's accessible and fairly quiet. Perfect Instagram material.

→
Novalja's pedestrianized waterfront bustling in summertime

After 1000 AD it was granted to the Templar Knights. It then passed to the Frankopans, and finally came under the direct rule of the King of Hungary. As defence against the Ottomans, the Habsburgs established the first station of the Military Frontier *(Vojna krajina)* here. This stronghold had a powerful outer wall that is now only partly preserved.

After the Battle of Mohács in 1526, many Uskoks from Sinj and Klis came to Senj, and were co-opted by the local Austrian governor in the fight against the Ottomans. Their presence is recorded in **Nehaj Castle**, a fortress constructed in 1553–8 by the Uskok captain Ivan Lenković on a hill a short distance from the town. The Museum of the Uskoks is on the first floor of the fort, and has an excellent view over the bay.

The narrow alleys of Senj's Old Town are grouped around the **Cathedral of St Mary** (Sv. Marija), built in the 13th century and altered in the Baroque period. It has tombstones with Renaissance reliefs and Baroque works, including an altar decorated with four marble statues.

A short distance from the square is the Vukasović Palace which houses the **Senj Town Museum** (Gradski muzej Senj), a museum of local history. The palace was once the residence of an Uskok captain. Flanking the roads of the town and in the Small Square (Mala placa), also known as Campuzia, are Renaissance buildings such as the Town Hall with its splendid loggia. Nearby is

↑ Senj's populated coastline, fringing the Adriatic Sea

Did You Know?

The Croatian kuna is named after the marten, whose sleek fur was used as payment in the Middle Ages.

the Leon tower (Leonova kula), dedicated to Pope Leo X, and the small, pretty Church of St Mary.

The small village of Jablanac lies 37 km (23 miles) south of Senj. This well-preserved village is a good starting point for the Velebit massif, and worth an unhurried visit in its own right. The castle, which is now in ruins, was built by the Ban (governor) Stjepan Šubić. Nearby, the port of Stinica is a departure point for ferries to the island of Rab.

To the east of Jablanac is the Sjeverni Velebit National Park *(p194)* on the slopes of Mount Zavižan, with stunning panoramic vistas.

Nehaj Castle

◈ ◲ Nehajeva bb ☎ (053) 885 277 ◷ May–Oct: 10am–6pm (Jul & Aug: to 9pm)

Cathedral of St Mary

◲ Župni ured Senj, Milana Ogrizovića 2 ◷ Daily ☒ zupasenj.com

Senj Town Museum

◈ ◲ Milana Ogrizovića 5 ☎ (053) 881 141 ◷ Jul–Aug: 7am–3pm & 6–8pm Mon–Fri, 10am–noon & 6–8pm Sat, 10am–noon Sun; Sep–Jun: 7am–3pm Mon–Fri

---

Novalja

🅰 B4 🚌 🚢 From Rab and Rijeka 🛈 Trg Briščići; www.visitnovalja.hr

Located at the beginning of the narrow peninsula of Lun, Novalja is the second town on Pag island *(p140)* and makes its living entirely from tourism, thanks to its beautiful beaches. Many of these are family-friendly, but Novalja is perhaps best known for its "party beach": Zrce. This boasts four clubs, with thumping tunes blaring from long-before-dusk till dawn. During the daytime, partygoers can take advantage of the numerous activities in the area, which include zip-lining, bungee jumping and jet skiing. In the centre of the town

are the remains of an early Christian basilica and a pre-Romanesque church dating from the 9th–10th centuries. The Novalja City Museum (Gradski Muzej Novalja) is also worth a visit, with displays on traditional Croatian living and the town's Roman aqueduct. A ferry service connects the island to the mainland.

Lun Peninsula

🅰 B4 🚌 From Novalja

The northernmost tip of the island of Pag *(p140)*, in Northern Dalmatia, protrudes into the waters of the Kvarner Area. Lun is verdant, with olive groves and weathered maquis that pre-date local settlements. The village of Lun is circled by dry-stone walls and nearby is the port of Tovrnele, where sun-soakers can be found on the beaches. Note that just one bus makes the journey from Novalja to Lun every day so independent transport is advised.

Sjeverni Velebit National Park

Atop dramatic Velebit, Croatia's most famous mountain range ↑

△B4 *i* National Park Visitor Centre: Krasno; www.np-sjeverni-velebit.hr

The Velebit mountain chain runs along the Adriatic coast for almost 100 km (62 miles), starting in the northwest just above Senj and culminating in the southeast just inland from Zadar. Large areas of the northern part of the chain lie within the Sjeverni Velebit National Park (Nacionalni park Sjeverni Velebit), which embraces the Northern Velebit's highest peaks as well as much of its most stunning scenery. At the heart of the park is the 1,676-m- (5500-ft-) high Mount Zavižan, which offers spectacular views of the coast. Beneath the peak is a mountain hut with refreshments and a unique Botanical Garden (Botanički vrt). The garden is the starting point for the Premužić Trail, a 57-km- (35-mile-) long hiking route that winds its way along the main Velebit ridge, offering stupendous views on either side. Most visitors sample the first section of the trail before heading back to Zavižan, or opting for one of the marked trails that head downhill to the coast. Note that the park isn't accessible by public transport.

Northeast of Zavižan, the logging village of Krasno contains the national park headquarters and the Velebit House, a four-floor exhibition space.

INSIDER TIP
Bear Care

Kutarevo's Velebit Sanctuary for Young Bears was established in 2002 to care for orphaned bear cubs who would not survive in the wild. During certain periods, visitors can observe the bears *(www. kuterevo-medvjedi.org)*.

Fužine

△B3 🚌🚆 From Rijeka *i* Ul sv. Križa 2; www.tz-fuzine.hr

The pretty village of Fužine emerged as a popular lake resort in the last century, thanks to the creation of two nearby reservoirs. Dating from the 1950s is Lake Bajer (Bajersko jezero), which sits right beside the village and is surrounded by a footpath. In summer it is popular with bathers, kayakers and canoeists. Lake Bajer is also very attractive in winter, when the reservoir freezes over and the surrounding pines are covered with snow. The larger, forest-shrouded Lake Lepenica (Jezero Lepenica), located to the northwest, was submerged in 1988 and is another good place to picnic, bathe and stroll in summer. The rock formations and subterranean pools of the Vrelo Cave (Špilja Vrelo), an atmospheric site just north of Fužine, can be visited during the summer months.

Skrad

△B2 🚌 From Delnice *i* Goranska bb; www.tz-skrad.hr

Just east of Delnice, the village of Skrad occupies a green ridge above two of the Gorski kotar region's most spectacular beauty spots. The first is Zeleni Vir ("Green Spring"), a large pool fed by a waterfall that covers a cave entrance in the rock face to the rear. It can be reached by a footpath from the Zeleni Vir mountain hut, which lies at the end of a rough asphalt road. This hut is also the starting point for the boardwalk trail into Vražji Prolaz ("Devil's Passage"), a spectacular, steep-walled canyon with a rushing stream at the bottom.

Brod na Kupi

△B2

Brod na Kupi is located on the banks of the Kupa, which here forms the border between Croatia and Slovenia. Flowing swiftly through steep green hills, this stretch of the river is a popular place for canoeing,

> Squeezed between wooded hill just south of the Risnjak National Park, Lovke is one of the most picturesque villages in Gorski kotar.

Did You Know?

Nicknamed the green lungs of Croatia, the region of Gorski kotar is 63 per cent forest.

kayaking and rafting. Standing squarely in the middle of Brod is the 17th-century **Zrinski Castle** (Kaštel Zrinski), a cube-like, pyramid-roofed structure now shorn of its defensive walls. It was erected in 1651, likely built on the foundations of an older Frankopan castle. Inside, a display explains traditional jobs of the region such as logging and fishing.

The pebbly beach at Pritske, 2 km (1 mile) west of town, is a cult spot for bathing and pic-nicking among locals, and gets lively on hot summer days.

Zrinski Castle

⌖ 🚹 Ul Kralja Tomislava 1
📞 (051) 629 301 🕐 9am-7pm Tue-Fri, 10am-6pm Sat & Sun

Sledgers in Delnice admiring Gorski kotar's snowy landscape

㉑ Delnice

🅰 B2 🚌 From Rijeka
🚹 Lujzinska cesta 47; www.tz-delnice.hr

Located on the main road and rail routes from Rijeka to Zagreb, Delnice is the largest settlement in the densely forested mountain massif known as Gorski kotar. On the outskirts of town, a marked trail leads through the Japlenški Vrh Forest Park (Park Šuma Japlenški Vrh), an unspoiled area of deciduous forest and tumbling streams. The Risnjak National Park, 10 km (6 miles) east of Delnice, is a protected area surrounding the 1,528-m (5,013-ft) peak of Mount Risnjak, Gorski kotar's highest point. The park has a range of forest, grassland, and karst features. Providing an introduction to this landscape is the Leska Trail, a circular two-hour walking route that begins at Crni Lug at the entrance to the park. Recreational fishing is permitted in the park for a fee, from the beginning of April to the end of October.

㉒ Lokve

🅰 B2 🚹🚌 From Rijeka
🌐 tz-lokve.hr

Squeezed between wooded hills just south of Risnjak National Park, Lokve is one of the most picturesque villages in Gorski kotar. There is a small but fascinating Ethnographic Collection (Zavičajna Zbirka) run by local heritage enthusiasts, which displays traditional textiles, crafts and musical instruments. Local honey, preserves and liqueurs can be sampled in the Lujzijana Gallery and Nature House (Kuća Prirode Galerija "Lujzijana"). There is also a small display devoted to the Louisiana Road (Lujzijana), which was built by the Austrians in 1809 to connect Rijeka and Karlovac, traversing Gorski kotar in the process.

Just east of the village is Lokvarka Cave (Špilja Lokvarka), with four dramatically lit chambers of rock formations. Beyond the cave lies the Golubinjak Forest Park, which is perfect for hikes and picnics.

ZAGREB

With a population approaching one million, Zagreb is the undisputed political, economic and cultural heart of the country, a place that has been at the centre of the nation's fortunes since becoming a cathedral city in the 12th century. Brimming with monuments and museums, it's also a relaxing city in which to stroll, take things easy and enjoy an unhurried cake and coffee.

The Upper Town (historic centre) is the result of a merger between two medieval communities sited on adjacent hilltops: Gradec, to the west, was a secular settlement of townspeople and merchants; Kaptol, to the east, was dominated by priests and religious orders. Part of the Habsburg Empire from the 16th century onwards, the city experienced a boom in the 19th century, when a swathe of elegant public buildings formed the so-called Lower Town and provided the centre with a distinctly Austrian appearance. The Zagreb of today is a vivacious open-air city of colourful central markets, pavement cafés and fountain-splashed parks.

Around Zagreb

Mirogoj Cemetery ㉕

Maksimir Park ㉔

Črnomerec

area of main Zagreb map ①

Lauba Gallery ㉙

Maksimir ○

D1026

D1033

D1035 D1035

Jarun

Museum of Contemporary Art ㉑

Jarun Lake ㉝

D1040

Sava

Novi Zagreb

Botinec

A3

0 km 3

0 miles 3

N

0 metres 250

0 yards 250

N

TUŠKANAC

DUBRAVKIN PUT

DEMETROVA

BASARIČEKOVA

Croatian Natural History Museum ⑧

VISOKA

Atelier Meštrović ⑥

Church of St Mark ⑨

Viceroy's Palace ⑪

MARKOV TRG

Croatian History Museum ⑫

MATOŠEVA

GORNJI GRAD

Museum of Broken Relationships ㉖

Croatian Museum of Naïve Art ⑭

KATARININ TRG

Grič Tunnel

Tower of Lotrščak ⑬

Church St Catherine

STROSSMAYEROVO

DEŽMANOVA

Art Park ㉗

TOMIĆEVA

ZAMENHOFOVA

IVANA GORANA KOVAČIĆA

TUŠKANAC

PANTOVČAK

VLADIMIRA NAZORA

ROKOV PERIVOJ

Museum of Illusions ㉘

⑨

ILICA

ILICA

⑧

ILICA

ILICA

PRIMORSKA

FRA ANDRIJE KAČIĆA MIOŠIĆA

MEDULIĆEVA

DALMATINSKA

FRANKOPANSKA

GUNDULIĆEVA

VARŠAVSKA

PRERADOVIĆ TRG

VARŠAVSKA

MIŠKECOV PROLAZ

PRILAZ GJURE DEŽELIĆA

PRILAZ GJURE DEŽELIĆA

MASARYKOVA

PRILAZ...

VJEKOSLAVA KLAIĆA

TRG MARŠALA TITA

DONJI GRAD

Museum of Arts and Crafts ⑳

KLAIĆEVA

Croatian National Theatre ⑯

HEBRANGOVA

ROOSEVELTOV TRG

Mimara Museum ⑰

⑱ Ethnographic Museum

TRG BRAĆE MAŽURANIĆ

GUNDULIĆEVA

ŽERJAVIĆEVA

IZIDORA KRŠNJAVOG

VUKOTINOVIĆEVA

MARULIĆEV TRG

SVAČIĆ TRG

ZAGREB

SAVSKA

KUMIČIĆEVA

VODNIKOVA

ANTUNA MIHANOVIĆA

CRNATKOVA

Botanical Garden of the Faculty of Science ⑲

ZAGREB

Must See

1 Strossmayer Gallery of Old Masters

Experience More

2 Stone Gate
3 Church of St Mary
4 Cathedral of the Assumption of the Blessed Virgin Mary
5 Tkalčićeva
6 Atelier Meštrović
7 Zagreb City Museum
8 Croatian Natural History Museum
9 Church of St Mark
10 Parliament Building
11 Viceroy's Palace
12 Croatian History Museum
13 Tower of Lotrščak
14 Croatian Museum of Naïve Art
15 Church of St Catherine
16 Croatian National Theatre
17 Mimara Museum
18 Ethnographic Museum
19 Botanical Garden of the Faculty of Science
20 Museum of Arts and Crafts
21 Museum of Contemporary Art
22 Modern Gallery
23 Archaeological Museum
24 Maksimir Park
25 Mirogoj Cemetery
26 Museum of Broken Relationships
27 Art Park
28 Museum of Illusions
29 Lauba Gallery
30 Image of War – War Photography Museum
31 Klovićevi Dvori Gallery
32 Art Pavilion
33 Jarun Lake

Eat

1 Noel
2 Plac
3 Vinodol

Drink

4 Craft Room
5 Mali Medo
6 Pod Starim Krovovima

Stay

7 Esplanade Zagreb
8 Hotel Jagerhorn
9 Swanky Mint

❶ 🏛️ 🏛️

STROSSMAYER GALLERY OF OLD MASTERS

📍 **D4** 🏛️ **Trg Nikole Šubića Zrinskog 11** 🕐 **For restoration** 🌐 **sgallery.hazu.hr**

Lining the walls of this grand neo-Renaissance palace are Old Master heavyweights – Tintoretto, Poussin, Bellini and Brueghel to name a few. The core collection once belonged to the museum's founder.

In 1880 Josip Juraj Strossmayer, the rich and powerful Bishop of Đakovo and one of the leading proponents of a pan-Slav movement, had this gallery built to house the Academy of Arts and Sciences and the Strossmayer Gallery of Old Masters (Galerija starih majstora). He donated his own impressive assemblage of about 250 works of art on its completion in 1886.

Today this is Croatia's foremost collection of Old Master works. The Neo-Renaissance building has a large internal porticoed courtyard and nine rooms on its upper floor, displaying around 200 works. These encompass the major European schools, from the 14th to the 19th century. The museum also holds the Baška Tablet, one of the oldest documents of Croat culture (11th century), writen in Glagolitic script. Behind the building is a large statue of Bishop Strossmayer, the gallery's founder, sculpted by artist Ivan Meštrović (*p205*) in 1926.

GALLERY GUIDE

The gallery rooms are on the second floor of the building. The Italian school occupies the first six rooms before continuing on to the Flemish, Dutch and German schools. The final room is dedicated to the French school. The historic Baška Tablet can be seen in the entrance hall. There isn't much information provided for artworks but the Old Masters speak for themselves.

Gallery Highlights

c 1100

▽ Unearthed on Krk island, this prized stone block shows a rare Glagolitic inscription, the oldest such example to be found.

c 1480

▽ *Virgin Mary with Jesus, John and an Angel* is by Jacopo del Sellaio (c 1441-1493), who belonged to the circle of Lippi and Botticelli.

c 1450

△ *Virgin with Child and St Francis and St Bernardine of Siena* is by Bartolomeo Caporali (c 1420-1505), an artist associated with Perugia.

c 1487

△ *St Augustine and St Benedict* reveals the expressive skill of great Venetian master Giovanni Bellini (1430-1516).

↑ Façade of the Strossmayer Gallery of Old Masters, a shrine to works of art set in spectacular surroundings *(inset)*

c 1510

▽ The lively oil painting *Adam and Eve* is by Florentine painter Mariotto Albertinelli (1474–1515) and shows the expulsion from paradise.

c 1555

▽ *Susanna and the Elders* by the Master of the Prodigal Son demonstrates the Flemish artist's great technical skill and vivid use of colour.

1514

△ *St Sebastian* by Venetian Vittore Carpaccio (1465–1525) uses vivid colours to express the drama of young Sebastian's martyrdom.

c 1825

△ This portrait by Antoine Jean Gros (1771–1835) shows Madame Recamier, a figure of notoriety in Parisian high society.

EXPERIENCE MORE

②

Stone Gate
Kamenita vrata

⑨ D2 ⛪ Kamenita

In the walls around Gradec, the part of the Upper Town built on a neighbouring hill to Kaptol, there were once five gates. Stone Gate is now the only one of these remaining. It was built in the 13th century, and stands beside a square tower dating from 1266. In 1731 a fire destroyed all the nearby houses, but the painting of *Mary with Child* on the gate was left undamaged. A chapel was established around this painting and a Baroque wrought-iron grille now protects the work, attributed to a local master from the 16th century.

On the west façade of the church is a statue of a woman, a character from a famous Croation novel and the work of the sculptor Ivo Kerdić in 1929. On the other side of the gate, on the corner of Kamenita and Habdelićeva, stands an 18th-century building. On its ground floor is a pharmacy

(Alighieri ljekarna) that has been there since 1350 and which, from 1399 onwards, belonged to Nicolò Alighieri, the great-grandson of the Italian writer Dante.

---

③

Church of St Mary
Sv. Marija

⑨ D2 ⛪ Dolac 2 ☎ (01) 481 49 59 ⏰ For Mass

Opatovina is a narrow street where some of the houses were built using parts of the late 15th-century fortifications. The street leads into the ancient district of Dolac, at the end of which stands the 14th-century Church of St Mary. It was rearranged in 1740 when several Baroque altars were built by Franjo Rottman, but the church of today dates back to rebuilding after the earthquake in 1880.

Nearby stands a statue by Vanja Radauš of the minstrel Petrica Kerempuh, playing to the figure of a hanged man. The large, picturesque Dolac

Market, first held in 1930, takes place around the church. Fruit, vegetables and meat are sold daily but Thursday and Friday are the best days to shop, with further fish, cheese and bread on sale. This is a characteristic district of the city where Baroque houses face narrow streets and lanes. A historic pharmacy is located at No 19 Kaptol.

---

④

Cathedral of the Assumption of the Blessed Virgin Mary
Katedrala Marijina Uznesenja

⑨ E2 ⛪ Kaptol ☎ (01) 481 47 27 ⏰ For restoration

Dedicated to the Assumption and St Stephen, this is the most famous monument in the city. Its present appearance dates from renovations carried out after the earthquake of 1880, which destroyed the dome, the bell tower and some of the walls. The rebuilding, which retained the medieval plan of the

↑ Cobbled, snowy street leading to the Stone Gate, passing the statue of St George

↑ Pedestrians wandering amid the pretty pastel houses on Tkalčićeva street

Did You Know?

Three chandeliers in Zagreb's cathedral are said to have originally been made for a Las Vegas casino.

cathedral, was just the latest in a series of alterations the building had undergone in its long history. The building was already in existence in 1094, when King Ladislaus transferred the bishopric here from Sisak. Destroyed by the Mongols in 1242, the cathedral was rebuilt by Bishop Timotej a few years later, with side aisles, statues and reliefs added in the centuries that followed.

The Neo-Gothic façade (1880) is flanked by twin spires. Its large, ornate doorway has sculpted decorations and is crowned by a tympanum. The interior has three aisles and a polygonal apse. During a late 19th-century reorganization, the Baroque and Rococo altars were transferred to other churches in the diocese, and as a result only a few Gothic and Renaissance works remain. These include a 13th-century statue of St Paul, wooden statues of the saints Peter and Paul from the 15th century, a triptych entitled *Golgotha* (1495) by Albrecht Dürer and a 14th-century *Crucifixion* by Giovanni da Udine. The cathedral also contains the tombs and votive chapels of bishops and important people in Croatian history, such as Petar Zrinski, Krsto Frankopan and the Blessed Cardinal Alojzije Stepinac, whose tomb is by Ivan Meštrović.

Of great interest are the frescoes from the Giotto-esque school in the sacristy, the oldest (12th century) in inland Croatia. In the basement of the bishop's sacristy, the Cathedral Treasury preserves a rich collection of religious objects, but is rarely open to the public. The treasures include illuminated manuscripts, finely crafted church ornaments and the so-called Sepulchre of God, which was made by the embroiderers of the village of Vugrovec, where Bishop Petar Petretić founded an embroidery school around 1650. Among the oldest works are a 10th-century ivory diptych and a bronze crucifix from the 11th–12th centuries.

⑤
Tkalčićeva

📍 D2 🏠 Ul Ivana Tkalčićeva

Occupying the former course of the Medveščak stream, pedestrianized Tkalčićeva is one of Zagreb's most vibrant and visually appealing streets. It is lined with pastel-painted 18th- and 19th-century houses, most of which now hold restaurants, boutiques, galleries and, above all, cafés. An umbrella-wielding female statue near the southern end of the street honours Marija Jurić Zagorka (1873-1957), the renowned journalist and author of historical novels who set many of her stories in Zagreb's Upper Town.

EAT

Noel

Just a five-minute walk from the main square, the Michelin-starred Noel serves modern European cuisine.

📍 B2 🏠 Ulica popa Dukljanina 1 🌐 noel.hr

Plac

With outdoor seating, this casual eatery does tasty homemade burgers and fresh, colourful salads.

📍 D3 🏠 Dolac 2 🌐 plac-zagreb.com

Ⓚ ⓚ ⓚ

Vinodol

You'll find all manner of Croatian cuisine in this restaurant's pleasant city-centre courtyard.

📍 D3 🏠 Teslina 10 🌐 vinodol-zg.hr

Some of the spectacular sculptures exhibited in the Atelier Meštrović

DRINK

Craft Room

Offering a range of craft beers from across the country, Craft Room is an ideal spot to indulge in serious tasting.

📍 D2 🏠 Opatovina ul 35

Mali Medo

Local brewery Pivovara Medvedgrad has been making beer since the 1990s, and Mali Medo is the liveliest of its city outlets.

📍 D2 🏠 Tkalčićeva 36 🌐 pivovara-medvedgrad.hr

Atelier Meštrović

Atelje Meštrović

📍 C2 🏠 Mletačka 8 🕐 10am-6pm Tue-Fri, 10am-2pm Sat & Sun 🌐 mestrovic.hr

The Meštrović building dates from the 17th century; the iconic Croatian sculptor Ivan Meštrović – who had also worked as an architect – adapted it himself to live in from 1922 to 1942. It now houses a comprehensive collection of his work. As such, it is part of The Museums of Ivan Meštrović, together with the Gallery and the Kaštilac in Split, as well as the burial chapel in Otavice *(p141)*. Here in Zagreb, there are almost 100 works on display, including exhibits in the courtyard: *History of Croatia, Laookon of our Days* and *Woman in Agony*. Works are also exhibited in what used to be Meštrović's studio. The drawings, models and sculptures in wood, stone and bronze testify to the expressive ability and great skills of the sculptor. His personal archives are kept here as well, along with photographic records and works by other artists associated with the master.

Zagreb City Museum

Muzej grada Zagreba

📍 D1 🏠 Opatička ulica 20 🕐 10am-7pm Tue-Sat, 10am-2pm Sun 🌐 mgz.hr

This absorbing museum is a great way to get a grasp on Zagreb's complex and fascinating history. Three historic buildings (the 17th-century nuns' convent of St Clare; a 12th-century tower; and a 17th-century granary) have been linked to form the museum. Founded by the Brethren of the Croatian Dragon Society in 1907, its collection comprises historical, cultural, military and domestic artefacts, many of which were donated by prominent townspeople. Items are arranged in themed displays illustrating every facet of the city's development, from scale models of early Zagreb and sacral art from the 17th century, to political posters from the turbulent 20th century.

Across the city, the museum also maintains the former residences of some of Croatia's most celebrated figures: that of the architect Viktor **Kovačić** (1878–1924); the writer Miroslav **Krleža** (1893–1981) and his wife Bela; and that of the poet and painter Cata **Dujšin-Ribar** (1897–1994) and her two husbands, the actor/theatre director Dubravko Dujšin and the politician Dr Ivan Ribar. The period furnishings, decor and works of art in each are perfectly preserved, making fascinating short tours. Visit the website for more information.

Kovačić Residence
⌂ Masarykova 21
🕐 10am–5pm Thu

Krleža Residence
⌂ Krležin Gvozd 23
🕐 11am–5pm Tue

Dujšin-Ribar Residence
⌂ Demetrova 3/II
🕐 11am–5pm Wed

Croatian Natural History Museum
Hrvatski prirodoslovni muzej

📍 C2 ⌂ Demetrova 1
🔧 For restoration until 2023 🌐 hpm.hr

↑ The "Museums outside the museum" project, Croatian Natural History Museum

The 18th-century Amadeo Palace, a theatre from 1797 to 1834, has been the home of natural history collections since 1868, when exhibits from the Department of Natural Science at the National Museum were transferred here. At the end of the 19th century there were three museums of natural history: Mineralogy and Petrography, Geology and Palaeontology, and Zoology. These merged in 1986 to form the present museum. There are over 2,500,000 exhibits, including minerals from all over the world and palaeontology collections containing some of the material found in Krapina.

IVAN MEŠTROVIĆ

Regarded as one of the most important sculptors of the 20th century, Ivan Meštrović was born in 1883 in Vrpolje. As a young boy he delighted in making figures out of wood. His work was noticed by the village mayor and by Lujo Marun, an archaeologist, who sent him to Split when he was 17 to study sculpture. Thanks to donors, he was able to attend the Academy of Fine Arts in Vienna. Here he met and became friends with the great French sculptor Auguste Rodin.

Around the World
In 1908 Meštrović moved to Paris and his first exhibition established his reputation. He worked in various cities, including Split - creating many of the works now on show in the Meštrović gallery there - and Zagreb. He also took up politics. During World War II he was imprisoned by the Nazi regime and freed on the Vatican's intervention. He then moved to Rome where he sculpted the *Pietà Romana*, now in the Vatican Museum. After the war he taught at universities in the US, where he died in 1962. He was buried in the burial chapel in Otavice that he designed for himself and his family.

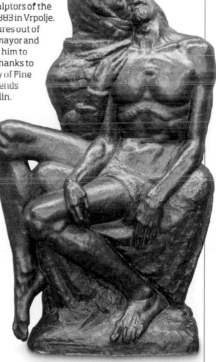

→ *Pietà* (1932), part of the Ivan Meštrović Museums, Zagreb

Church of St Mark
Sv. Marko

📍C2 🏛Markov trg
📞(01) 485 16 11 🕐For restoration

Today this is the Upper Town's parish church. St Mark's was first mentioned in 1256, when King Bela IV granted the town of Gradec permission to hold a market fair in front of the church. The fair lasted for two weeks and was held to celebrate the saint's day.

The church has undergone various alterations over the centuries. All that is left from the original construction is a Romanesque window and a splendid Gothic doorway, created by the sculptor Ivan Parler between 1364 and 1377. The 15 niches on the door contain statues of Jesus, Mary, St Mark and the 12 apostles. Some of these were replaced by wooden copies in the Baroque era.

On various occasions, fires and earthquakes have been responsible for changes in the church's appearance. Its present look dates from 1882, when the colourful glazed tiles on the roof were added. The tiles bear the coats of arms of Croatia, Dalmatia, Slavonia and the city of Zagreb. The church has been refurbished with several statues by the sculptor Ivan Meštrović. On the high altar is a large *Christ on the Cross*, while a bronze statue of

Mary with Child adorns an altar dedicated to the Virgin Mary. The modern frescoes depicting Croat kings in action were painted by Jozo Kljaković.

Parliament Building
Sabor

📍C2 🏛Markov trg 📞(01) 456 96 07 🕐Groups only, by appointment

Built in Neo-Classical style in 1908 after several 17th- and 18th-century Baroque structures were razed, this building holds an important place in the story of Croatia. Historic proclamations have been issued from the balcony, such as the seceding of the nation from the Austro-Hungarian kingdom (29 October 1918) and the country's independence from Yugoslavia after a referendum in 1991. Today the Sabor is still the centre of Croat politics.

Viceroy's Palace
Banski dvori

📍C2 🏛Markov trg 📞(01) 456 92 22 🕐By appt

The parliament chamber, the central archives, the law courts, the President of the Republic's residence and government offices are all housed in this building in front of St Mark's, which

was badly damaged in an airstrike in 1991. The palace is similar in design to the parliament building and is made up of two long 18th-century structures. In the 19th century, two two-storey wings were added.

Croatian History Museum
Hrvatski povijesni muzej

📍C2 🏛Matoševa ulica 9 🕐For restoration 🌐hismus.hr

The museum, founded in 1846, illustrates the history of Croatia from the Middle Ages to the present day, by

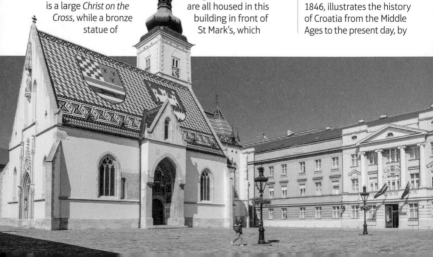

↑ The imposing medieval Tower of Lotrščak

means of all kinds of historical mementoes and literature. The exhibitions are not permanent but change frequently due to limited space.

The museum has been housed here since 1959. The building itself is a Baroque Vojković-Oršić-Kulmer-Rauch Palace, dating from the second half of the 18th century.

Tower of Lotrščak
Kula Lotrščak

♥ C2 ⬛ **Strossmayerovo šetalište 9** ☎ **(01) 485 17 68** ⏱ **10am–8pm Tue–Sun**

Since the middle of the 19th century, the inhabitants of Zagreb have set their clocks by the cannons fired from this tower at noon. Dating from the 13th century, it is one of the oldest buildings in the city.

At one time the tower had a bell, which announced the closing of the city gates each evening. Its name

←

The Church of St Mark, with its roof of brightly coloured tiles

is taken from the Latin *campana latruncolorum* – bell of thieves; anyone left outside at night ran the risk of being robbed.

The tower originally stood alongside the southern side of the walls of Gradec. The walls, nearly 2 m (6 ft) thick, were built with chains inside them as an anti-earthquake measure.

The tower now houses a gallery. It is worth climbing to the top for spectacular views over the city.

---

⑭

Croatian Museum of Naïve Art
Hrvatski muzej naivne umjetnosti

♥ C2 ⬛ **Sv Ćirila i Metoda 3** ⏱ **10am–5pm Mon–Fri** ⊘ **Public hols** 🌐 **hmnu.hr**

This is the oldest museum in the world to specialize in Naïve art. The museum was established in 1952, and since 1967 it has been housed within this 19th-century building with its beautiful Neo-Baroque façade. The collection contains about 1,900 artworks, with around 80 of them on public display. Alongside works by artists of the Hlebine School, such as Ivan Generalić, Mirko Virius, Ivan Večenaj and Mijo Kovačić, are the poetic landscapes of Ivan Rabuzin, the cityscapes of Emerik Feješ, the allegorical scenes of Matija Skurjeni and the sculptures of Petar Smajić.

---

⑮

Church of St Catherine
Sv. Katarina

♥ C2 ⬛ **Katarinin trg** ☎ **(01) 485 19 50** ⏱ **For restoration**

The Jesuits built this church in around 1630, on the site of a Dominican building, and it is now considered to be one of the most beautiful religious buildings in Zagreb.

The white façade has a doorway and four niches with statues and six prominent pilasters. Above is a niche with a statue of Mary.

The single-nave church is home to numerous Baroque works of art. Of particular interest are the stucco reliefs (1721–3) by Antonio Quadrio, the *Scenes of the Life of St Catherine* by the Slovenian artist Franc Jelovšek (1700–64) in the medallion on the ceiling, the beautiful *Altar of St Ignatius* by the Venetian sculptor Francesco Robba (1698–1757) and, on the main altar (1762), *St Catherine among the Alexandrian Philosophers* by Kristof Andrej Jelovšek (1729–76).

In the nearby square called Jezuitski trg, there is a fountain with a statue of a *Fisherman with a Serpent* by Simeon Roksandić (1908). Facing this is a 17th-century Jesuit Monastery and a large building from the same period that was the Jesuit seminary, before later becoming a boarding school for boys of noble parentage.

 INSIDER TIP
Summer in the City

Summer brings out the best in Zagreb's open spaces. The parks and the main square host a string of fetes and food fairs, while the Upper Town comes to life with outdoor cinema projections and open-air concerts on the Strossmayerovo šetalište promenade.

Croatian National Theatre
Hrvatsko narodno kazalište

C4   **Trg Republike Hrvatske**   **For performances only**   **Public hols**   **hnk.hr**

The Croatian National Theatre stands in the square marking the beginning of a U-shaped series of parks that form a "green horseshoe", the design of the engineer Milan Lenuci (1849–1924). The theatre was completed in 1895 and is a blend of Neo-Baroque and Rococo. It was designed by the Viennese architects Hermann Helmer and Ferdinand Fellner.

In the area in front of the National Theatre stands a masterpiece by Ivan Meštrović, *The Well of Life*, which consists of a group of bronze figures huddled around a well.

The theatre's interior is richly decorated with works by Croatian and Viennese artists.

> In the area in front of the National Theatre stands a masterpiece by Ivan Meštrović, *The Well of Life*, which consists of a group of bronze figures huddled round a well.

Mimara Museum
Muzej Mimara

B4   **Rooseveltov trg 5**   **For restoration until 2022**   **mimara.hr**

In 1973, Croatian businessman Ante Topić Mimara donated his extensive personal art collection to Croatia, and the Mimara Museum was set up for its display. The museum is housed in an enormous Neo-Renaissance building, built in 1895 by the German architects Ludwig and Hülsner.

The artworks here are displayed chronologically, from the prehistoric era to the present day. The archaeological section of the museum is particularly fascinating, with important finds from Ancient Egypt,

pre-Columbian America and Mesopotamia, as well as the Middle and Far East.

The icon collection not only contains Russian pieces, but also has icons from Palestine, Antioch and Asia Minor dating from the 6th to the 13th cen-turies. There are ancient carpets, and about 300 exhibits cover more than 3,500 years of Chinese art, from the Shang to the Qing dynasties.

Around 1,000 objects of applied arts and pieces of furniture give a good overall picture of European craftsman-ship from the Middle Ages to the 19th century. There is also a wide-ranging collection of 200 sculptures, which date from ancient Greece to the time of the Impressionists.

The museum also has paintings by the English artists John Constable and JMW Turner, the French painters Edouard Manet, Pierre-Auguste Renoir and Camille Pissarro, and an excellent collection by the Dutch and Flemish masters.

The lavish interior and ornate façade *(inset)* of the Croatian National Theatre

Ethnographic Museum
Etnografski muzej

B4 **Trg Mažuranića 14** **10am-6pm Tue-Fri, 10am-2pm Sat** **Public hols** **emz.hr**

This is the most important museum of its kind in Croatia. It was founded in 1919 and set up in this harmonious domed building, constructed in 1902 in the Art Nouveau style by the architect Vjekoslav Bastl.

The statues decorating the central part of the façade are by the sculptor Rudolf Valdec and the frescoes on the dome inside were painted by Oton Iveković. Just under 3,000 of the 80,000 exhibits owned by the museum are on display. Croatian culture is illustrated through exhibits of gold and silver jewellery, musical instruments, splendid embroidery and beautiful traditional costumes. A reconstruction of a farmhouse illustrates the way of life of Croat farmers and fishermen.

There is also a fascinating collection of dolls dressed in traditional costumes, called the Ljeposav Perinić collection.

The valuable collection of pieces from non-European civilizations was assembled from donations made by scholars and explorers, among them Dragutin Lerman.

Botanical Garden of the Faculty of Science
Botanički vrt Prirodoslovno matematičkog fakulteta

C5 **Marulićev trg 9a** **May-Nov: 10am-2:30pm Mon & Tue, 10am-6pm Wed-Sun** **Dec-Apr** **botanickivrt.biol.pmf.hr**

Part of the "green horseshoe", this English-style garden was created in 1889 by Antun Heinz, a professor of botany, and now belongs to the Faculty of Science at Zagreb University.

The garden, covering an area of 50,000 sq m (540,000 sq ft), is a popular place to stroll. There are about 5,000 plant species here from all over the world, including around 1,500 tropical plants. Plants are arranged according to their phylogenetic relationships. Paths link the conifer woods, and aquatic plants are cultivated in special ponds.

↑ A 19th-century clock on display in the Museum of Arts and Crafts

Museum of Arts and Crafts
Muzej za umjetnost i obrt

B4 **Trg Republike Hrvatske** **10am-7pm Tue-Sat, 10am-2pm Sun** **muo.hr**

This museum was first established in 1880 to house collections of artworks by craftsmen and artists. The building was designed by Hermann Bollé and was built between 1887 and 1892. More than 3,000 objects, from the Gothic period to the present day, provide an overview of Croatia's cultural history and its ties to the rest of Europe.

The collections housed in the museum offer an insight into the Croatian and European production of arts and crafts and include religious art, Judaica, and items including clocks, ivories, metalwork, glass, ceramics and textiles. As the museum is supported by international backing, impressive temporary exhibitions from abroad occasionally take place here. The adjacent library has a total of 65,000 books on arts and crafts.

↑ Marija Ujevic's *Target 2* sculpture at the Museum of Contemporary Art

Museum of Contemporary Art
Muzej suvremene umjetnosti

📍A2 🏛Avenija Dubrovnik 17 🕐11am-7pm Tue-Fri, 11am-6pm Sat & Sun 🌐msu.hr

This superb exhibition space displays more than 600 works by 200 contemporary artists. Highlights include the experimental films of Ivan Ladislav Galeta and Tomislav Gotovac, and conceptual pieces from Goran Trbuljak, Sanja Iveković and Atelier Kožarić. Works such as Miroslav Balka's *Eyes of Purification* and Carsten

246

The number of street lamps in Zagreb's Upper Town, each lit by hand every night.

Höller's *Double Slide*, also shown in Tate Modern's Turbine Hall in London, add to the heavyweight credentials of the museum.

Modern Gallery
Moderna galerija

📍D4 🏛Andrije Hebranga 1 🕐11am-7pm Tue-Fri, 11am-2pm Sat & Sun 🚫Public hols 🌐moderna-galerija.hr

The richest national museum of Croatian arts, housed in the Vranyczany Palace (1883), holds works by the most eminent Croatian painters and sculptors of the 19th–21st centuries. The collection dates from 1905, when the first works of Ivan Meštrović, Mirko Rački and others were acquired. Later purchases and donations brought the current total to some 9,800 pieces.

The permanent display of 750 works includes modern classics from painters such as

Vlaho Bukovac and Josip Račić, sculptors such as Meštrović and Frano Kršinić, alongside contemporary artists working in photography, video and other new media. The innovative, multi-sensory MG Tactile Gallery is designed for the visually impaired.

Archaeological Museum
Arheološki muzej

📍D3 🏛Trg Nikole Šubića Zrinskog 19 🕐For restoration 🌐amz.hr

The 19th-century Vranyczany-Hafner Palace has housed the Archaeological Museum since 1945. The institution itself, however, was founded in 1846.

Around 400,000 pieces from all over Croatia, particularly Zagreb, are on display here. The museum has five main sections: prehistoric, Egyptian, ancient and medieval, plus a part devoted to coins and medals.

One significant exhibit is the bandage used to bind the Mummy of Zagreb. This bandage has mysterious origins and bears text in the Etruscan language, which has not yet been completely deciphered.

The museum's ancient collection is undoubtedly its most important. This includes the Lapidarium, which can be found in the courtyard, and comprises a collection of stone monuments that date from the Roman period. The valuable *Head of Plautilla*, from the Roman town of Salona (*p106*), is the emblem of the museum.

On site, there is also an archaeological conservation laboratory dedicated to preserving the exhibits. In addition the museum has developed several educational projects aimed at schoolchildren. The archaeological library next door houses over 45,000 volumes, some of which are extremely rare.

24

Maksimir Park
Park Maksimir

🇶 B1 🇦 Maksimirski perivoj bb 🇨 Daily 🇼 park-maksimir.hr

The largest park in the city is considered one of Croatia's living monuments. It is named after Bishop Maksimilijan Vrhovac, who initiated the project in 1794. The park was finally completed in 1843, and is landscaped in the English style with wide lawns, flower beds and lakes. The Zoološki vrt (zoo) has hundreds of different animals. Among the park's many follies, the Vidikovac (Belvedere) offers great views and a small café.

25

Mirogoj Cemetery
Groblje Mirogoj

🇶 A1 🇦 Mirogoj 🇨 Apr-Oct: 6am-8pm daily; Nov-Mar: 7:30am-6pm daily

Situated at the foot of Mount Medvednica, 4 km (2 miles) from the city centre, is the Mirogoj Cemetery, built in 1876 by Hermann Bollé. The cemetery covers an area of 28,000 sq m (7 acres) and the tombs of the most illustrious figures in the political, cultural and artistic life of Croatia lie here.

An imposing façade forms the entrance to the Catholic and Orthodox chapels. From here branch two long Neo-Renaissance arcades, where the most important families are buried. The area is divided into squares of trees and bushes. Among these patches of greenery stand funerary monuments by leading Croatian sculptors and engravers, such as Ivan Meštrović, Ivan Rendić, and Robert Frangeš-Mihanović.

As well as the tombs of notable personalities there is also a monument dedicated to the memory of the soldiers who died during World War I, and a monument to the Jews who died in World War II. There is a separate monument for the German military.

The well-preserved cemetery is an open-air museum and is often visited by locals, who keep the tombs of great past Croats topped with fresh flowers and candles.

Attractive, ivy-covered arcades *(inset)* at the imposing Mirogoj Cemetery ↓

↑ Unique items on display at the intriguing Museum of Broken Relationships

26

Museum of Broken Relationships
Muzej prekinutih veza

📍**C2** 🏛**Ćirilometodska 2** 🕐**10am–9pm daily** 🌐**brokenships.com**

Featuring mementoes of break-ups donated by the public, Zagreb's Museum of Broken Relationships began as an art installation in 2006, intended to last only a few weeks. It struck a profound chord with the public, however, and became a permanent institution four years later. Far from being a gimmicky attraction, the display offers a moving record of human experience, presented with warmth and humour. The museum has frequently mounted international touring exhibitions, becoming a recognizable Croatian cultural brand in the process.

27

Art Park

📍**C3** 🌐**artparkzagreb.com**

A team of local graffiti artists combined forces to revitalize this patch of derelict ground between the Upper Town and Zagreb's main shopping street, Ilica. They painted new murals on the surrounding walls and tidied up the sloping terrain

to produce a unique, semi-hidden relaxation space in the middle of the city. In the summer there is an open-air bar here and a programme of events, ranging from children's playgroups to food festivals.

28

Museum of Illusions
Muzej iluzija

📍**B3** 🏛**Ilica 72** 🕐**9am–10pm daily** 🌐**muzejiluzija.com**

Displaying a collection of optical illusions and visual tricks, the Museum of Illusions demonstrates that things are not always as they seem. Two floors of imaginative exhibits play with the mind's understanding of proportion and perspective, providing plenty of opportunities to take mind-boggling selfies. There is also a hands-on section devoted to tantalizing toys and games.

29

Lauba Gallery

📍**A1** 🏛**Baruna Filipoviča 23a** 🕐**11am–8pm Mon–Fri, 11am–10pm Sat** 🌐**lauba.hr**

This pre-World War I cavalry barracks, 4 km (2 miles) west of the centre, was repurposed in 2011 and now holds the city's most significant private art collection, with contemporary Croatian painters particularly well represented. Sheathed in a matt-black coating on the outside, the building has preserved its raw, red-brick interior. Part of the permanent collection is usually on display alongside one or two temporary exhibitions. Locally referred to as the "House for People and Art", the gallery regularly hosts unusual events in its unique, sprawling space.

30

Image of War - War Photography Museum

📍 **D4** 🏛 **Ul Andrije Hebranga 4** 🕐 **10am-8pm daily** 🌐 **imageofwar.hr**

A private museum initiated by local enthusiasts, Image of War presents photographs conveying the cost of conflict, especially among civilians. Croatia's 1991-5 Homeland War naturally forms a core element of the display, with temporary exhibitions concentrating on other conflicts around the globe. The museum, which opened in 2018, gains added poignancy by frequently displaying the work of professional photographers alongside images recorded by members of the public, who just happened to be caught up in dramatic events.

 31

Klovićevi Dvori Gallery
Galerija Klovićevi dvori

📍 **D2** 🏛 **Jezuitski trg 4** 🕐 **11am-7pm Tue-Sun** 🌐 **gkd.hr**

Zagreb's principal venue for international art and history exhibitions, this gallery

occupies a former monastery built for the Jesuits in the 17th century. The building's late-Baroque appearance is best admired from the inner courtyard. The gallery's name comes from Julije Klović, a Croatian-born miniaturist who found fame in Italy during the 16th century. Just south of the gallery is the so-called plateau, a large open space with splendid views towards Zagreb Cathedral.

32

Art Pavilion
Umjetnički paviljon

📍 **D4** 🏛 **Trg kralja Tomislava 22** 🕐 **For restoration until 2023** 🌐 **umjetnicki paviljon.hr**

In 1896, the Art Pavilion represented Croatia at an international exhibition in Budapest. Its iron skeleton was then transported to Zagreb and rebuilt on this site in 1898, to fit the designs of Ferdinand Fellner and Hermann Helmer. It is now used for diverse, large-scale art exhibitions. A monument to Renaissance painter Andrija Medulić by Ivan Meštrović stands outside.

The Pavilion faces onto a square, Trg Kralja Tomislava, which is dedicated to the first Croatian king, Tomislav. An equestrian statue by Robert Frangeš-Mihanović stands here in commemoration.

33

Jarun Lake
Jasrunsko jezero

📍 **A2**

Just southwest of the city centre, the artificial Jarun Lake was created in 1987 to serve

 ←
Contemporary art displayed at Zagreb's ultra-cool Lauba Gallery

↑ Swans gathering at sunrise on Zagreb's Jarun Lake

as a rowing venue for the World Student Games. It's now one of the city's prime recreation spots, circled by a foot- and cycle-path and with a pebble beach at one end. Beyond the beach is a cluster of appealing cafés. The southern shores of the lake are backed by meadows and woodland, perfect for picnics. Just beyond the eastern end is the Sava Embankment, a riverside dyke popular with walkers and cyclists.

🔍 HIDDEN GEM
Grič Tunnel

Passageways built beneath Zagreb's Upper Town during World War II were reopened in 2016, and became an unexpected hit with locals and tourists alike. Usually left eerily bare, they are occasionally used for exhibitions or decorative displays, especially during December's season of Advent.

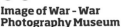

A SHORT WALK
THE UPPER TOWN (GORNJI GRAD)

Distance 700 m (766 yds)
Time 15 minutes

This area has historically been the heartbeat of the capital, and the sense of energy remains today. Institutions that have played a significant part in Croatia's complex story can be found here, from the presidency of the Republic and the Parliament Building to the State Audit Court and several government ministries. Museums based in ancient noble palaces and grand churches further contribute to the Upper Town's sense of history and culture. It's historic institutions aside, this area makes for a delightful stroll thanks to its tangle of narrow streets and leafy squares, perfect for relaxing in after a busy day of sightseeing. And don't foget to pay your respects at the Stone Gate's shrine to the Virgin Mary, claimed to have miraculous powers.

*The **Croatian Natural History Museum** (p205) houses finds that date human life back to the Palaeolithic era.*

DEMETRO

▶ START

*The **Viceroy's Palace** (p206) dates from the 17th century and was built after the city became the seat of the governor of Croatia in 1621.*

*The **Croatian History Museum** (p206) has works of art and documents collected since 1959.*

MESNIČKA ULICA

*A wonderful collection of paintings and sculptures is on display at the **Croatian Museum of Naive Art** (p207).*

MATOŠEVA ULICA

CIRILOMETOD

0 metres	50	N ↑
0 yards	50	

Did You Know?

The Cable car that runs from Lotrščak Tower is the shortest in the world.

*Built by Orthodox Christians in the first half of the 19th century, the **Church of SS. Cyril and Methodius** was designed by Bartol Felbinger, and has a fine iconostasis.*

*At noon every day a cannon is fired from the **Tower of Lotrščak** (p207), which dates from the 12th century.*

The Church of St Mark, with its intricately tiled roof

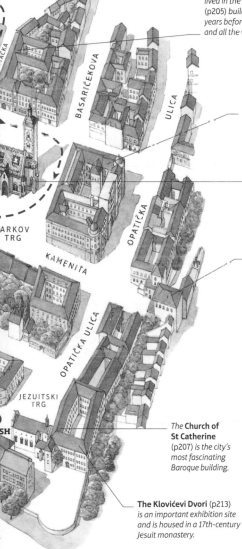

The great Croatian sculptor Ivan Meštrović lived in the 18th-century **Atelier Meštrović** (p205) building from 1922 to 1941. About ten years before his death he donated his home and all the works of art in it to the state.

The **Parliament Building** (p206) dates from 1911, when the provincial administration offices were enlarged. The independence of Croatia was proclaimed from the central window of the building in 1918.

The coloured tiles on the roof of the Gothic **Church of St Mark** (p206) form the coats of arms of Croatia, Dalmatia, Slavonia and Zagreb.

The **Stone Gate** (p202) is all that remains of the five original gates constructed around the Gradec area in the 13th century.

The **Church of St Catherine** (p207) is the city's most fascinating Baroque building.

The **Klovićevi Dvori** (p213) is an important exhibition site and is housed in a 17th-century Jesuit monastery.

Worshippers at the Stone Gate's shrine to the Virgin Mary

CENTRAL AND NORTHERN CROATIA

A mixed region of prosperous market towns, agricultural plains and vineyard-covered hills, Central and Northern Croatia is easily accessible from Zagreb. Most tourist interest focuses on the rolling hills of the Zagorje, rich in romantic castles, hilltop churches and thermal spas. Baroque Varaždin is one of the architectural jewels of Inland Croatia, while Samobor, near Zagreb, is one of its most evocative small towns.

The area served as the heartland of the Croatian state from the 8th century onwards. While Eastern Croatia fell to the Ottoman Empire in the 16th century, Central and Northern Croatia came under Habsburg rule. The Habsburgs developed castles and fortifications at towns including Čakovec, Varaždin, Sisak and Karlovac, turning them into major centres of Austrian power. In order to guard against Ottoman raids, the Habsburgs established the so-called Military Frontier along Central Croatia's southern margins, bringing in Serb, Croat and other settlers in order to defend it. The southern parts of the region suffered significant material damage during the Homeland War of 1991–95. In December 2020 a terrible earthquake struck near Petrinje, leaving extensive damage in nearby Sisak and as far afield as Zagreb.

CENTRAL AND NORTHERN CROATIA

Must See
1. Varaždin

Experience More
2. Samobor
3. Ozalj
4. Ogulin
5. Karlovac
6. Sisak
7. Jasenovac
8. Lonjsko Polje Nature Park
9. Štrigova
10. Vinica
11. Čakovec
12. Trakošćan
13. Krapina
14. Klanjec
15. Veliki Tabor
16. Kumrovec
17. Koprivnica
18. Marija Bistrica
19. Belec

0 kilometres 15

0 yards 15

N

KVARNER AREA
p170

↑ Some of the unique Baroque buildings that have made the Old Town of Varaždin famous

❶

VARAŽDIN

◉D1 🚌Frane Supila, (042) 210 444 🚍Kolodvorska 17, (060) 333 555 🛈 Local: Ivana Padovca 3, (042) 210 987; regional: Trg bana Josipa Jelačića 12; www.tourism-varazdin.hr

Traces of occupation from the Neolithic period onwards have been found around Varaždin, but the town remains absent from the records until the Middle Ages. From the late 14th century onwards it passed from the hands of the Celjskis to the Frankopans, the Brandenburgs and the Erdödys. In 1446 it was destroyed in a fire, and in 1527 the Turks attacked. In 1776 another fire destroyed the houses, but spared its famous Baroque buildings.

Castle and Museum
Stari grad & Gradski muzej

🏛Strossmayerovo šetalište 3 ☎(042) 658 754 🕒9am-5pm Tue-Fri, 9am-1pm Sat & Sun

Varaždin Castle is thought to date from around the 12th century. In the 15th century, two towers were added. It was rebuilt in 1560 with arcades and corridors facing courtyards. The Erdödy counts later added the bastions and a moat. It is now the Civic Museum, which has collections of weapons, furniture and handicrafts.

The ancient walls and Lisak Tower to the east are all that is left of the original buildings.

Gallery of Old and Modern Masters
Galerija starih i novih majstora

🏛Stančićev trg 3 ☎(042) 214 172 🕒9am-5pm Tue-Fri, 9am-1pm Sat & Sun

The gallery has a large collection of works by artists from all over Europe, particularly landscapes by Flemish and Italian artists, and portraits by German and Dutch painters.

③

Varaždin Cemetery
Hallerova aleja

🕒Feb: 7am-6pm daily; Mar & Oct: 7am-7pm daily; Apr & Sep: 7am-8pm daily; May-Aug 7am-9pm daily; Nov-Jan 7am-5pm daily

Founded in 1773, Varaždin Cemetery was given a totally new appearance in 1905 when its manager Herman Haller decided to turn it into a French-style park. He planted thousands of thuja plants in neat rows, and trimmed them to form towering wedges of evergreen hedge. Augmented by a higher level of tree cover, the overall effect is of one huge horticultural sculpture. Among the greenery are Art Nouveau grave memorials.

 INSIDER TIP
Špancirfest

Croatia's biggest street festival takes place in Varaždin at the end of August. With street performances, crafts, and live music, people come from all over Croatia to participate (www.spancirfest.com).

Tomislav Square

Trg kralja Tomislava

This square is the heart of the town. Facing it is the 15th-century Gothic Town Hall (Gradska vijećnica), one of the oldest buildings in Varaždin. It is guarded in summer by the Purgers, who wear decorative uniforms and bearskin hats. To the east stands Drašković Palace, built in the late 17th century with a Rococo façade.

↑ Lights streaming down from the trees in Tomislav Square during Advent

Cathedral of the Assumption

Uznesenja Marijina

📍 Pavlinska ulica 4
📞 (042) 210 688 🕐 9:30am–12:30pm, 4–7pm daily

The tall facade of this 17th century cathedral is enlivened by pillars. The interior is a triumph of the Baroque. The main altar has gilded columns, stuccoes and engravings. At the centre of the altar is an *Assumption of the Virgin*, reminiscent of Titian's work in Venice. Baroque music concerts are held here in the evenings.

World of Insects

📍 Franjevački trg 6 📞 (042) 658 760 🕐 9am–5pm Tue–Fri, 9am–1pm Sat & Sun

Housed in the Classicist style Hercer Palace, the methodically organized entomological section of the Civic Museum was founded by the naturalist Franjo Koščec (1882–1968), who donated his collection to the town in 1959. This became the permanent collection titled "World of Insects", widely considered one of the finest collections in Europe. The museum also has a herbarium.

Church of St John the Baptist

Sv. Ivan Krstitelj

📍 Franjevački trg 8
📞 (042) 213 166 🕐 8:30am–noon, 5:30–7pm daily

The church, built in 1650, has a Renaissance doorway with a tympanum and statues of St Francis of Assisi and St Anthony of Padua. In front of the church is one of the copies of the Monument of Bishop Gregory of Nin by Ivan Meštrović. The pharmacy has works of art, among them some allegorical frescoes by Ivan Ranger.

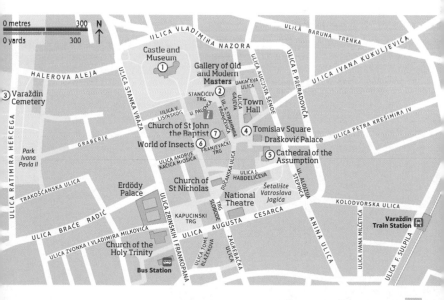

EXPERIENCE MORE

② Samobor

⚠C2 ☎(01) 336 72 76
ℹTrg kralja Tomislava 5;
www.samobor.hr/visit

Samobor is built below the ruins of what was once a large fort (Stari Grad). Throughout the city, remains from Stone and Iron Age settlements can be seen. In 1242 it was granted the status of a royal free town, and became an important trading centre. Today it is one of the capitals of Croatian gastronomy, and prides itself on its traditional local dishes.

In Taborec, the oldest area, stands the Gothic Church of St Michael (Sv. Mihalj), rebuilt in the Baroque period. Dating from the same time is the Church of St Anastasia (Sv. Anastazija) and a Franciscan monastery with the Church of St Mary (Sv. Marija); the *Assumption* behind its main altar was frescoed by Franc Jelovšek in 1752, while the left altar was decorated by Valentin Metzinger (1734). The adjacent monastery is laid out around a beautiful quadrangular cloister and has Baroque frescoes in the refectory and library.

The history of the city and local area is well documented in the **Civic Museum** (Muzej grada Samobora), which was inaugurated in 1948 and is housed in the 18th-century Livadić Palace. The section dedicated to the history of Croatian mountaineering is especially interesting.

Civic Museum

♿🚻🅿 ⬛Livadićeva 7
☎(01) 336 10 14 🕐8am–4pm Tue–Wed & Fri, 8am–7pm Thu, 10am–6pm Sat & Sun

---

EAT

Gabrek 1929

Named after the year of its foundation, this traditional restaurant offers typically north Croatian and meat-heavy dishes. Forest mushrooms, a local speciality, flavour the legendary soup.

⚠C2 ⬛Ul Starogradska 46 Samobor ⬛gabrek.hr

⟨Kn⟩⟨Kn⟩⟨Kn⟩

---

③ Ozalj

⚠C2 ☎(047) 731 158
🚌Karlovac, (060) 338 833; Ozalj, (047) 731 107
ℹKurilovac 1; www.tzp-kupa.com

This small town is located on the edge of the Kupa River. Its most famous draw is a 13th-century royal **castle** (Stari Grad) that was built on this rocky spur to monitor the roads and traffic on the river below. The castle was strengthened by the Babonić counts and was later the property of the Frankopan family and of Juraj Zrinski *(p228)*. After the Ottoman threat had passed, a village grew up around the castle, which had since become a residential manor.

Parts of the fortress remain visible: two encircling walls with five semicircular towers. Next to these are some more recent buildings: the 16th-century granary *(palas)* and a Gothic family chapel. For a time the building was abandoned but in 1971 it became a **museum**. Exhibits explain the history of the fort.

Did You Know?

Karlovac is unique for having a birthday (13 July) and couples waltz at the birthday ball in its main square.

Castle and Museum

 Cesta Zrinskih i Frankopana 2 (047) 732 271 Apr-Oct: 8am-8pm Mon-Fri, 10am-8pm Sat & Sun (Nov-Mar: to 4pm daily)

4
Ogulin

C3 (047) 525 001 Kardinala A Stepinca 1; www.tz-grada-ogulina.hr

When Marshal Tito was imprisoned here in 1927 and in 1933, this town became renowned throughout Croatia. The prison was part of a castle built by the Frankopan counts in the 15th century. Its walls enclosed a large building with two tall towers at the ends, a Gothic chapel and several houses that were built when Ogulin became a staging post on the *Vojna krajina* (Military Frontier) in 1627. Part of the structure is given over to the Regional Museum, which has sections on archaeology, folklore and mountaineering. It also comprises Ivana's House of Fairy Tales, a unique, inter-active visitor's centre that celebrates fairy tales – both Croatian and international – and their creators.

A short distance from the fortified town is the Old Castle (Zulumgrad) situated near the Đula abyss, a chasm formed by the Dobra River.

Walking along a tree-lined avenue in charming Samobor

5
Karlovac

C2 (060) 333 444 (060) 338 833 Ulica Petra Zrinskog 3; www.visitkarlovac.hr

Karlovac is an industrial city and an important junction for roads to Slovenia. It originated as a bulwark against Turkish raids, but was actually founded in 1579 by the Archduke of Austria, Charles of Habsburg, from whom it gets its name.

Karlovac was planned by the Italian N Angelini as a city-fort at the confluence of the rivers Korana and Kupa. The layout was based on a six-pointed star with bastions and moats that have now been transformed into public gardens. The interior contained 24 similar buildings, all of which are still preserved today.

Strossmayer Square is the heart of the city, with the **Civic Museum** (Gradski muzej) housed in Baroque Frankopan Palace. The archaeological and ethnographic collections document the city's history. In the square Trg Bana Jelačića is a Franciscan monastery.

The **Vjekoslav Karas Gallery** was built in 1975 in the New Centre and uses its attractive display space for both visual art pieces and museum exhibitions.

The Catholic **Church of the Holy Trinity** (Presvetoga Trojstvo) dates mainly from 1683–92 with an 18th-century clock tower. The church has an elaborate black marble altar made by Michele Cussa in 1698. The Orthodox Church of St Nicholas (Sv. Nikola) dates from 1786.

Also worth a visit is **Aquatika**, a modern, fresh-water aquarium that presents the biological diversity of Croatia's waters.

To the east, the city now extends as far as the medieval Dubovac Castle. Formerly a hotel, it is now being restored to its original design.

↑ Richly adorned drinking fountain in Karlovac

Civic Museum

 Strossmayerov trg 7 8am-4pm Tue, Thu & Fri, 8am-7pm Wed, 10am-4pm Sat, 10am noon Sun gmk hr

Vjekoslav Karas Gallery

Ljudevita Šestića 3 (047) 615980 During exhibitions: 8am-4pm Tue & Thu, 8am-7pm Wed & Fri, 10am-4pm Sat, 10am-noon Sun

Church of the Holy Trinity

Trg bana Jelačića 7 (047) 615 950/1 Before Mass; other times by appt

Aquatika

Branka Čavlovića Čavleka 1a Summer: 9am-7pm daily; winter: 9am-5pm daily aquarium karlovac.com

> INSIDER TIP
> **Samoborska kremšnita**
>
> The kremšnita, or cream slice, is a favourite in Croatian patisseries, but those produced in Samobor are said to be the best. With fluffy custard sandwiched between pastry layers, these sweet treats are sold in all the main cafés.

Battered building in historic Karlovac

The round fortress at Sisak, reflected in the still waters of the River Kupa

Fortress
 Tome Bakača Erdödyja ☎(044) 811 811 🔄For restoration until 2022

Civic Museum
♿ 🏛Kralja Tomislava 10 🔄For restoration until late 2021 🌐muzej-sisak.hr

---

7

Jasenovac

🅰E3 🚂🚌From Sisak 🛈Trg kralja Petra Svačića 19; (044) 672 490

This town is remembered as the place where, during World War II, tens of thousands of prisoners of war, Jews, Gypsies, Serbs and Croats perished in

> **STONE FLOWER**
>
> Unveiled in 1966, this monument is the focus of remembrance at the Jasenovac Memorial Site. Designed by Bogdan Bogdanović, it was one of many moving memorials built by the Communist regime to honour World War II victims and the exploits of anti-fascist partisans. Abstract in style, it aims to express hope and a break with past national divisions.

6

Sisak

🅰D2 🚂(044) 524 724 🚌(060) 330 060 🛈Rimska ul bb; www.sisakturist.com

The city of Sisak, located where the rivers Kupa and Odra flow into the Sava, has always played an important role in Croatian history. Its name has changed many times over the course of its 2,000 years of existence. It originated as the Illyrian-Celtic Segestica, becoming Siscia with the Romans, and later Colonia Flavia Siscia. After the conquest of the Balkans, Emperor Augustus made it the capital of the Pannonia Savia province and it became a trading centre.

It was destroyed by Attila in 441, and in the 6th century it was raided by the Avars and the Slavs. The town was finally rebuilt by the Croats and became Sisak. Despite being destroyed again by the Hungarians in the 10th century, Sisak later rose nearby and began to enjoy a long period of prosperity, thanks to tolls on river traffic. It still has some Baroque buildings, including the old and new town halls.

A park surrounds a **fortress** (Stari Grad) on the River Kupa, south of the city. The fortress was built in the 16th century, at the time of the Turkish invasions. It has a triangular ground plan, with three large round brick towers (1544–55), connected by a high wall with openings for firearms. The **Civic Museum** (Gradski muzej) displays exhibits that trace the city's development from its origins to the present day. Material from the Roman settlement is a highlight. On 29 December 2020, a devastating earthquake hit the area, centring on nearby Petrinje. Sisak experienced considerable damage and reconstructions are underway.

About 20 km (12 miles) southwest of Sisak is Gora, which, in the Middle Ages, was the centre of a Županija (county) of the same name. The county seat was a castle that appears in documents from 1242, but which was destroyed by the Turks in 1578. Gora's Gothic Church of the Assumption of the Blessed Virgin Mary (Uznesenja Blažene Djevice Marije) was also damaged, but was restored in the 18th century in the Baroque style. The church resembles a castle, with a marble altar and pulpit inside.

the concentration camp that was located here. To commemorate this terrible genocide, a large stone flower – designed by Bogdan Bogdanović (1922–2010) who served as mayor of Belgrade in the 1980s – now stands in what was formerly the camp's centre *(see box)*. This impressive monument and the **Memorial Museum** are part of Jasenovac Memorial Site. Many such monuments across the country were left to decay after the fall of Yugoslavia, but have since been rediscovered by a 21st-century audience appreciative of commemorative art.

Memorial Museum

🏛 Jasenovac Memorial Site
🕐 Mar–Nov: 9am–5pm Mon–Fri, 10am–4pm Sat & Sun; Dec–Feb: 9am–4pm Mon–Fri
🌐 jusp-jasenovac.hr

8

Lonjsko Polje Nature Park

📍 D2 🏛 Park office (Krapje)
🕐 Apr–Oct: 8am–4pm Mon–Fri, 9am–5pm Sat & Sun; Nov–Mar: by appt 🌐 pp-lonjsko-polje.hr

The wide bend in the River Sava between Sisak and Stara Gradiška has been an ornithological reserve since 1963. It became a nature reserve in 1990 to protect an area of 506 sq km (195 sq miles). This vast region was regularly flooded by the river and its tributaries during the thaw. Since the 1960s parts of the wetlands have been drained, but they still remain some of Europe's most important areas of marshland.

Woods of oak, poplar, ash and willow trees grow along the banks of the river, while the dry fields are used as grazing for sheep in the summer months. Wild boar and deer live here, as well as Turopolje pigs and Posavina horses, both of which are protected species.

The park is also a stopping place for black storks, which arrive in spring and leave in autumn after nesting, and for numerous other bird species.

> **Woods of oak, poplar, ash and willow trees grow along the banks of the river, while the dry fields are used as grazing for sheep in the summer months.**

9

Štrigova

📍 D1 🚌 From Čakovec
📍 Štrigova 29; www.strigova.info

Numerous finds of Roman origin have been discovered in this village, leading historians to believe that it was built on the site of the Roman city of Stridon, the birthplace of St Jerome.

The counts of Štrigovčak lived here, but their castle was destroyed during a raid by the Turks. Nearby, the Bannfy counts also built a castle, which was transformed into a palace in the 17th century. The palace was once famed for its rich furnishings, its art collections, and for the fact that the Hungarian king, Matthias Corvinus, was often a guest here.

The Church of St Jerome (Sv. Jerolim) stands on a hill at the edge of the village. Restoration has uncovered frescoes above the doorway and in the niches on the façade, which is flanked by two harmonious bell towers and culminates in a curvilinear tympanum.

In the church are numerous *trompe-l'œil* paintings by the Tyrolean artist Ivan Ranger, which depict *Angels*, the *Evangelists* and the *Life of St Jerome*. There are also statues representing the fathers of the Church.

↑ Horses grazing in the fields of Lonjsko Polje Nature Park

↑ Abandoned ruin and climbing foliage in Vinica's arboretum

⑩ Vinica

🅰 D1 🚌 From Varaždin
🅸 Trg bana Josipa Jelačića
12, Varaždin; (042) 210 096

This small town lies at the foot of vine-covered hills. It was first mentioned in documents of 1353 as the site of a medieval fortress. At one time it was known for its large palace, built by the Patačić counts on the site of their old castle. The palace is now in ruins, as is that of the Drašković counts, which was situated in the centre of a large park.

In the late 19th century, Count Marko Bombelles created Opeka Park, 2 km (1 mile) south of Vinica. At that time, this large arboretum was the only one of its kind in the country. Bombelles planted exotic trees and plants from around the world over an area of flat and hilly ground.

Next to this wonderful park, declared a protected nature reserve in 1961, a school of horticulture has been set up. The school has several glasshouses and a large garden of flowering plants.

⑪ Čakovec

🅰 D1 🚇 (040) 384 333
🖥 Masarykova ulica (040)
313 947 🅸 Kralja Tomislava
1; www.visitcakovec.com

In the second half of the 13th century, on a site once inhabited by Romans, Count Demetrius Chaky, a magistrate at the court of King Bela IV, built a tower here that was called Chaktornya. In the following century, the main defensive structure in the Međimurje – a frontier region that borders Slovenia and Hungary – was built around the tower. In 1547 Emperor Ferdinand gave it to the Ban (governor) of Croatia, Nikola Zrinski, together with a large estate, to settle a debt and as a reward for the victory against the Turks. Nikola Zrinski died heroically while defending Siget against the Ottomans, and became a national hero.

ZRINSKI AND FRANOPAN DYNASTIES

Dujam, count of Krk, died in 1163 and his descendants took the name Frankopan. They were allied with Venice until 1480, when they were forced to surrender the island, but they kept the vast estates given to them by Hungary. The Šubić family became counts of Bribir in 1290 and counts of Zrinski in 1347. The execution of Petar Zrinski and his brother-in-law Fran Krsto Frankopan, in 1671, ended Croatia's powerful dynasties.

Timeline

1508–66

▽ Nikola Zrinski. Fought against the Turks and was a defender of Christianity.

1621–71

▽ Petar Zrinski. Leader of the movement to limit Habsburg activity in Croatia.

1480–1527

△ Krsto Frankopan. He died fighting for the independence of Hungary, of which Croatia was part.

1643–71

△ Fran Krsto Frankopan. He was publicly executed for his part in a plot against the Empire.

On 29 May 1579, one of his successors, a member of the Zrinski family of Siget, guaranteed tax privileges to whoever went to live in the city that was developing around the fort. This date is considered the founding of Čakovec and is celebrated with a festival. Bastions and a moat were added in this period as defence against cannon fire. Inside the walls, a four-storey palace was built around a square courtyard.

In 1671, Petar Zrinski led a plot to separate Croatia from the Kingdom of Hungary. The plot was discovered and Zrinski and his co-conspirator Fran Krsto Frankopan were beheaded on 30 April 1671. Čakovec then came under the direct rule of the Emperor.

The Renaissance Old Castle, of which only the first floor remains, and the Baroque New Castle face each other inside the medieval walls. For a long time the Old Castle was used as a prison, but it has since been restored and now houses the **Medimurje Civic Museum**. On display here are exhibits of prehistoric material, many Roman finds, and ethnographic collections. There is also an exhibition dedicated to local composer J Slavenski (1896–1955), who was known for his love of the region's traditional music.

Čakovec is the main administrative centre of the Medimurje. The western part of the region is hilly with broad valleys, and is renowned for its wines, while the fertile plains of the eastern part produce cereal crops.

In the village of Šenkovec, around 2 km (1 mile) from Čakovec, stands the Church of St Helen (Sv. Jelena). What little remains of its original Gothic form has been integrated into an overall Baroque appearance. The church is the only surviving part of the monastery founded here by the Paulines in 1376. It has been rebuilt at various times, firstly after a Protestant revolt, then because of a fire and finally after an earthquake. Inside the church are the tombstones of the powerful Zrinski family: that of Nikola Zrinski and his wife Catherine Frankopan, and that of Petar Zrinski.

The church also contains a number of tombs belonging to members of the Kneževič family, who became the successors to the Zrinskis.

Medimurje Civic Museum
ⓐⓕⓒ ◨ Trg Republike 5
🕐 7am–6pm Mon–Fri (Oct–Mar: to 3pm); 10am–2pm Sat & Sun 🌐 mmc.hr

↑ A section of Čakovec's historic Old Castle, home to the Civic Museum

↑ Snowy road leading to the hilltop Castle of Trakošćan

 12

Trakošćan

🅰D1 🚌For Trakošćan
ℹ️Trakošćan; www.
trakoscan.hr

The pretty surroundings of the **Castle of Trakošćan** and its excellent state of conservation make this one of the most visited tourist sights in Zagorje. Originally built to guard the road that descends from Ptuj towards the valley of the River Sava, the castle was listed in 1434 as one of the properties granted by Sigismund of Austria to the Count of Celje. It was used for defence purposes until the end of Turkish rule. In 1568 it became the property of the Drašković counts.

During the second half of the 19th century, it was transformed into a splendid Neo-Gothic residence by Juraj Drašković. He also added an

Did You Know?

A girl's body is said to be built into Veliki Tabor Castle, her punishment for a romance with the castle lord's son.

artificial lake, a park and gardens, while still preserving some of the military aspects of the castle. It stands on a wooded hilltop and is surrounded by a high wall with a tower, which encircles the imposing palace.

All 32 of the rooms of the castle are now a **museum**, where furniture, armoury, vestments, paintings and a rare series of portraits of the Drašković family, are on display.

Castle and Museum

🖼🖼🖼 🏠Trakošćan 1
📞(042) 796 422 🕐Apr-Oct:
10am-6pm daily; Nov-Mar:
9am-5pm daily

 13

Krapina

🅰C1 🏠(049) 328 028
🖨(049) 328 028
ℹ️Magistratska 28; www.
tzg-krapina.hr

This town is well known in the scientific field because of the remains of Krapina man, *Homo krapinensis*, who lived in the Palaeolithic age, that were found nearby. The Neanderthal skeleton, discovered in 1899 in a hillside cave, is now in the Archaeological Museum in Zagreb. The **Museum of Krapina Neanderthal Men**

is one of the most modern museums in Croatia, with multimedia presentations and exhibits exploring the life and culture of Neanderthal man.

Krapina is first documented in 1193 as the site of a castle, now destroyed, built to guard the river of the same name. After the danger of Turkish attack had passed, it was conceded to the Keglević counts and became an important administrative town.

It also became a religious centre: in the mid-17th century, a Franciscan monastery and the Baroque Church of St Catherine were built here. The sacristy and some of the monastery rooms are decorated with vivid frescoes by Ivan Ranger.

In one of the town squares is a monument to Ljudevit Gaj, born in Krapina in 1809. During

→ Statue from the Museum of Krapina Neanderthal Men

the first half of the 19th century he was a prominent figure in a movement that promoted the revival of Croatian politics and culture.

Just northeast of Krapina in Trški Vrh is the sanctuary of the Madonna of Jerusalem, a magnificent example of Baroque art in Croatia. Built in 1750–61, the façade has a bell tower with an onion dome. Inside is an arched portico and four chapels similar to the tower. The interior is covered with a cycle of frescoes of biblical subjects and scenes from Mary's life by the Styrian artist Anton Lerchinger. The ornate main altar (with a statue of the Virgin brought from Jerusalem in 1669) is by sculptor Filip Jacob Straub of Graz, while the pulpit and the other three altars are the work of Anton Mersi.

Museum of Krapina Neanderthal Men

 ◍Šetalište V Sluge bb ◍9am–7pm Tue–Sun (Nov–Mar: to 5pm) ◍mkn.mhz.hr

Klanjec

◍C1 ◍From Zagreb, Krapina, Zabok ◍Trg A Mihanovića 3; www.biserzagorja.hr

Antun Augustinčić (1900–79) is one of the most important Croatian sculptors of the 20th century, and his works can be seen around the world. He was born in this town, and the **Antun Augustinčić Gallery** displays his work.

Also of interest are the Franciscan Monastery and the annexed Church of St Mary. Both were built in the 17th century by the powerful Erdödy family, whose tombs lie here. Tours can be arranged by the tourist office.

In the square is a monument by Robert Frangeš-Mihanović dedicated to the poet Antun Mihanović, who wrote the Croatian national anthem.

EAT

Vuglec Breg
This is one of the best rural eateries in the locality. Vuglec Breg sits on a vineyard-cloaked hilltop and serves traditional favourites such as *štrukli* (dough pockets filled with cheese) and generous slabs of locally reared pork. The restaurant's views across rippling green hills are not to be missed.

◍C1 ◍Škarićevo 151, Krapina
◍vuglec-breg.hr

Ⓚ Ⓚ ⓚ

Another memorial to this poet is the 9-m- (29-ft) high memorial stone that stands in Zelenjak, 3 km (2 miles) north of Klanjec towards Kumrovec.

Antun Augustinčić Gallery

◍Trg A Mihanovića 10 ◍Apr–Sep: 9am–5pm daily; Oct–Mar: 9am–3pm Tue–Sun ◍gaa.mhz.hr

Veliki Tabor

◍C1 ◍From Krapina or Zagreb for Desinić ◍Košnički Hum 1, Desinić; www.veliki-tabor.hr

One of the most famous and best-preserved castles in Croatia, Veliki Tabor stands on a bare hilltop, making it visible from a great distance. It was royal property in the 14th century at the time of King Matthias Corvinus I, which justified its imposing appearance. The castle was granted to the family of the Ratkaj counts, who transformed it into a sumptuous residential palace in the 16th century.

Walls with four semicircular towers encircle the main body of the castle, which is built on a pentagonal ground plan. Two floors with porticoes face the central courtyard. The bastions (no longer extant) made Veliki Tabor a fortress to be feared. The castle is included on Croatia's UNESCO Tentative list, and now houses a museum.

Miljana, just to the south-west of Veliki Tabor, is home to one of the most picturesque Baroque castles in Croatia. Construction began in the 17th century but was not completed until the mid-19th century. This time span resulted in a variety of styles; there are striking 18th-century Rococo frescoes in a number of rooms, as well as some delightful artworks.

Castle

◍Košnički Hum 1, Desinić ◍(049) 374 970 ◍Apr–Sep: 9am–5pm Tue–Fri, 9am–7pm Sat & Sun; Mar & Oct: 9am–4pm Tue–Fri, 9am–5pm Sat & Sun; Nov–Feb: 9am–4pm Wed–Sun

↑ Central area of the historic Veliki Tabor castle

↑ Flower beds bordering pathways in the city of Koprivnica

Kumrovec

Ⓐ C1 ▦ From Zagreb
🛈 Ulica Josipa Broza 12; www.kumrovec.hr

This was the birthplace of Marshal Tito, born Josip Broz in 1892. His house, which dates from 1860, was turned into a museum in 1953. On display are the furniture and household goods that belonged to his family. In the square in front of the house is a monument to Tito, the work of Antun Augustinčić in 1948. Along with other village houses, Tito's birthplace is now part of a folk museum, the **Ethnological Museum – Staro Selo**, which means "old village". The thatched houses are furnished with utensils and household goods of the time. Reconstructed workshops have been set up to demonstrate crafts such as hemp- and flax-weaving.

Ethnological Museum - Staro Selo
⊛ⓈⒶ Kumrovec bb
Ⓒ Apr-Sep: 9am-7pm daily; Mar & Oct: 9am-4pm Mon-Fri, 9am-6pm Sat & Sun; Nov-Feb: 9am-4pm daily
Ⓦ mss.mhz.hr

Koprivnica

Ⓐ E1 🚉 Kolodvorska 31, (060) 305 040
🚌 Zagrebačka ulica, (048) 621 282 🛈 Trg bana Jelačića 7; www. koprivnicatourism.com

Koprivnica (originally known as Kukaproncza) was founded by the powerful Ernust family and was a key trading centre for the Podravina area as well as a royal city from 1356. It was burned down by the Turks in the 16th century, destroying one of Croatia's first free towns.

Slowly rebuilt in the 17th century, the town took on a Baroque appearance with a wide avenue flanked by the main buildings. Many Serbian immigrants settled here, hence the Orthodox Church of the Holy Spirit (Sveti Duh), dating from the late 18th century.

In 1685 a Franciscan Monastery and the Church of St Anthony of Padua were established. The monastery was a source of culture and learning for the whole region and it has resumed this role in recent times.

Nearby is the **Civic Museum** (Gradski muzej), with archaeological, historical and cultural collections, and the **Koprivnica Gallery**, which houses a collection of Naïve works linked to the Hlebine School. Next door, in a former brewery, is the Kraluš beer hall, much loved by the locals.

Hlebine, 13 km (8 miles) east of Koprivnica, owes its fame to the peasant painters fostered by the artist Krsto Hegedušić. In the 1930s this group founded the so-called Hlebine School of Naïve art: the core of a trend in painting that represented the landscape and people of this region in a simple and original way. Their work is exhibited in both the **Hlebine Gallery** and the Koprivnica Gallery.

Civic Museum
Ⓐ Trg Leandera Brozovića 1
Ⓒ (048) 642 538 Ⓒ 8am-3pm Mon-Fri, 10am-1pm Sat & Sun

Koprivnica Gallery
⊛ Ⓐ Zrinski trg 9/1 Ⓒ (048) 622 307 Ⓒ 8am-3pm Mon, 10am-6pm Tue-Fri, 10am-2pm Sat & Sun

Hlebine Gallery
⊛ Ⓐ Trg Ivana Generalića 15
Ⓒ 099 733 6026 Ⓒ 10am-6pm Tue-Fri, 10am-2pm Sat & Sun

Marija Bistrica

 D1 🚂 Zlatar Bistrica, 5 km (3 miles) 🚌 From Zagreb ℹ️ Zagrebačka bb; www.tz-marija-bistrica.hr

This small village is home to the **Sanctuary of St Mary of Bistrica** (Majke Božje Bistričke), one of the best-known pilgrimage sites in Croatia. There has been a church on this site since 1334. In the mid-16th century, when a Turkish invasion seemed imminent, a wooden statue of the *Black Madonna with Child* was hidden in the church. Some decades later, it was miraculously rediscovered, and still inspires tremendous devotion today.

The church was the first to be declared a Sanctuary of Croatia by Parliament (1715). It was rebuilt from 1879 to 1883 by the architect Hermann Bollé, who combined a number of distinctive styles.

Some important objects from the sanctuary's rich collection are now on display in the Diocesan Museum in Zagreb.

Sanctuary of St Mary of Bistrica

📍 Trg pape Ivana Pavla II 32 🕐 Daily 🌐 svetiste-mbb.hr

19
Belec

D1 🚌 From Zabok ℹ️ Magistratska 3, Krapina; (049) 233 653

Among the rolling hills of Zagorje is the village of Belec, on the outskirts of which is the small Church of St George (Sv. Jurja), one of the few Romanesque buildings preserved in inland Croatia. The bell tower takes up nearly all of the façade (it resembles a defensive tower rather than a campanile).

Lower down the hillside is the beautiful **Church of St Mary of the Snow** (Sv. Marija Snježna), constructed in 1674. It is considered a masterpiece of Croatian Baroque, because of its sumptuously decorated interior with intricate stucco work and figurative sculptures. The monk and artist Ivan Ranger painted some of his *trompe-l'œil* masterpieces here, including *Scenes from the Old Testament*.

Church of St Mary of the Snow

📍 49250, Belec 📞 (049) 460 040 🕐 By appt

STAY

Villa Zelenjak-Ventek

This intimate pension sits in a lovely wooded valley, just southeast of Kumrovec. As well as cosy rooms, there's a restaurant serving traditional food, plus an attractive garden, a fish pond, a children's play-park, and an abundance of picturesque country walks.

C1 📍 Risvica 1, Kumrovec 🌐 zelenjak.com

The façade *(inset)* and Baroque interior of Belec's Church of St Mary of the Snow

EASTERN CROATIA

Wedged between Hungary, Serbia and Bosnia-Herzegovina, Eastern Croatia is one of the most fertile regions of the country. Carpeted with maize fields, orchards and vineyards, it's also famous for its paprika plantations, which give the cuisine of the region a rich, piquant character. The main city of Osijek is one of the best preserved Baroque towns in Central Europe; highlights elsewhere include the historic town of Vukovar and any number of quaint villages and ruined castles.

Eastern Croatia was one of the cradles of European civilization, with Neolithic cultures around Vukovar and Vinkovci smelting metals and producing decorative pottery. Part of the Croatian (subsequently Hungaro-Croatian) kingdom from the 10th century, Eastern Croatia fell to the Ottoman Empire after the Battle of Mohács in 1526. It was reconquered by the Habsburgs in the late 17th century, who repopulated it with migrants from Central Europe and endowed loyal aristocrats with vast agricultural estates. Significant pockets of Serbian language and culture grew up around Vukovar, Osijek and Požega. In 1991 the Yugoslav People's Army used this as a pretext to carve out areas of occupation in these areas, subjecting both Vukovar and Osijek to murderous bombardments. The occupied areas were peacefully reintegrated into an independent Croatia in 1998, and much of the wartime damage was rebuilt.

EASTERN CROATIA

Must Sees
1 Osijek
2 Kopački Rit Nature Park

Experience More
3 Slavonski Brod
4 Daruvar
5 Lipik
6 Kutjevo
7 Požega
8 Đakovo
9 Vinkovci
10 Ilok
11 Našice
12 Batina
13 Valpovo
14 Virovitica
15 Vukovar

CENTRAL AND
NORTHERN
CROATIA
p216

↑ Early morning fishing on the River Drava, Osijek

❶

OSIJEK

🅰G2 ✈20 km (12 miles) Vukovarska 67, www.osijek-airport.hr 🚊Trg Ružičke, (031) 205 155 🚌Bartola Kašića, (060) 334 466 ℹLocal: Županijska 2, (031) 203 755; regional: Županijska 4; www.tzosijek.hr

The capital of Slavonia sits in the middle of a fertile plain. It is a centre of industry, a university city and a lively Central European metropolis with wide roads linking three districts: the Fort (Tvrđa), Lower Town (Donji grad) and Upper Town (Gornji grad). The city grew in 1786 when the three areas merged. Due to its position on the River Drava, Osijek has always played a strategic role. In 1809 Emperor Francis I declared it a Royal Free Town (this document is now in the Museum of Slavonia). In 1991, after Croatia declared independence, the city was bombed for over a year by Yugoslav forces, and much of the old centre (Upper Town) was damaged. Liberated in 1995, in 1998 Osijek became part of the Croat state again.

①

Church of St Michael
Sv. Mihovil

🅰Trg Jurja Križanića, Tvrđa
📞(031) 208 990
🕐Before Mass

Standing a little way back from the square is the 18th-century Church of St Michael, built by the Jesuits in the high- and late-Baroque style and showing inspiration from Budapest and Vienna. The bright yellow façade is flanked by two bell towers, and a splendid wooden doorway leads inside. Below street level the foundations of the 16th-century Kasimpaša mosque on which the church was built are still visible, a relic of the Ottoman era. With a polite and timely request, you may be granted an informal tour by the resident priest.

②

Museum of Slavonia
Muzej Slavonije

🅰Trg sv. Trojstva 6, Tvrđa
📞(031) 250 730 🕐10am-6pm Tue-Sat 🌐mso.hr

On Tvrđa central square, the old Town Hall, the oldest public building in Osijek, has housed the Museum of Slavonia since 1946. Some 500,000 geological, prehistoric, Greek, Illyrian and Roman objects are included in the museum's 160 collections. One section is dedicated to the ancient Roman settlement of Mursa on which Tvrđa was built, with statues, tombstones, architectural pieces and a coin collection. Other sections are devoted to folklore, with exhibits of richly decorated costumes. Today these clothes provide models for a flourishing handicrafts industry making silk fabrics.

Did You Know?

The word Osijek comes from the Croatian word *oseka*, which means "ebb tide".

③
Church of SS Peter and Paul
Sv. Petar i Pavao

📍 Trg Marina Držica, Gornji grad 📞 (031) 310 020 🕐 8am-noon & 3-6pm Mon-Fri, 8am-noon Sat

This imposing Neo-Gothic church is known as *katedrala* (cathedral) by the locals by virtue of its sheer size. It was designed and built by Franz Langenberg in the late 19th century. The 40 stained-glass windows and some of the sculptures are by the Viennese artist Eduard Hauser. Most of the windows were bombed out but have been restored.

↑ Bell dome of the Church of SS Peter and Paul

④
Church of the Holy Cross
Sv. Križ

📍 Franjevačka ulica, Tvrđa 📞 (031) 302 733 🕐 8am-noon, 3-8pm daily

Northeast of the main square, on the site of a sacred medieval building, stands the Church of the Holy Cross, built by the Franciscans in 1709–1720. Next to this is the monastery, which housed the first printing press in Slavonia (1735), and from the mid-18th century also housed schools of philosophy and theology. The interior of the church is complemented by a statue of the Virgin from the 15th century and a variety of liturgical furnishings.

⑤
Europe Avenue
Europska avenija

This is the main road of Osijek, linking Tvrđa to the Upper Town, and possibly the finest Art Nouveau avenue in Croatia. It crosses some of the city's parks, one of which is Kralja Državnica slava, home to a striking bronze memorial to the fallen of the 78th Infantry Regiment regarded as the first modern sculpture in Croatia.

⑥
Museum of Fine Arts
Muzej likovnih umjetnosti

📍 Europska avenija 9 📞 (031) 251 280 🕐 10am-8pm Tue-Fri, 10am-1pm Sat & Sun 🌐 mlu.hr

The Museum of Fine Arts was founded in 1954 in an elegant 19th-century townhouse. It has collections from the 18th and 19th centuries, as well as works by contemporary Croatian artists. There is also a section dedicated to the Osijek School.

⑦
Archaeological Museum
Arheološki muzej

📍 Trg svetog Trojstva 2 🕐 10am-6pm Tue-Sat 🌐 amo.hr

Located in the City Guard House (Glavna straža), this museum is a former annex to the Museum of Slavonia. On the ground floor is a lapidarium containing relics from Roman Mursa, including a relief of a satyr chasing a nymph. On the first floor is a Neolithic section rich in decorated pottery, and a large display of jewellery and medieval weapons.

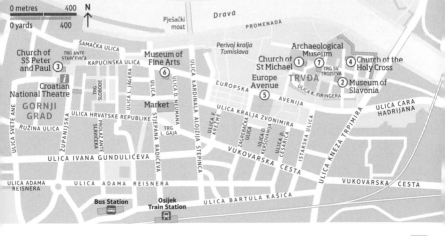

A SHORT WALK
THE FORT (TVRĐA)

Distance 1.5 km (1 mile) **Time** 20 minutes

The fortified centre of Osijek (Tvrđa) is a historic stronghold and a charming place to meander. It was built on the site of the Roman settlement of Mursa before it was destroyed by the Avars and rebuilt by the Croats. It remained a military and administrative centre until it was attacked and burned by the Turks in 1526, who then rebuilt their own fort here. Tvrđa now houses the Town Hall, the university faculties, and the Museum of Slavonia, which together give the area a sense of an open-air musuem.

On the western side of the square stands the Building of the Guard, with a clock tower from the 18th century. It now houses the **Archaeological Museum** *(p239).*

Constructed by Jesuits in the first half of the 18th century, the **Church of St Michael** *(p238) has a Baroque façade flanked by two towers.*

Croatian Academy of Science and Arts

0 metres 50 N
0 yards 50

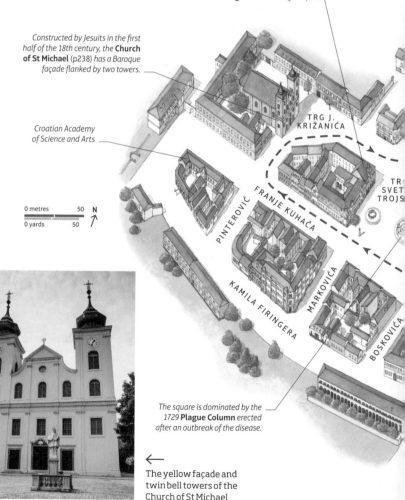

TRG J. KRIŽANIĆA

TR SVET TROJS

FRANJE KUHAČA

PINTEROVIĆ

KAMILA FIRINGERA

MARKOVIĆA

BOSKOVIĆA

The square is dominated by the 1729 **Plague Column** *erected after an outbreak of the disease.*

←
The yellow façade and twin bell towers of the Church of St Michael

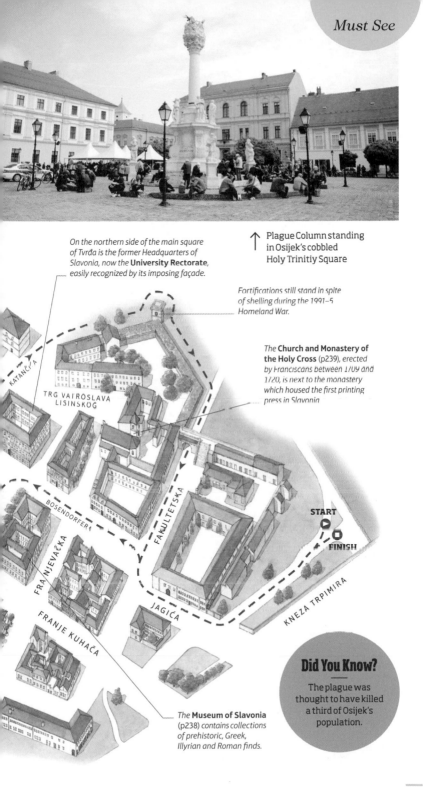

↑ Plague Column standing in Osijek's cobbled Holy Trinitiy Square

On the northern side of the main square of Tvrđa is the former Headquarters of Slavonia, now the **University Rectorate**, easily recognized by its imposing façade.

Fortifications still stand in spite of shelling during the 1991–5 Homeland War.

The **Church and Monastery of the Holy Cross** (p239), erected by Franciscans between 1709 and 1720, is next to the monastery which housed the first printing press in Slavonia

KATANČIĆA

TRG VATROSLAVA LISINSKOG

BOSENDORFER

FAKULTETSKA

FRANJEVAČKA

JAGIĆA

FRANJE KUHAČA

KNEZA TRPIMIRA

START ▶

■ FINISH

Did You Know?

The plague was thought to have killed a third of Osijek's population.

The **Museum of Slavonia** (p238) contains collections of prehistoric, Greek, Illyrian and Roman finds.

290

Species of birds live
in the wetlands.

2

KOPAČKI RIT
NATURE PARK

G2 **Mali Sakadaš 1, Kopačevo, (031) 445 445** **Nov-Mar: 8am-4pm
daily; Apr-Oct: 9am-5pm daily** **pp-kopacki-rit.hr**

This is one of the largest wetlands in Europe, home to legions of
birds and wildlife. The nature park wonderfully showcases Croatia's
changing seasons – watch herons and storks feed here in spring,
ducks and geese migrate in autumn, and deer graze in winter.

This triangular piece of land is bordered by the
final stretch of the river Drava before it meets
the Danube. The area covers 177 sq km (68 sq
miles) and can turn into an immense wetland
marsh when the Danube floods. At other times
it is a vast grassland plain with pools and ponds.
There are also dry areas which support
enormous willows and tall oak trees. A nature
reserve since 1967, it has a rich and varied
fauna and for many months of the year
provides a sanctuary for hundreds of different
species of bird, both migratory and domestic.
A high embankment on the western side stops
the further spread of the flood waters.

On top is a road which allows cars to cross
this part of the park. Information on boat rides
and bike hire is available at the park entrance.
Insect repellent is recommended in summer.

↑ Flooded white willow forest in Kopački Rit, a photogenic wetlands park *(inset)*

↑ Wild boar roaming grassland in the nature park

→ Grey heron hunting fish in Kopački Rit, a common sight in the park's marshland in springtime

TOP 5 RESIDENT ANIMALS

Deer
Thousands of deer live in the park and can be spotted wandering the surrounding woodland.

Cormorants
There are many nests in the park's willow and poplar trees. You can see them feeding spring through autumn.

Great Crested Grebe
The mating display of these birds is one of the more spectacular sights of the park.

Storks
The white stork is one of the park's symbols and the birds are especially visible during the breeding season. Black storks are much rarer; only a few dozen pairs live here.

Wild Boar
During the spring, it is sometimes possible to see whole families of this shy animal in the park's oak woods.

EXPERIENCE MORE

3
Slavonski Brod

 F3 🚂 Osijek or Zagreb 🚌 (060) 333 444 🚏 Trg Hrvatskog proljeća, (060) 310 310 🛈 Trg Ivane Brlić Mažuranić 7a; www.tzgsb.hr

Built on the site of the Roman town Marsonia, this town was placed so as to monitor the traffic on the River Sava, which forms the border with Bosnia-Herzegovina. The town belonged to the Ottomans from 1536 until 1691, when it fell to the advancing Austrians.

In the 18th century, the Austrians built the huge star-shaped Brod Fortress (Tvrđava Brod) in the centre of town, containing barracks and administrative buildings, and surrounded by concentric moats. One barrel-vaulted former arms depot now houses the Ružić Gallery (Galerija Ružić), which displays contemporary Croatian art. Just east of here, is an 18th-century Franciscan Monastery and a Baroque church.

The town's **Regional Civic Museum** (Muzej Brodskog Posavlja) contains historic documents and archaeological, geological and ethnological finds from the region.

Croatian children's writer Ivana Brlić-Mažuranić (1874–1938) spent much of her life in Slavonski Brod. Her former home on the main square now contains the Vladimir Becić Art Gallery (Likovni Salon Vladimir Becić), with contemporary exhibitions. The town is also known for its annual June folklore festival (Brodsko kolo).

Regional Civic Museum
⊘ ⊘ 🏛 Ulica Ante Starčevića 40 📞 (035) 447 415 🕙 10am–1pm Mon, Wed & Fri, 5–7pm Tue & Thu, 10am–1pm Sun 🗓 Public hols 🖥 muzejbp.hr

4
Daruvar

 E2 🚂 Osijek or Zagreb 🚌 🚏 🛈 Trg kralja Tomislava 12; www.visitdaruvar.hr

This spa town was known as Aquae Balissae in the time of the Roman Empire for the quality of its hot water spring.

In 1760, the area was bought by a Hungarian count, Antun Janković, who built a Baroque castle – that he named Daruvar – and the first **spa**. Today, Daruvar has many locations offering the spa waters, as well as a thermal water park, Aquae Balissae.

The town is also a centre for the Czech people in Croatia, who maintain the Czech language and customs.

Daruvar Spa
🏛 Julijev Park 🖥 daruvarske-toplice.hr

Did You Know?

Slavonski Brod and its train station feature in Agatha Christie's novel *Murder on the Orient Express*.

5
Lipik

 E2 🚂 Osijek or Zagreb 🚌 🚏 From Zagreb 🛈 Trg kralja Tomislava 3; www.tz-lipik.hr

In the late 18th century a hot water spring, rich in minerals, was rediscovered in this region, and Lipik became one of the most famous spas in Croatia. It was especially popular between the two world wars. Lipik was damaged in the 1991 war, but a new spa (**Toplice Lipik**) has since been built and the hotels and medical centres restored. Lipik is also known for breeding the famous Lipizzan horses, a valuable breed most closely associated with the Spanish Riding School in Vienna. There are many popular riding trails in the area.

Toplice Lipik
🏛 Marije Terezije 13 🖥 bolnica-lipik.hr

6

Kutjevo

A Г2 **Osijek Našice
Trg graševine 1; www.tzkutjevo.hr**

A wine-producing centre, this town is famed for a winery founded by the Cistercians. In 1232, the order built a monastery here and encouraged the cultivation of vines. After Turkish rule, at the end of the 17th century, the monastery was taken over by Jesuits and wine-making resumed. The Cistercian cellars are still intact

and wine remains an important industry in the area.

The Jesuits also built the Church of the Nativity of the Blessed Virgin Mary (Crkva rođenja Blažene Djevice Marije) in 1732, which houses a painting of the *Madonna with Child* by A Cebej (1759).

7

Požega

A E3 **Osijek or Zagreb
(034) 273 911 (034) 273 133 Trg Sv Trojstva 11; www.pozega-tz.hr**

The Romans founded this city as a halfway settlement between Sisak and Osijek. In the 11th century the heretical movement of the Bogomili spread from here; after their repression in the 12th century, properties around the city were granted to the Templars by King Bela IV.

In 1285 the Franciscans founded a monastery, the church of which was used as a mosque during the Turkish occupation. In the 18th and 19th centuries the city was called the "Athens of Slavonia" for the cultural events held to commemorate the expulsion of the Turks in 1691. Every year on 12 March Požega still holds an event called Grgurevo, to commemorate a local victory won over the Turks in 1688.

In the main square stands a memorial to plague victims by Gabrijel Granicije (1749). The renovated 18th-century Church of St Francis (Sv. Franjo) also stands in the square;

↑ Interior of the Church of St Theresa, Požega's cathedral

the monastery alongside it still houses a community of Franciscan monks.

Dating from 1763, the **Church of St Theresa** (Sv. Terezija Avilska) became a cathedral in 1997. Its frescoed walls are by Celestin Medović and Oton Iveković.

The Church of St Lawrence (Sv. Lovro, 14th century) was renovated in Baroque style in the early 18th century. It houses tombstones testifying to the city's glory; one tombstone is for the poet Antun Kanižlić (1699–1777).

The **Civic Museum** (Gradski muzej) contains an assortment of Romanesque reliefs, archaeological finds and Baroque paintings.

Church of St Theresa
Trg sv Terezije 13
(034) 274 321 8am-noon, 3-6pm daily

Civic Museum
Matice hrvatske 1
(034) 272 130
9am-noon & 4-6pm Mon-Fri, 10am-noon Sat

←

Brod Fortress, standing in the centre of Slavonski Brod town

⑧ Đakovo

△F3 ✈ Osijek, 48 km
(22 miles) 🚍 (031) 811 360
🚌 (060) 302 030 **🛈** Kralja
Tomislava 3; www.
tzdjakovo.eu

In medieval times this town was known by the name of Civitas Dyaco, and later as Castrum Dyaco. Late in the 13th century it became a bishopric, and its influence extended over most of Slavonia and Bosnia. Conquered and destroyed by the Turks in 1536, it became a Muslim centre and a mosque was built. After Turkish rule, the city was renovated. Only the mosque, at the end of the central avenue, was retained. It was converted into the parish Church of All Saints (Svi Sveti) in the 18th century.

The **Cathedral of St Peter** (Sv. Petar), built between 1866 and 1882 by Bishop Josip Juraj Strossmayer, dominates the central square. The project was the work of the Viennese architects Karl Rösner and Friedrich von Schmidt. The imposing façade is flanked by two 84-m (275-ft) belfries. The interior has frescoes by Maksimilijan and Ljudevit Seitz, sculptures by Ignazio Donegani and Tomas Vodcka, and decorations by Giuseppe Voltolini from the 19th century. The crypt houses the tombs of the bishops Strossmayer and Ivan de Zela. Next to the church is the 18th-century Bishop's Palace, which has an ornate Baroque doorway.

The Festival of Embroidery of Đakovo (Đakovački vezovi) is held at the beginning of July with displays of traditional costumes, folk dancing and wine tasting.

Đakovo has a long-standing tradition of horse-breeding. The State Stud Farm was established here in 1506,

The towering spires *(inset)* and sumptuous interior of the Cathedral ↓ of St Peter in Đakovo

which makes it one of the oldest stud farms in Europe. Lipizzan horses have been bred at this farm since the beginning of the 18th century.

Cathedral of St Peter

🏛 Strossmayerov trg 6
🕻 (031) 802 200 ⏰ 6:30am–
noon, 3–7pm daily

⑨ Vinkovci

△G3 ✈ Osijek, 43 km
(27 miles) 🚍 (032) 308 215
🚌 (060) 332 233 **🛈** Trg
bana Josipa Šokčevića 3;
www.tz-vinkovci.hr

A settlement existed here as far back as 6000 BC; the Romans named it Aurelia Cibalae. It was the birthplace of the emperors Valens and Valentinian, and a bishop's see from the 4th century. In the Middle Ages it was called Zenthelye, because of the presence of the (now abandoned) Church of St Elias (Sv. Ilija). The 12th-century church is one of the oldest monuments in Slavonia.

The **Vinkovci Municipal Museum** (Gradski muzej), situated in the 18th-century

Façade of the Church
and Monastery of
St John of Capistrano, Ilok ↑

former Austrian barracks in the main square, holds finds from the Roman necropolis and has a folklore collection. One of the museum's most interesting exhibits is the Orion Vessel, the world's oldest Indo-European calendar. Large Roman sarcophagi are also displayed in the museum's lapidarium.

Each September a festival of music and popular traditions is held in the town and groups from all over the country take part. The streets are decorated, stallholders sell local produce, and artists perform.

Vinkovci Municipal Museum

🅐 📍Trg bana Šokčevića 16
📞(032) 332 504 🕐Jan & Feb: 9am–3pm Mon–Fri; Mar–Jul & Sep–Dec: 9am–7pm Tue–Fri, 9am–2pm Sat; Aug: 9am–3pm Tue–Fri

---

Ilok

🅰G3 🚆Osijek, 62 km (38 miles) 🚌Vukovar, 35 km (22 miles) ℹTrg Nikole Iličkog 2; www.turizamilok.hr

Overlooking a wide loop in the River Danube, Ilok is the easternmost city in Croatia

and the centre of the region of Srijem, famous since Roman times for its wine.

In the Middle Ages Ilok was a *castrum* with fortified buildings. The defences were reinforced in 1365, and the town was given to Nikola Kont, whose family later acquired the title of counts of Ilok.

Around the middle of the 15th century, the **Church and Monastery of St John of Capistrano** (Sv. Ivan Kapistran) were built inside the fort. The saint was a Franciscan famed for uniting Christian forces against the Turks; he died here in 1456. When Ilok became a major Turkish administrative and military centre in the 16th century, mosques and baths were added to the fortress.

Both the church and the monastery have been renovated and between them, long stretches of the ancient walls can still be seen.

In 1683, after his role in winning the battle of Vienna,

Commander Livio Odescalchi was given the town of Ilok by the Austrian emperor. He built a U-shaped mansion, **Odescalchi Manor**, which today houses the town's **Civic Museum** (Gradski muzej) with superbly arranged archaeological and ethnographic collections. The Old Cellars next door are some of the biggest and oldest in this part of Europe, best known for their production of a dry white wine called Traminac. The cellars are open daily for wine tastings from 10am to 9pm.

Church and Monastery of St John of Capistrano

🅐O M Barbarića 4 📞(032) 590 073 🕐By appt or before Mass

Odescalchi Manor and Civic Museum

🅐🅐🅐 📍Šetalište oca Mladena Barbarića 5 📞(032) 827 410 🕐Civic Museum: 9am–6pm Fri, 9am–3pm Tue–Thu, 11am–6pm Sat

---

VINKOVCI ORION

The Vinkovci Orion is the name given to a mysterious ceramic bowl excavated in the centre of Vinkovci in 1976 and dated to around 2600 BC. It is covered in pictograms, thought to refer to the changing seasons and the constellations of the night sky. One of the pictograms represents Orion, whose appearance marked the beginning of the spring agricultural cycle. Local archeologists believe that the bowl is Europe's earliest calendar. The original is kept in Vinkovci Municipal Museum and its beguiling icons are reproduced throughout the town, notably in the paving stones of the Trg bana Josipa Šokčevića road.

→

The Neo-Classical Pejačević Castle and its gardens in Nasice

Našice

F2 ✈**Osijek** 🚌**(060) 333 444** 🚌**(060) 334 030** 🅸**Trg dr Franje Tuđmana 4; www. tznasice.hr**

The town of Našice is set on a small plateau, surrounded by pretty vineyards and woods. Built on the site of an ancient settlement, it changed hands many times before being occupied by Turkish forces in 1532.

After the expulsion of the Turks, the Franciscans returned and restored the Church of St Anthony of Padua (Sv. Antun Padovanski). They also rebuilt their monastery, originally founded here at the start of the 14th century.

A short distance away is a 19th-century Neo-Classical manor house where the musician Dora Pejačević (1885–1923) lived. The

Did You Know?

The Romans called the Baranja region 'Vallis Aurea' (Golden Valley) because of the wine produced here.

building has been restored, and now houses the town's informative **Civic Museum**.

Civic Museum

 Trg dr. Franje Tuđmana 📞**(031) 613 414** 🚫**For restoration until spring 2023** 🆆**zmn.hr**

Batina

G2 ✈**Osijek** 🚍**From Osijek**

Located in the northeastern corner of Baranja, the small town of Batina is celebrated for the huge war memorial that looms above the Danube riverbank just north of town. It was built in 1947 to honour the Soviet Red Army, who crossed the river here in November 1944, incurring huge losses – an estimated 2,000 men in only a few days. Erected before the Yugoslav-Soviet split of 1948, it is one of the Soviet-inspired Social-Realist monuments in the country. Its centrepiece is the 20-m- (66-ft-) obelisk bearing a bronze female allegory of Victory. This sculpture is the work of one of the great Croatian artists of the 20th century, Antun Augustinčić (1900–79), and it was built between 1945 and 1947.

INSIDER TIP
To the Spa

Southeast of Valpovo, the pools of Bizovačke Toplice spa have long been popular among locals in search of a soak. The pools are fed from warm local springs, with a higher salt and mineral content than usual.

Valpovo

F2 ✈**Osijek** 🚌**(060) 390 060** 🅸**Trg kralja Tomislava 2; www.tz.valpovo.hr**

The centre of Valpovo stands on the remains of the fort of Lovallia, one of many fortified settlements established by the Romans on the Pannonian plain. In the Middle Ages, a castle was erected to keep a look-out over the nearby Drava River. This castle was later granted to the Morović, Gorjanski and Norman families. After the Turkish conquest in 1526, the castle was used as a garrison.

In 1687, after the expulsion of the Turks, the area was handed over to the Hilleprand Prandau family. At the beginning of the 19th century the castle was destroyed by fire and then extensively rebuilt

as a larger building, which today houses the **Valpovo Museum** (Muzej Valpovštine). The museum contains period furniture and interesting archaeological finds. The complex stands in a large park and a moat surrounds the medieval walls.

Valpovo Museum

🏛Dvorac Prandau-Normann 📞(031) 650 639 🕐4–7pm Mon & Thu, 10am–noon Tue, Wed & Fri

---

⑭ Virovitica

🗺E2 🚆Osijek 🚍Ulica Stjepana Radića, (033) 730 121 🚍Trg fra B Gerbera 1, (033) 721 113 🛈Trg Bana Jelačića 23; www.tz-virovitica.hr

Documents from the end of the first millennium give the town its original name of Wereuche. It was declared a free town by King Coloman in 1234 and it developed into an agricultural and trading centre. Later it fell under the rule of the Turks, until 1684.

→

Attractive street of shops in the city of Vukovar

The Baroque Church of St Roch (Sv. Rok), decorated by the sculptor Holzinger and the painter Göbler, dates from the 18th century. On the site of the ancient Wasserburg Castle stands the imposing Pejačević Manor (1800–4), now the **Civic Museum** (Gradski muzej) with archaeological and folklore collections and an art gallery.

Civic Museum

 🏛Dvorac Pejačević, Trg bana Jelačića 23 📞(033) 722 127 🕐9am–2pm Mon, 9am–7pm Tue–Fri, 10am–2pm & 4–7pm Sat 🌐muzej virovitica.hr

---

⑮ Vukovar

🗺G3 🚆Osijek 🚉Priljevo 2 🚍From Vinkovci 🛈JJ Strossmayera 15; www.turizam vukovar.hr

This Baroque city was once known for its churches, elegant 18th-century buildings, and numerous museums. However, Vukovar has come to symbolize the war that raged in Slavonia in 1991, when it was bombed by the JNA (Yugoslav People's Army) and the Serbs. Many years have been spent restoring the historic nucleus from the damage it sustained.

The Baroque Eltz family mansion was nationalized after World War II and then housed the **Vukovar Municipal Museum** (Gradski muzej Vukovar). Badly damaged in 1991, its contents were taken to Novi Sad and Belgrade, but since 2001 have been returned and gradually restored. The new permanent exhibits explore the rich archaeological history of the area, its ethnic heritage and the development of the city and the chronology of the recent war.

On the right bank of the River Danube, 4 km (3 miles) from Vukovar, stands the **Vučedol Culture Museum** (Muzej Vučedolske Kulture). The exhibition here takes you through the development of the local prehistoric culture, covering farming, fishing, hunting, handcrafts and religion. The exhibits include jewellery, ceramics, tools, the oldest Indo-European calendar and a reconstruction of a typical wattle-and-daub dwelling. Opened in 2015, the museum's building has been cleverly incorporated into the existing landscape and has won prizes for its elegant contemporary design.

Vukovar Municipal Museum

🏛Županijska 2 📞(032) 441 270 🕐10am–6pm Tue–Sun

Vučedol Culture Museum

🏛Vučedol 252 🕐10am–6pm Tue–Sun 🌐vucedol.hr

NEED TO KNOW

Boats moored in a Dalmatian marina

BEFORE
YOU GO

Things change, so plan ahead to make the most of your trip. Be prepared for all eventualities by considering the following points before you travel.

AT A GLANCE

CURRENCY
Croatian
Kuna (HRK)

AVERAGE DAILY SPEND

SAVE
400Kn

SPEND
900Kn

SPLURGE
1500+Kn

BOTTLED WATER
8Kn

COFFEE
15Kn

BEER
17Kn

DINNER FOR TWO
400Kn

ESSENTIAL PHRASES

Hello	Bok
Thank you	Hvala
Please	Molim
Goodbye	Zbogom
Do you speak English?	Govorite li engleski
I don't understand	Ja ne razumijem

ELECTRICITY SUPPLY

Power sockets are type F, fitting two-pronged plugs. Standard voltage is 230 volts.

Passports and Visas

For entry requirements, including visas, consult your nearest Croatian embassy or check the **Ministry of Foreign and European Affairs** website. UK and EU nationals and citizens of the US, Canada, Australia and New Zealand do not need a visa for a stay of up to 3 months.
Ministry of Foreign and European Affairs
W mvep.hr

Government Advice

Now more than ever, it is important to consult both your and the Croatian government's advice before travelling. Visitors can get up-to-date travel safety information from the **UK Foreign and Commonwealth Office**, the **US State Department**, and the **Australian Department of Foreign Affairs and Trade**.
Australia
W smartraveller.gov.au
UK
W gov.uk/foreign-travel-advice
US
W travel.state.gov

Customs Information

You can find information on the laws relating to goods and currency taken in or out of Croatia on the **Ministry of Finance Customs Administration** website.
Ministry of Finance Customs Administration
W carina.gov.hr

Insurance

We recommend that you take out a comprehensive insurance policy covering theft, loss of belongings, medical care, cancellations and delays, and read the small print very carefully.

UK citizens are eligible for free emergency medical care in Croatia provided they have a valid European Health Insurance Card (**EHIC**) or Global Health Insurance Card (**GHIC**). Visitors from outside the EU must arrange their own private medical insurance.

EHIC
W ec.europa.eu
GHIC
W ghic.org.uk

Vaccinations

No inoculations are needed for travellers visiting Croatia.

Booking Accommodation

Croatia offers a wide variety of accommodation to suit any budget. Prices are often inflated during peak season (July and August), and lodgings along the coast tend to fill up, so it's essential to book well in advance.

Money

Major credit, debit and prepaid currency cards are accepted in many shops and restaurants, but certainly not all. Contactless payments are becoming more widely accepted but it is always advisable to carry some cash. Cash machines are widespread in towns and cities; less so in rural areas. A tip of 5–10 per cent is customary if service is particularly good.

Travellers with Specific Requirements

The old cobbled streets and ancient buildings of the majority of Croatia's towns and cities, along with its hilly countryside, are ill-equipped for visitors with limited mobility. Many sights do not have wheelchair access or lifts, however the situation is improving; some transport terminals in big cities are now wheelchair-friendly and public toilets at bus stations, train stations, airports and large public venues are usually wheelchair-accessible.

Travelling to the islands requires forward planning. Wheelchair access to the smaller ferries and catamarans is problematic due to their narrow gangways, so you should enquire at the ticket desk as to which vessels are accessible.

Specific resources for sight-impaired and hearing-impaired travellers are rare, but the **Association of Organizations of Disabled People in Croatia** and **Hsuti** both provide useful information.

Association of Organizations of Disabled People in Croatia
W soih.hr
Hsuti
W hsuti.hr

Language

Croatian is the official language. English is commonly spoken and Italian and German are also widely used. Outside large towns you may encounter staff who have basic English or German. Italian is officially the second language in Istria.

Opening Hours

COVID-19 Increased rates of infection may result in temporary opening hours and/or closures. Always check ahead before visiting museums, attractions and hospitality venues.

Mondays Museums and attractions are closed.
Weekends Many shops and small businesses close at 2pm on Saturdays and all day Sunday.
Public holidays Schools, post offices and banks are closed for the entire day. Shops are normally closed, while museums and attractions usually remain open.

PUBLIC HOLIDAYS	
1 Jan	New Year's Day
6 Jan	Epiphany
Mar/Apr	Easter Sunday
Mar/Apr	Easter Monday
1 May	Labour Day
30 May	Statehood Day
Jun	Corpus Christi
22 Jun	Day of Antifascist Resistance
5 Aug	Thanksgiving Day
15 Aug	Assumptio Day
8 Oct	Independence Day
1 Nov	All Sants' Day
18 Nov	Vukovar Remembrance Day
25 Dec	Christmas Day
26 Dec	St Stephen's Day

GETTING AROUND

Forward planning is essential for any successful trip. Prepare yourself for any eventuality by brushing up on the following points before you set off.

PUBLIC TRANSPORT COSTS

ZAGREB

10Kn

Single bus or tram journey in city centre

DUBROVNIK

12Kn

Single bus journey in city centre

SPLIT

11Kn

Single bus journey in city centre

SPEED LIMIT

EXPRESS ROADS

110 km/h (70 mph)

RURAL ROADS

90 km/h (56 mph)

MOTORWAYS

130 km/h (80 mph)

URBAN AREAS

50 km/h (30 mph)

Arriving by Air

Croatia's most important airports are Zagreb, Zadar, Split and Dubrovnik. These are all served by national carriers as well as many budget airlines such as Ryanair and easyJet. In addition there are hundreds of charter flights in the summer months. Zagreb is connected to many European capitals year-round; flights to other destinations in Croatia are seasonal. Croatia Airlines is the country's flag carrier, linking Croatia with many destinations across Europe.

Train Travel

Due to Croatia's terrain, the rail network isn't as developed as its European counterparts, and trains mainly run inland rather than along the coast. As a rule, trains are less frequent and more prone to delays than buses but they are arguably more comfortable, and are particularly popular with those interrailing around Europe.

International Train Travel

There are at least daily rail services to Zagreb from several European cities, particularly those in neighbouring countries. Flying is cheaper when coming from further afield, especially in low season. You can buy tickets and passes for international journeys via **Eurail** and **Interrail**.
Eurail
W eurail.com
Interrail
W interrail.eu

Domestic Train Travel

There are two main types of domestic trains in Croatia. The first is passenger, or *putnički*, which is generally slow and stops at numerous stations. The second is intercity, or ICN, which is faster and more expensive as a result. The entire network is run by **Croatian Railways** and tickets should be purchased at the station before boarding the train; tickets purchased on board might incur a surcharge. It's also worth asking if you're eligible for any kind of discount.
Croatian Railways
W hzpp.hr

GETTING TO AND FROM THE AIRPORT

Airport	Distance to City	Taxi Fare	Public Transport	Journey Time
Brač	15 km (9 miles)	150Kn	none	25 mins
Dubrovnik	20 km (12 miles)	260Kn	bus	30 mins
Osijek	18 km (11 miles)	100Kn	none	20 mins
Pula	8 km (5 miles)	120Kn	bus	15 mins
Rijeka	31 km (19 miles)	255Kn	bus	40 mins
Split	23 km (14 miles)	220Kn	bus	30 mins
Zadar	11 km (7 miles)	220Kn	bus	20 mins
Zagreb	17 km (10 miles)	155Kn	bus	25 mins

ROAD JOURNEY PLANNER

This useful map will help you plan your journey around Croatia. Be aware that there are tolls on Croatia's motorways and that any route north out of Dubrovnik passes through a tiny stretch of Bosnia where there are full passport and customs checks.

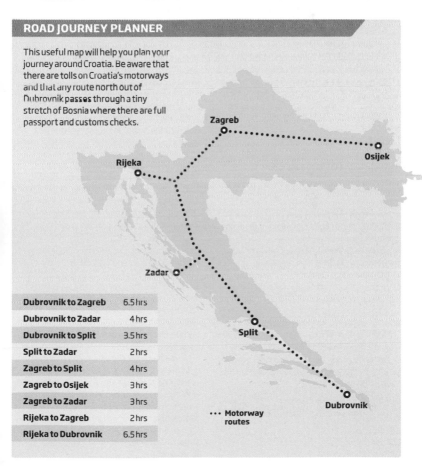

Dubrovnik to Zagreb	6.5 hrs
Dubrovnik to Zadar	4 hrs
Dubrovnik to Split	3.5 hrs
Split to Zadar	2 hrs
Zagreb to Split	4 hrs
Zagreb to Osijek	3 hrs
Zagreb to Zadar	3 hrs
Rijeka to Zagreb	2 hrs
Rijeka to Dubrovnik	6.5 hrs

··· Motorway routes

Zagreb

Osijek

Rijeka

Zadar

Split

Dubrovnik

Public Transport

The transport system within Croatia is efficient. Connections to the islands are good and, thanks to an extensive bus network, small towns can be easily reached. Many historic centres are fairly compact and can be easily covered on foot.

When planning a journey the best place to start is the website of the transport company for the town or province you are in. In Zagreb this is **Autobusni kolodvor Zagreb**. Public transport in the Split region is provided by **Promet Autobusni kolodvor**. Safety and hygiene measures, ticket information, timetables, transport maps and more can be obtained online.

Autobusni kolodvor Zagreb
Ⓦ zet.hr

Promet Autobusni kolodvor (Split)
Ⓦ promet-split.hr

Buses and Trams

Croatia's buses are a reliable way to get around and ticket prices are generally in line with the rest of Europe. Tickets are normally bought at the bus station before departure, although you can buy tickets from a newstand *(tisak)*. It is wise to buy well in advance in the summer months, especially on busy routes out of Dubrovnik, Split and Zadar. If travelling to the islands by bus, your ticket includes the ferry.

Zagreb and Osijek have tram systems. Tickets can be purchased at a *tisak* or from the driver. Validation machines are found on board.

Long-Distance Bus Travel

International coaches connect Croatia with the rest of Europe. There are regular services from major German cities to Zagreb and coastal cities, covering the stretch from Rijeka to Split. Many Italian cities are also connected to Zagreb by coach. **Arriva Udine** runs services four times a day in the summer, and twice in winter, from Trieste to Pula. From Trieste you can also get to Rijeka by a coach that runs four times a day. **Eurolines** and **Flixbus** also run various services into Croatia with the occasional coach from the UK, though journey times are long. Suitcases and larger rucksacks will need to go into the luggage storage compartments below the bus, and these are likely to incur a surcharge.

Croatia's domestic coach services are divided into intercity, which offer direct connections between the larger cities, and regional services, which provide connections between the smaller towns and the main cities.

Arriva Udine
Ⓦ arrivaudine.it

Eurolines
Ⓦ eurolines.hr

Flixbus
Ⓦ flixbus.hr

Taxis

Taxis can be booked by phone or found at designated taxi ranks outside hotels or stations in Croatia's larger cities. Only accept rides in licensed, metered taxis and always confirm the price with the driver before getting in. It's generally expected that passengers will round up the final metered price in place of a tip.

Ferries

With so many islands, ferries constitute a major part of Croatia's infrastructure. They make the islands accessible from the mainland while also cutting journey times by road. Ferry tickets can be bought in advance online or at the port.

The majority of ferries and catamarans are run by the state-owned company **Jadrolinija**. These ferries transport passengers and vehicles. Timetables and fare information can be found online. Note that some ferries only run in summer. **Krilo** operates fast catamarans between Split and Dubrovnik during summer only, with stops at several islands en route.

Croatia's public ferry network is divided into five districts: Rijeka, Zadar, Šibenik, Split and Dubrovnik. In the Rijeka district, Cres and Lošinj are connected to the mainland by the Valbiska–Merag and Brestova–Porozina routes. There is also a ferry running from Rijeka to Mali Lošinj, with stops at Cres, Unije and Susak en route. The island of Rab is connected to the coast by the Stinica–Mišnjak route and with the island of Krk by the Lopar–Valbiska route. The island of Pag is connected to the coast by the Prizna–Žigljen route, while Novalja on Pag is connected to Rijeka with a stop at Rab Town en route.

In the district of Zadar, there are connections to the cities of Preko, on the island of Ugljan, Bribinj and Zaglav, on the island of Dugi Otok and from Biograd to Tkon on the island of Pašman.

In the district of Šibenik, Šibenik town is connected to the islands of Zlarin and Prvić.

In the Split district there are connections between Split and the islands of Brač (Supetar), Korčula (Vela Luka and Korčula Town), Hvar (to Starigrad and Hvar Town), Šolta (Rogač), Vis (to the port of the same name) and Lastovo (to Ubli). There are connections between Makarska and Sumartin (island of Brač), between Ploče and Trpanj on the Pelješac peninsula, between Orebić and Dominče (on the island of Korčula) and between Drvenik and Sućuraj (on Hvar).

In the district of Dubrovnik, the main connection is between Dubrovnik and the island of Mljet (Sobra), while there are also small ferries running between Dubrovnik and the Elaphite islands of Koločep, Lopud and Šipan.

Jadrolinija
Ⓦ jadrolinija.hr

Krilo
Ⓦ krilo.hr

Driving

Croatia has some stunning stretches of road so it's worth seeing the country by car. A driving licence issued by an EU country is valid. If visiting from outside the EU, you may need to apply for an International Driving Permit. Check with your local automobile association before you travel.

Emergency road services are provided by the local automobile club **HAK**, which can be reached 24 hours a day by dialling 1987. The service offers repairs (a charge will apply) on the spot or in a garage (subject to transport), the removal of damaged cars and transport up to 100 km (62 miles) distance. HAK also provides useful information on road and maritime traffic, motor-way tolls, any temporary diversions, fuel prices, approximate waiting times at borders, possible alternative routes and general assistance for those travelling by car.

Service stations are open daily from 7am to 7 or 8pm, but in summer they are often open until 10pm. On the main roads in the larger towns and cities and on major international routes service stations are open 24 hours a day

HAK
W hak.hr

Rules of the Road

Cars drive on the right-hand-side of the road and safety belts should be worn in both the front and back seats. Children under 12 must sit in the back. Cars towing caravans must not exceed 80 kmph (50 mph). Road signs are generally more or less identical to those found in the rest of Europe. Note that it is illegal to drive with more than 0.5 per cent blood alcohol limit in the blood.

Car Rental

Car hire firms such as **Avis**, **Hertz** and **Sixt Rent-a-Car** can be found at airports and railway stations. Drivers need to produce their passport, driving licence and a credit card with enough capacity to cover the excess. Most rental agencies require drivers to be over the age of 21 and to have an international licence. Book online in advance for the best deals. Beware hidden charges levied by small local companies.

Avis
W avis.com.hr
Hertz
W hertz.hr
Sixt Rent-a-Car
W sixt.co.uk

Parking

As elsewhere in Europe, car parking is an ever-increasing problem in most Croatian cities. Likewise, in many smaller coastal towns, parking is much reduced, with seafront promenades closed to traffic through the summer season. Where indicated, a parking ticket must be clearly displayed inside the windscreen. If you park in a no-parking area, your vehicle can be forcibly removed by officials.

Some hotels have parking spaces reserved for guests. If you are travelling by car it is worth checking this in advance.

Roads and Tolls

Croatia's motorways are regarded as among the safest in Europe. There are plans to extend the motorway further down the coast to Dubrovnik. On certain stretches drivers pay a toll (by cash or credit card). There is also a toll for the bridge to the island of Krk and the Učka Tunnel.

Bicycle

Hilly Dubrovnik and crowded Split are far from ideal destinations for the urban cyclist. It is a very different story on the islands. With easy cycling in the coastal towns, wellmarked trails in the hinterland, and plenty of places to rent bikes from, Croatia's islands are ideal for bikes.

Walking and Hiking

With a vast network of clearly way-marked footpaths both on the coast and further inland, Croatia is a fantastic destination for walkers and hikers. Rural areas are fairly easy to reach and weather is generally pleasant. Ensure you have good hiking boots, plenty of water, a map and a compass – and stick to your route. Tell someone where you're going and when you plan to return.

Walking is also an enjoyable way to explore compact city centres such as Dubrovnik, Split and Zagreb, where most of the key sites are within a short distance of one another.

FERRIES FROM ITALY

Jadrolinija
This Croatian company runs overnight ferry services between Ancona and Split, Ancona and Zadar and Bari and Dubrovnik *(www.jadrolinija.hr)*.

SNAV
This Italian company operates over night ferries between Ancona and Split, running from mid-June to late September *(www.snav.com)*.

Venezia Lines
High-speed catamarans link the Northern Adriatic towns of Poreč, Rovinj, Pula and Rabac with Venice *(www.venezialines.com)*.

PRACTICAL
INFORMATION

A little local know-how goes a long way in Croatia. Here you will find all the essential advice and information you will need during your stay.

AT A GLANCE

EMERGENCY NUMBERS

GENERAL EMERGENCY	POLICE
112	**192**

FIRE SERVICE	EMERGENCY AT SEA
193	**195**

TIME ZONE
CET/CEST
Central European Summer Time (CEST) runs 31 Mar–27 Oct 2019

TAP WATER
Unless otherwise stated, tap water in Croatia is safe to drink.

WEBSITES AND APPS

National Tourist Board
Check out Croatia's national tourist board for useful travel tips and advice (www.croatia.hr).

Central Dalmatia
If you are visiting this region the Split-Dalmatia County Tourist Board is a great resource (www.dalmatia.hr).

Zagreb Airport
Keep up-to-date with arrivals and departures online (www.zagreb-airport.hr).

Personal Security

Croatia's crime rate is low. There is little street crime, although visitors should take the usual precautions in busy places to protect valuables from pickpockets – particularly on public transport or in busy tourist areas. It is worth using a money belt or other means of hiding your money and documents.

While the country holds conservative Catholic values, Croatians are generally accepting of all people, regardless of their race, gender or sexuality. Homosexuality was legalized in Croatia in 1977, and in 2015 Croatia was rated 5th in terms of LGBTQ+ rights out of 49 European countries. Gay venues can mainly be found in Zagreb and there are same-sex beaches in Hvar, Lokrum, Rovinj and Poreč. Zagreb has its own Gay Pride Day, which is gaining more attention every year. However, despite the many freedoms the LGBTQ+ community enjoy in Croatia, acceptance is not always a given. Rural communities may be less tolerant of public displays of affection and same-sex couples travelling together. If you do at any point feel unsafe, the **Safe Space Alliance** pinpoints your nearest place of refuge.

Visitors should be aware that de-mining along former lines of confrontation inland is not yet complete. As a result, travellers should not stray from known safe routes in these zones.
Safe Space Alliance
w safespacealliance.com

Health

Croatia's public health services meet the high standards of those elsewhere in Europe. Tourists run no serious health risks, though they should be careful to avoid over-exposure to the sun.

Emergency medical care in Croatia is free for all UK and EU citizens. If you have an EHIC or GHIC (p252), present this as soon as possible. You may have to pay after treatment and reclaim the money later.

For those visiting from other areas, payment of medical expenses is the patient's responsibility. As such it is important to arrange comprehensive

medical insurance before travelling. If your travel plans include extreme sporting activities, such as rock climbing and some water sports, make sure the policy covers rescue services.

Seek medicinal supplies and advice for minor ailments from a pharmacy (ljekarna), which can be identified by the green cross above the door. Pharmacies are usually open all day (8am to 8pm) or in the morning or afternoon, depending on the day. Although it is easy to find all the more common over-the-counter medicines in pharmacies without too much difficulty, it is best to carry an adequate supply of any prescription medicines you may need. Some medicines are not known by the commercial names given to them in their country of origin, but by the active ingredients contained in them. It is useful if you can produce a prescription issued by your own doctor as proof that you are authorized to take a particular medicine.

Smoking, Alcohol and Drugs

Croatia has a strict smoking ban in all enclosed public spaces as well as open ones such as bus stations and stadiums. The fine for smoking where you shouldn't is 1,000Kn. There is a strict 0.5 per cent blood-alcohol limit for drivers

ID

It's a good idea for visitors to carry ID, especially if driving. If you are stopped by the police and don't have your passport with you, the police may escort you to wherever it is being kept so that you can show it to them.

Local Customs

Croatians are generally fairly conservative. Noisy or drunken behaviour is frowned upon. Some towns in Croatia now have local laws about how tourists should behave. For example, Zadar, Split, Hvar Town and Dubrovnik have ruled that people cannot walk around the cities in swimwear without incurring a fine.

The conflict of the 1990s is still very recent, and many locals were affected. Some may wish to discuss it, while others will not. Do not force the matter. Read up before you go, and treat the subject sensitively. Note that many Croatians don't appreciate it being called a "civil war".

Visiting Places of Worship

It is advisable to dress respectfully when visiting places of worship: cover your torso and upper arms, and ensure shorts and skirts cover knees. Hats should be removed.

Mobile Phones and Wi-Fi

Wi-Fi hotspots are widely available in big cities like Zadar, Dubrovnik and Zagreb. Cafés and restaurants are usually happy to permit the use of their Wi-Fi on the condition that you make a purchase. Wi-Fi is free in most hotels. Visitors from the EU can use their devices abroad without being affected by data roaming charges.

Post

The national postal company **HP** operates a network of post offices, with branches in all towns. If you are sending ordinary post, stamps (marke) can also be bought at a newsagents. Note that unless airmail is specifically requested, postcards and letters will be sent overland. Letters and cards can be posted at post offices or the roadside yellow post boxes. Post offices are open 7am–7pm Monday–Friday, and to 1pm Saturday. In summer, some post offices in tourist resorts extend their opening times until 10pm.
HP
W posta.hr

Taxes and Refunds

VAT ranges between 13 per cent and 25 per cent. Non-EU residents are entitled to a tax refund on purchases over 740Kn. To make a claim you must request a tax receipt and export papers when you purchase goods. Then, when leaving the country, present these papers, along with the receipt and your ID.

Discount Cards

Discount cards are not common in Croatia. An International Student Identity Card is the best proof of age for those under 26, while the **European Youth Card Association** offers discounts at selected shops, restaurants and sights.
European Youth Card Associaion
W eyca.orf

INDEX

Page numbers in **bold** refer to main entries.

PHRASE BOOK

PRONOUNCIATION

c – "ts" as in rats
č – "chi" as in church
ć – "t" is a soft t
đ – "d" is a soft d
g – "g" is a hard g as in get
j – "y" as in yes
š – sh
ž – shown here as "zh", sounds like the "J" in the French name, Jacques
"aj" – shown here as "igh", sounds like "I" or the "igh" in night.

IN EMERGENCY

Help!	Pomoć!	pomoch
Stop!	Stani!	stahnee
Call a doctor!	Zovite doktora!	zoveetey doktorah
Call an ambulance!	Zovite hitnu pomoć!	zoveetey heetnoo pomoch
Call the police!	Zovite policiju!	zoveetey poleetseeyoo
Call the fire brigade!	Zovite vatrogasce!	zoveetey vatrohgastsay
Where is the nearest telephone?	Gdje je najbliži telefon?	gdyey yey n-igh-bleezhee telefon
Where is the nearest hospital?	Gdje je najbliža bolnica?	gdyey yey n-igh-bleezhah bolnitsa

COMMUNICATION ESSENTIALS

Yes	da	dah
No	ne	ney
Please	molim vas	moleem vas
Thank you	hvala	hvahlah
Excuse me	oprostite	oprosteetey
Hello	dobar dan	dobar dan
Goodbye	dovidenja	doveedjenya
Goodnight	laku noc	lakoo noch
Morning	jutro	yootroh
Afternoon	popodne	popodney
Evening	večer	vecher
Yesterday	jučer	yoocher
Today	danas	danas
Tomorrow	sutra	sootrah
Here	tu	too
There	tamo	tahmoh
What?	što?	shtoh
When?	kada?	kada
Why?	zašto?	zashtoh
Where?	gdje?	gdyey

USEFUL PHRASES

How are you?	Kako ste?	kakoh stey
Very well, thank you	Dobro, hvala	dobroh, hvahlah
Pleased to meet you	Drago mi je!	dragoh mee yey
See you soon	Vidimo se	veedeemoh sey
That's fine	U redu	oo redoo
Where is/are...?	Gdje je/su?	gdyey yey/soo
How far is it to...?	Koliko je daleko do...?	kolikoh yey dalekoh doh...
How can I get to...?	Kako mogu doći do...?	kakoh mogoo dochee doh...
Do you speak English?	Govorite li engleski?	govoreetey lee engleskee
I don't understand	Ne razumijem	nay razoomeeyem
Could you speak more slowly please?	Molim vas, možete li govoriti sporije?	moleem vas, mozhetey lee govoreetey sporiyey
I'm sorry	Žao mi je	zhaoh mee yey

USEFUL WORDS

big	veliko	veleekoh
small	malo	mahloh
hot	vruć	vrooch
cold	hladan	hlahdan
good	dobar	dobar
bad	loš	losh
enough	dosta	dostah
well	dobro	dobroh

open	otvoreno	otvohrenoh
closed	zatvoreno	zatvohrenoh
left	lijevo	leeyevoh
right	desno	desnoh
straighton	ravno	ravnoh
near	blizu	bleezoo
far	daleko	dalekoh
up	gore	gorey
down	dolje	dolyey
early	rano	ranoh
late	kasno	kasnoh
entrance	ulaz	oolaz
exit	izlaz	eezlaz
toilet	WC	Veytsey
more	više	veeshey
less	manje	manyey

SHOPPING

How much does this cost?	Koliko ovo košta?	kolikoh ovoh koshta
I would like...	Volio bih...	volioh bee...
Do you have...?	Imate li...?	eematey lee...
I'm just looking	Samo gledam	Samoh gledam
Do you take credit cards?	Primate li kreditne kartice?	preematey lee credeetney carteetsey
What time do you open?	Kad otvarate?	kad otvaratey
What time do you close?	Kad zatvarate?	kad zatvaratey
This one	Ovaj	ov-igh
That one	Onaj	on-igh
expensive	skupo	skoopoh
cheap	jeftino	yefteenoh
size (clothes)	veličina	veleechinah
size (shoes)	broj	broy
white	bijelo	beeyeloh
black	crno	tsrnoh
red	crveno	tsrvenoh
yellow	žuto	zhootoh
green	zeleno	zelenoh
blue	plavo	plavoh
bakery	pekara	pekarah
bank	banka	bankah
books hop	knjižara	knyeezharah
butcher's	mesnica	mesnitsah
cakes hop	slastičarna	slasteecharnah
chemist's	apoteka	apohtekah
fishmonger's	ribarnica	reebarnitsah
market	tržnica	trzhneetsah
hair dresser's	frizer	freezer
news agent's/ tobacconist	trafika	trafeekah
post office	pošta	poshtah
shoe shop	prodavaonica cipela	prodavaonitsa tseepelah
supermarket	supermarket	soopermarket
travel agent	putnička agencija	pootneechka agentseeyah

SIGHTSEEING

art gallery	galerija umjetnina	galereeyah oomyetneenah
cathedral	katedrala	katedralah
church	crkva	tsrkvah
garden	vrt	vurt
library	knjižnica	knyeezhneetsah
museum	muzej	moozey
tourist information centre	turistički ured	tooreesteechkey oored
town hall	gradska vijećnica	gradskah veeyechneetsa
closed for holiday	zatvoreno zbog praznika	zatvorenoh zbog praznikah
bus station	autobusni kolodvor	aootoboosnee kolodvor
railway station	željeznički kolodvor	zhelyeznichkih kolodvor

STAYING IN A HOTEL

Do you have a vacant room?	Imate li sobu?	eematey lee soboo
double room	dvokrevetna soba	dvokrevetnah sobah

single room	**jednokrevetna soba**	**yed**nokrevetnah sobah
room with a bath	**soba sa kupatilom**	**sobah** sah koopateelom
shower	**tuš**	toosh
porter	**portir**	portir
key	**ključ**	klyooch
I have a reservation	**Imam rezervaciju**	**ee**mam rezervatseeyoo

EATING OUT

Have you got a table for...?	**Imate li stol za...?**	**ee**matey lee stol zah
I want to reserve a table	**Želim rezervirati stol**	**Zhe**leem rezer**vee**ratee stol
The bill please	**Molim vas, račun**	**mo**leem vas, **ra**choon
I am a vegetarian	**Jasam vegeterijanac**	**yah**sam vegetereeyanats
waiter/waitress	**konobar/ konobarica**	**kono**bar/ **kono**baritsah
menu	**jelovnik**	**yel**ovneek
wine list	**vinska karta**	**veen**skah kartah
glass	**čaša**	**chash**ah
bottle	**boca**	**bot**sah
knife	**nož**	nozh
fork	**viljuška**	**veel**yooshkah
spoon	**žlica**	**zhlee**etsah
breakfast	**doručak**	**do**roochak
lunch	**ručak**	**roo**chak
dinner	*večera*	**ve**cherah
main course	**glavno jelo**	**glav**noh yeloh
starters	**predjela**	**pred**yelah

MENU DECODER

bijela riba	**bee**yelah reebah	"white" fish
blitva	**bleet**vah	Swiss chard
brudet	**broo**det	fish stew
čevapčići	che**vap**cheechee	meatballs
crni rižot	**tsrn**ee reezhot	black risotto (prepared with cuttlefish ink)
desert	**des**ert	dessert
glavno jelo	**glav**noh yeloh	main course
grah	grah	beans
gulaš	**goo**lash	goulash
jastog	**yas**tog	lobster
juha	**yoo**hah	soup
kuhano	**koo**hanoh	cooked
maslinovo ulje	**mas**leenovoh **oo**lyey	olive oil
meso na žaru	**mes**oh nah zharoo	barbecued meat
miješano meso	mee**yesh**anoh **mes**oh	mixed grilled meats
na žaru	nah zharoo	barbecued
ocat	**ot**sat	vinegar
palačinke	pala**cheen**kay	pancakes
papar	**pap**ar	pepper
paški sir	**pash**kih seer	sheep's cheese from Pag
pečeno	**pech**enoh	baked
piletina	**pee**leteenah	chicken
plava riba	**plav**ah reebah	"blue" fish
predjelo	**pred**yelnh	starters
prilog	**pree**log	side dish
pršut	**pr**shoot	smoked ham
pržene lignje	**pr**zhene **leeg**nyey	fried squid
prženo	**pr**zhenoh	fried
ramsteak	**ram**steyk	rump steak
ražnjići	razh**nyee**echee	pork kebabs
riba na žaru	**reeb**ah nah zharoo	barbecued fish
rižot frutti di mare	**reez**hot **froo**tee dee **mar**ey	seafood risotto
rižot sa škampima	**reez**hot sa **shkam**peemah	scampi risotto
salata	**sal**atah	salad
salata od hobotnice	**sal**atah od **ho**botneetsey	octopus salad
sarma	**sar**mah	cabbage leaves
sir	seer	cheese
sladoled	**sla**doled	ice cream
slana srdela	**slan**ah **srd**elah	salted sardines
škampi na buzaru	**shkam**pee nah **boo**zaroo	scampi in tomato and onion

školjke na buzaru	**shkol**kay nah **boo**zaroo	shellfish in tomato and onion
špageti frutti di mare	**shpag**etee **froo**tee dee **mar**ey	spaghetti with seafood
sol	sol	salt
tjestenina	**tjest**eneenah	pasta stuffed with meatandrice
ulje	**oo**lyey	oil
varivo	**var**eevoh	boiled vegetables

DRINKS

bijelovino	**bee**yeloh **vee**noh	white wine
čaj	ch-igh	tea
crno vino	**tsrn**oh **vee**noh	red wine
gazirana mineralna voda	**gaz**eeranah **meen**eralnah **vod**ah	sparkling mineral water
kava	**kav**ah	coffee
negazirana mineralna voda	**ney**gazeeranah **meen**eralnah **vod**ah	still mineral water
pivo	**pee**voh	beer
rakija	**rak**eeyah	spirit
tamno pivo	**tam**noh **pee**voh	stout (dark beer)
travarica	**trav**areetsah	spirit flavoured with herbs
voda	**vod**ah	water

NUMBERS

0	**nula**	**noo**lah
1	**jedan**	**ye**dan
2	**dva**	dvah
3	**tri**	tree
4	**četiri**	che**tee**ree
5	**pet**	pet
6	**šest**	shest
7	**sedam**	**sed**am
8	**osam**	**os**am
9	**devet**	**dev**et
10	**deset**	**des**et
11	**jedanaest**	**yed**anest
12	**dvanaest**	**dvah**nest
13	**trinaest**	**tree**nest
14	**četrnaest**	**chetr**nest
15	**petnaest**	**pet**nest
16	**šestnaest**	**shest**nest
17	**sedamnaest**	**sed**amnest
18	**osamnaest**	**os**amnest
19	**devetnaest**	**dev**etnest
20	**dvadeset**	**dvah**deset
21	**dvadesetijedan**	**dvah**desetee yedan
22	**dvadesetidva**	**dvah**deseteedvah
30	**trideset**	**tree**deset
31	**tridesetijedan**	**tree**deseteeyedan
40	**četrdeset**	**chetr**deset
50	**pedeset**	**ped**eset
60	**šezdeset**	**shez**deset
70	**sedamdeset**	**sed**amdeset
80	**osamdeset**	**os**amdeset
90	**devedeset**	**dev**edeset
100	**sto**	stoh
101	**stoijedan**	**sto**heeyedan
102	**stoidva**	**sto**heedvah
200	**dvjesto**	**dvee**stoh
500	**petsto**	**pet**stoh
700	**sedamsto**	**sed**amstoh
900	**devetsto**	**dev**etstoh
1,000	**tisuću**	**tee**soochoo
1,001	**tisućuijedan**	**tee**soochoo eeyedan

TIME

One minute	**jedna minuta**	**yed**na meenootah
One hour	**jedan sat**	**yed**an saht
Half an hour	**pola sata**	**pol**ah sahtah
Monday	**ponedjeljak**	pone**dyel**yak
Tuesday	**utorak**	**oo**torak
Wednesday	**srijeda**	**sree**jedah
Thursday	**četvrtak**	**chetv**rtak
Friday	**petak**	**pet**ak
Saturday	**subota**	**soo**botah
Sunday	**nedjelja**	**ned**yelyah

ACKNOWLEDGMENTS

DK would like to thank the following for their contribution to the previous editions: Jonathan Bousfield, Marc Di Duca, Jane Foster

The publisher would like to thank the following for their kind permission to reproduce their photographs:

Key: a-above; b-below/bottom; c-centre; f-far; l-left; r-right; t-top

123RF.com:
Ilijaa 228tl; Mato Papic 245tr.

4Corners:
Lucie Debelkova 128t; Justin Foulkes 86–7b.

Alamy Stock Photo:
AF archive 46bl; AGE Fotostock 22crb, 31cl; allOver images 34tr 43b, 50–51t, 50–51b; Giuseppe Anello 166tl; Archive PL 101tr; ART Collection 56tl; Artokoloro Quint Lox Limited 57bl; Ilija Ascic 21bl, 200–201, 222b, 234–5; Zvonimir Atletić 200cra, 209tr, 233b; Aurora Photos 48crb; Joachim Bago 137br; Nedim Bajramovic 77br; Dario Bajurin 230t; Ivica Batinic 112tl; Dalibor Brlek 78t, 144–5b, 152br, 188–9b, 223tr; Daniella Cesarei 115br; Chronicle 55cra; Emanuele Ciccomartino 40-1b; Ivan Coric 18tl, 116–17, 138–9b, 194–5t; dbimages 92–3t; dleiva 72bl; DOD Photo 59tr; DPA Picture Alliance 58cla; dreamer4787 122–3b; Rainer Drexel 32b; John Elk III 126clb, 233clb; Eye35 8–9b, 73br; Falkensteinfoto 54crb; FL Historical 1D 58br; Funkyfood London - Paul Williams 140–41t, 179tr, 182br, 215br; Ian Furniss 51cl; Janos Gaspar 37cr; Dubravko Grakalic 58clb, 230bl; Alen Gurovic 52tl, 53clb, 205tr, 241t; Terry Harris 161bl; Juergen Hasenkopf 38tl; Hemis 4, 39t, 204t, 205br; hemis.fr / Bertrand Rieger 45crb, / Fabien Olart 220t; Heritage Image Partnership Ltd 56–7t, 58tl; James Hodgson 243cra; Peter Horree 89br; Dragan Ilic 228clb; imageBROKER 32–3t, 153t, 190tl; Interfoto 58cb; Ivica Jandrijević 34b, 211b, 226br, 227b, 238t; Dave Jepson 200bl; Jevgenija 154cl; John Warburton-Lee Photography 151bl; Jon Arnold Images Ltd 60-61; Bjanka Kadic 43cl, 78cl, 210tl, 240bl; Věra Kailová 192b; Matej Kastelic 162–3b; Pawel Kazmierczak 31tr; John Kellerman 75tr; Gunter Kirsch 215tl; Larum Stock 121cra; Constantino Leite 51br; Andrew Lloyd 49br; LOOK Die Bildagentur der Fotografen GmbH 160t; Blazej Lyjak 49cl; Nino Marcutti 37cla, 56cr, 74–5b, 114t, 189tr, 190–191b, 202b, 213tr; 226tl; Borislav Marinic 142bl; Igor Markov 224–5; Stefano Politi Markovina 53crb; Itsik Marom 141br; Mauritius Images

Gmbh 28clb, 33clb, 42–3t, 203tr; Mezzotint_Alamy 49t; Hilary Morgan 201crb; Muddymari 76t; Nikreates 89cr, 106–107b, 111br; Samantha Ohlsen 52cr; Panther Media GmbH 95tr; Sanela Plisko 47cr, 53cl; Sebastijan Polak 91t; Emil Pozar 52tr; Paul Prescott 42bl; Peter Ptschelinzew 24cl, 212–13b; Alex Ramsay 27tr, 163tr; Robertharding 68tr, 84t, 143tr; DE ROCKER 178bl; Boaz Rottem 30cra; Denis Rozhnovsky 28cl; Rudi1976 24t; Goran Šafarek 35cl, 157br, 195br, 242–3t, 243clb, 243bc; Andrej Safaric 26cr; Sensi Images 168cra; Antony Souter 52crb; Really Easy Star / Toni Spagone 130bc, 131b, 133cla, 133cra; Martin Strmiska 12clb; Luka Tambaca 143cra, 169tr; The History Collection 228bc, 228br; The Picture Art Collection 228cb; TravelCollection 24bl; Travelfile 93crb, 192–3tr; Eye Ubiquitous 52clb; Učka ti materina 157clb; UtCon Collection 157tr; Janez Volmajer 186t; Wanderworldimages 134br; Wenn UK 41cb, 46–7t, 47cl, 52cl; Tim E White 212tl; Jan Wlodarczyk 28t; 106tl; Xinhua 33cl, 53tr; Philipp Zechner 177tr; ; Zoonar GmbH 20, 196–7; ZUMA Press; Inc. 105br.

Bridgeman Images:
Osterreichische Nationalbibliothek, Vienna, Austria / *Detail of Italy from the Peutinger map copy* 54t.

Depositphotos Inc:
TTstudio 208clb.

Dorling Kindersley:
Lucio Rossi 90br, 177br, /Archaeological Museum of Istria, Pula, Croatia 152tl.

Dreamstime.com:
Darren Baker 39clb; Valery Bareta 168–9b; Sinisa Botas 45cla; Boris15 207tl; Daniel M. Cisilino 89tr; Dbajurin 208b; Deymos 182t; Dennis Dolkens 124–5b, 133tr; Dreamer4787 229b; Dziewul 176b; Freesurf69 112-13b; GoranJakus 40–41t, 44–5t; Maurie Hill 155t; Kasto80 178–9t; Kuhar 11br; Masar1920 94–5b; Zdeněk Matyáš 36–7t; Gabriel Murad 185tr, Aleksej Orel 130tl, Oriontrail 246clb, Phant 231br, Rndmst 104, Fesus Robert 19, 170–171; Tetiana Rozhnovska 128bc; Shufu 53cr; Zoran Stojiljkovic 246b; Studioclover 39br; Tcerovski 55tr; Toldiu74 183cra; Vaclav Volrab 134–5t; xbrchx 124tl; Zatletic 200cb, 200crb, 200bc, 201cb, 201bl.

This edition updated by
Contributer Jane Foster
Senior Editor Alison McGill
Senior Designers Laura O'Brien,
Stuti Tiwari
Project Editors Parnika Bagla,
Danielle Watt
Editors Nayan Keshan,
Anuroop Sanwalia
Picture Research Coordinator
Sumita Khatwani
Assistant Picture Research Administrator
Vagisha Pushp
Jacket Coordinator Bella Talbot
Jacket Designer Laura O'Brien
Senior Cartographer
Subhashree Bharti
Cartography Manager Suresh Kumar
DTP Designer Tanveer Zaidi
Senior Production Editor Jason Little
Production Controller Rebecca Parton
Deputy Managing Editor Beverly Smart
Managing Editors Shikha Kulkarni,
Hollie Teague
Managing Art Editors Bess Daly,
Priyanka Thakur
Art Director Maxine Pedliham
Publishing Director Georgina Dee

First edition 2003

Published in Great Britain by Dorling Kindersley Limited,
One Embassy Gardens, 8 Viaduct Gardens, London, SW11 7BW

The authorised representative in the EEA is
Dorling Kindersley Verlag GmbH. Arnulfstr.
124, 80636 Munich, Germany.

Published in the United States by DK Publishing,
1450 Broadway, Suite 801, New York, NY 10018

Copyright © 2003, 2021 Dorling Kindersley Limited
A Penguin Random House Company
21 22 23 24 10 9 8 7 6 5 4 3 2 1

The publishers cannot accept responsibility for any consequences
arising from the use of this book, nor for any material on third
party websites, and cannot guarantee that any website address
in this book will be a suitable source of travel information.

A CIP catalog record for this book
is available from the British Library.

A catalog record for this book is available
from the Library of Congress.

ISSN: 1542 1554
ISBN: 978 0 2414 7212 5

Printed and bound in China.

www.dk.com

MIX
Paper from
responsible sources
FSC™ C018179

A NOTE FROM DK EYEWITNESS

The rapid rate at which the world is changing is
constantly keeping the DK Eyewitness team on our
toes. While we've worked hard to ensure that this
edition of Croatia is accurate and up-to-date, we
know that opening hours alter, standards shift, prices
fluctuate, places close and new ones pop up in their
stead. So, if you notice we've got something wrong
or left something out, we want to hear about it.
Please get in touch at travelguides@dk.com